VULNERABLE
COMMUNITIES

VULNERABLE COMMUNITIES

Research, Policy, and Practice
in Small Cities

**Edited by James J. Connolly,
Dagney G. Faulk, and Emily J. Wornell**

CORNELL UNIVERSITY PRESS   ITHACA AND LONDON

This book was published with assistance from the Center for Business and Economic Research and the Sponsored Projects Administration, Ball State University.

First published 2022 by Cornell University Press

Library of Congress Cataloging-in-Publication Data

Names: Connolly, James J., 1962– editor. | Faulk, Dagney Gail, 1969– editor. | Wornell, Emily J., 1983– editor.
Title: Vulnerable communities : research, policy, and practice in small cities / edited by James J. Connolly, Dagney G. Faulk, and Emily J. Wornell.
Description: Ithaca [New York] : Cornell University Press, 2022. | Includes bibliographical references and index.
Identifiers: LCCN 2021039543 (print) | LCCN 2021039544 (ebook) | ISBN 9781501761324 (hardcover) | ISBN 9781501761546 (paperback) | ISBN 9781501761331 (pdf) | ISBN 9781501761348 (epub)
Subjects: LCSH: Small cities—United States. | Small cities—Economic aspects—United States. | Small cities—Social aspects—United States. | City planning—United States.
Classification: LCC HT153 .V85 2022 (print) | LCC HT153 (ebook) | DDC 307.76—dc23
LC record available at https://lccn.loc.gov/2021039543
LC ebook record available at https://lccn.loc.gov/2021039544

All photographs are by the chapter authors unless otherwise noted.

For all those working to improve America's small cities,
and for the people living in them

Contents

Acknowledgments

This book is one of the outcomes of the 2018 Small Cities Conference at Ball State University, which drew together scholars and policy practitioners from around the country to consider the current challenges facing small cities and rural communities. The Center for Business and Economic Research, the Center for Middletown Studies, and the Indiana Communities Institute jointly organized the conference. It also received support from Accelerate Indiana Municipalities, the Indiana Philanthropy Alliance, and the RUPRI Center for State Policy. We wish to thank these organizations for making the conference, and this book, possible.

The chapters in this book represent only a selection of the work presented at the conference. We are grateful to all the presenters and attendees for their contributions to the discussion about the issues facing vulnerable communities in the United States. Special thanks go to Greg Goodnight and Charles Fluharty for their keynote addresses and to Geoffrey Mearns for his opening remarks. Invaluable insight and support also came from David Terrell. Thank you.

The editors of this book, along with Michael Hicks and Lisa Goodpaster, formed the conference committee, but many other people played a role. Victoria Meldrum, Kaylie McKee, Kera Fenimore, Silvey Shamsi, Ben Delisle from the Center for Business and Economic Research, Angie Popplewell and Candy Dodd from the Indiana Communities Institute, and Sean Godfroy from the Center for Middletown Studies provided valuable assistance in staging the conference, and for that they have our deep gratitude.

Thanks also go to the editorial the team at Cornell University Press, particularly Jim Lance and Clare Jones, for shepherding the book through to completion. We appreciated the thorough comments and advice from three anonymous reviewers, which made the book far stronger. Sean Weiss, Cade Deckard, and Megan Vohs provided editorial assistance as we produced the manuscript.

Finally, Ball State's Sponsored Projects Administration provided necessary financial support for the book, and we thank the members of its Intellectual Property and Publications Committee for their support of the project.

VULNERABLE COMMUNITIES

VULNERABLE COMMUNITIES

An Introduction

James J. Connolly, Dagney Faulk, and Emily J. Wornell

Social and political concerns about wide differences in regional economic performance have beset Americans for more than a generation. Diminished opportunity due to economic globalization and automation along with the rapid growth of major metropolitan areas have had especially dramatic effects on small cities, towns, and rural communities. Although geographic variation in economic growth is not new to the United States, it seems more pronounced today than in the past. Research suggests that many smaller communities may experience further job loss, population decline, and associated social problems as these trends accelerate (see, e.g., Moretti 2013). The to-be-determined effects of the COVID-19 pandemic that emerged in 2020 are likely to fuel their deterioration.

This book examines a subset of these vulnerable American communities: small cities. Like larger metropolitan centers, small cities are now compelled to reimagine their role within a globalized economic and cultural order. Many of them have lost their identities as industrial or commercial centers and face a complex and distinctive mix of economic, social, and civic challenges as they struggle to change course. Some of the difficulties they confront mirror those that afflict larger cities. Others are the product of smallness. Even when the challenges are comparable, small cities usually have fewer resources as well as different strengths and weaknesses, all of which differentiate their experiences from those of bigger communities.

By *small cities*, we mean municipalities with populations between twenty thousand and two hundred thousand people. That definition is to some extent arbitrary. There are no precise criteria for determining what constitutes a small city. For instance, Jon Norman, in *Small Cities USA* (2013), defines his subject as cities with populations between one hundred thousand and two hundred thousand. We cast our net more widely, in part for opportunistic reasons, in part because these chapters arose from a conference devoted to communities of various sizes in a population range that includes most of the places we cover in this book, and in part because the problems that we consider here are spread broadly across urban settlements of varying sizes and character. The national and historical contexts in which we write also matter. In another time and place, a community with two hundred thousand people might have been a behemoth. Today, a city of that size would rank as the 116th largest city in the United States, slotting in between Grand Rapids, Michigan, and Amarillo, Texas, according to 2018 estimates (US Census 2019). More importantly, such a city would occupy a subordinate place in the American urban hierarchy, a position that limits and shapes its ability to solve its own problems.

By casting our net widely, we can capture the range of challenges facing economically and socially vulnerable small cities. Many of the places examined here are *legacy cities*, the current term used to label once-thriving industrial centers that have fallen on hard times. Most are located in the Rust Belt, the region stretching from the Northeast through the Midwest that industrialized during the nineteenth and early twentieth centuries. But similar struggles can be found in the South, as the subsequent discussions of places such as Bessemer, Alabama, or micropolitan Louisiana demonstrate. These struggles also arise in aging inner-ring suburbs, as this book's case study of the Cleveland region makes clear. The path forward for places residing in the orbit of a larger city may differ from those locations that are more geographically distinct, but in at least some respects they also confront a common set of difficulties and limitations as they strive to reinvent themselves and return to prosperity.

Deliberations on how best to redevelop America's diminished small cities raise the question of whether such places even warrant the effort and expense. Human settlements, including quite large ones, have come and gone across millenia. If the geographic or economic reasons for a community's development disappear, the argument goes, we should not invest scarce resources in the vain hope of bolstering a place that cannot sustain itself. There are several problems with such thinking, not least of which is the number of people in question. More than 92 million Americans live in the nation's 1,718 cities with populations between twenty thousand and two hundred thousand. Half of them—more than 46 million—reside in municipalities experiencing either slow growth (where the population is growing more slowly than the national average) or outright decline. By comparison, fewer people—about 45 million—live in the nation's *forty* largest cities. (US Census 2019). Zeroing in reveals that upward of 15.6 million Americans live in small cities that have shrunk since 2010, a figure that exceeds the combined populations of New York, Los Angeles, and Chicago. It is also worth noting that many smaller cities serve as commercial and cultural hubs for agricultural regions. The fortunes of these places are intimately bound up with those of rural America and the millions who live there (Arnosti and Lui 2018). Beyond purely empirical grounds, substantial numbers of people living in these communities have formed deep attachments to place that are often intertwined with kinship and communal ties. Proposals that envision them pulling up stakes and relocating as we allow their communities to wither will face strong resistance. Taken together, these considerations make a course of abandonment and neglect unfeasible as a practical political matter, to say nothing of the ethical issues it raises.

Despite the growing necessity of tackling small-city redevelopment, many academics, policy analysts, and journalists have been slow to address the topic. Even initial descriptions of the American Rust Belt, where dozens of once-thriving industrial centers struggled, dwelled primarily on larger cities such as Detroit, Cleveland, and Pittsburgh, while mostly neglecting smaller cities, save for a few prominent examples such as Youngstown or Flint. Some of the earlier research neglect of smaller cities and towns can be attributed to the lure of the metropolis. As David Bell and Mark Jayne (2009) have aptly observed, urbanists "have been too dazzled by the spectacular urbanism of big cities" and have thus failed to pay attention to smaller, seemingly less exciting places. The prevailing assumption seems to have been either that such locales simply reproduced metropolitan patterns on a smaller scale or were provincial backwaters of little significance.

The pattern of neglect began to diminish during the first decade of the 2000s when a series of think-tank studies addressed the plight of smaller and midsized communities (Erickcek and McKinney 2004; Hoyt and Leroux 2007; Vey 2007; Fox and Axel-Lute 2008; Vey and McGahey 2008). A few academics trained their sights on small cities as well, but scholarly interest remained limited (Mahoney 2003; Garrett-Petts 2005; Connolly 2010; Tumber 2012). Generally optimistic in tone, these analyses called for new state-level policies while advising smaller, formerly industrial communities to build on their remaining strengths, attract "creative class" workers, and capitalize on the move away from carbon-based energy. Despite these prescriptions for improvement, generating prosperity in deindustrializing small cities has remained difficult.

A new sense of urgency has emerged as Americans recognize the persistent decline of many smaller cities and nonmetropolitan regions. There is now a consensus, as Alan Berube (2019) has argued, "that place matters for economic policy," and it has grown increasingly evident that "the largest places are succeeding while smaller ones are not." In the wake of the surprising result of the 2016 presidential election, a growing number of observers have concluded that the troubles besetting once-prosperous small industrial cities "threaten the social fabric on which a healthy democracy depends" (Berube and Murray 2018). Others have highlighted the divide between globalized superstar cities and the rest, noting a severing of connections between metropolitan centers and their hinterland (Badger 2017; Longworth 2017). Spurred by such concerns, journalists now regularly venture into "flyover country," a genre of reporting that very quickly became a cliché. Smaller cities have also attracted the interest of commentators such as Paul Krugman (2017), who foresees an inevitable demise for many of them, and Noah Smith (2017), who pins hopes for revival on immigration and an expanded role for educational institutions.

Interest in small cities among academics developed more slowly but over time has generated a substantial body of scholarship that approaches such places as something other than the metropolis writ small. The difficulties that many small cities face have earned attention and in some instances prescriptions for revival, from sociologists (Rich 2013; Norman 2013), geographers (Ofari-Amoah, 2006; Breitbart 2016), and urban planners (Miraftab 2016; Burayidi 2013), as well as multidisciplinary researchers (Bowen 2014; Mallach 2018). Broadly speaking, this body of work argues that struggling communities should seek to build their supply of human capital and take advantage of their presumably deep reservoir of social capital while striving to become more attractive places to live. Employment growth will follow from these changes rather than precede them. Economic development efforts should thus focus on creating amenities that will draw educated workers; attracting immigrants; reviving downtowns as walkable retail, residential, and cultural centers that create a sense of place; improving schools; and undertaking other measures that aim to draw people to the city. Attempts to lure businesses through tax breaks and direct forms of support are judged to be less effective, although that tactic remains a staple of redevelopment programs in many places.

Those focused on improving the fortunes of urban communities, both large and small, are increasingly concerned with generating inclusive growth. Amenities that attract professionals and the middle class are necessary, they acknowledge, but not sufficient. There is also a need to address pervasive inequality within cities and between cities and their suburbs. Doing so will require a wide array of initiatives, including programs that broaden access to well-paying jobs, improve human capital through educational initiatives ranging from preschool to postsecondary programs, pay attention to housing and spatial justice, and increase collective efficacy in impoverished neighborhoods (Mallach 2018, chap. 11). Racial discrimination in housing, employment, education, and policing has stamped itself indelibly on many small cities, as it has on large metros, leaving a legacy of inequality that functions as a drag on economic growth. Those crafting growth strategies face the challenge of incorporating the interests of low-wage workers, racial minorities, and others left out of earlier prescriptions for urban revival.

Vulnerable Communities extends many of the arguments advanced in recent research on small cities while calling attention to the difficulties that arise in moving from plans to projects. One challenge for those seeking to understand the fate of nonmetropolitan places is to recognize and account for their social and political complexity. Much of the prescriptive literature emanating from both scholars and policy writers approaches these communities as monolithic entities, assuming that they can and will enact the policy agendas laid out by think tanks and academics in a straightforward, coherent manner. But smaller cities are nevertheless urban and thus diverse. They have an intersecting set of social tensions; geographies segregated by race, class, and ethnicity; political rivalries; and cultural divides. As with larger cities, these place-specific rifts tend to be deeply rooted and have tangled histories. They inevitably shape the ways in which a community strives to revive itself. Redesigning a downtown as an upscale retail destination, for instance, may attract middle-class shoppers but ignore long-neglected demands from nearby blue-collar residents and thus generate resistance to further redevelopment initiatives.

Greater attention to the internal dynamics of nonmetropolitan places raises questions about what many scholars see as a key characteristic of small cities: their social cohesiveness. If smaller cities and towns have any advantage, some scholars suggest, it is the manner in which they can combine big-city amenities with a small-town sense of community. Put in social scientific terms, analysts and theorists assume that nonmetropolitan places have more social capital than the anomie-laden metropolis, including both the *bonding* social capital that unites groups and neighborhoods and the *bridging* social capital that results from strong links between segments of the community. Several of the case studies assembled here raise doubts about that proposition. They point to cleavages across many lines, including class, race, ethnicity, political outlook, and even whether one is a newcomer or an old timer. Recent economic, demographic, and cultural trends have only deepened these divides, eroding the civic trust necessary for decisive community action. At the very least, it seems likely that few small cities have developed or sustained a sufficient level of bridging capital to enable creative responses to the challenges produced by economic change (Safford 2009).

There are structural obstacles to small-city revival as well, as the contributions assembled in the second part of this book make clear. Cities in the United States have relatively little power, a situation unlikely to change in the current political environment in which polarization tracks closely with the urban-rural divide (Schragger 2016; Rodden 2019; Wilkinson 2018). Nonmetropolitan places are increasingly dependent on federal and state support and are often hamstrung by limits on their ability to tax, spend, annex, and regulate economic behavior. The conservative policy regimes that have emerged in many states tend to push these places toward self-help strategies, which is a problematic approach for communities with limited and declining resources. Along with internal divisions, these political impediments limit or distort the capacity of small cities to execute even the best-laid plans.

As the circumstances of the numerous cities discussed in this book indicate, the relationship between a small city and its region's metropolitan core matters. For geographically distinct communities located well beyond the gravitational pull of a large city, routes to redevelopment are more limited. They have little chance of becoming suburban bedroom communities or even exurban alternatives to life in a costly metropolis. Instead, they have to rely on revival strategies built around local or regional assets, perhaps an anchor institution such as a college or hospital or perhaps some kind of locational advantage tied to natural resources, regional attractions, or transportation networks. For communities situated closer to the metropolitan core, opportunities for growth are often tied to the principal city's economic vitality, although patterns of discrimination and neglect often exacerbate the economic and social difficulties these places experience. Rust Belt cities such as Cleveland or Detroit create challenges for older suburbs that do not apply to communities adjacent to prosperous, tech-oriented coastal cities. On the other hand, fierce debates that have arisen in prosperous metros about displacement of the poor through gentrification may be less relevant in struggling small cities where investment is desperately needed.

Much of the thinking that informs small-city rejuvenation efforts originated as responses to metropolitan conditions. Two sets of ideas have been particularly influential. The first, new urbanism, represented a revolt among architects and planners against the combination of automobile-era sprawl and inner-city decline. Bolstered by arguments for "smart growth," its prescriptions have worked their way into proposals to reconfigure small-city downtowns and neighborhoods as compact, walkable retail and residential centers (Burayidi 2001, 2013; Robertson 1999). The second concept is Richard Florida's (2002) argument that luring the "creative class" to a city by offering cultural amenities and promoting tolerance generates economic benefits. His claims have been sharply contested on grounds that include their applicability to smaller cities, but they have nevertheless proven influential among economic development officials in such locales (Rich 2013). In both cases, it seems unlikely that approaches devised for metropolitan settings will apply in a straightforward way to the troubles evident in the smaller communities of the United States. In placing too much of the burden for revival on small cities themselves, we may also lose sight of the larger political and economic changes necessary to restore these communities to prosperity.

Vulnerable Communities explores these issues in two sections. The first considers the interior dynamics of cities and towns as they navigate changing economic and social forces. It includes chapters examining the social conflicts and clashing visions that arise even in a relatively prosperous community, efforts to strengthen local civic cultures in New England, the frictions and opportunities that follow an influx of refugees, and revitalization efforts in a majority-black southern steel town. Not only does this collection of case studies offer representative examples of the challenges facing smaller urban communities, it also provides ample evidence of the multidimensional character of such places.

The second part of the book investigates broader structural developments impacting economically weakened communities. It includes an analysis of the increasing reliance on transfer payments from the federal government in cities with shrinking economic bases, an examination of the Census Bureau's criteria for defining metropolitan and micropolitan areas and the challenges and opportunities that process offers for entrepreneurial civic leaders, an investigation of how planners and other officials in the inner-ring suburbs of Cleveland conceive of their communities, a close look at how Indiana's property tax caps have reshaped municipal behavior, and a discussion of employment multipliers with implications for our understanding of conventional economic development incentives. These chapters include detailed analyses of data capturing underlying forces that affect growth in struggling communities and regions. They highlight the extent to which smaller cities are at the mercy of state and federal agencies, both as suppliers of desperately needed revenues and as rule makers limiting the capacity of small cities to address their problems.

The first section of the book digs into the interior complexities of small cities. It opens with Henry Way's account of growth-induced tensions in Harrisonburg, Virginia. Although the city's recent expansion distinguishes it from most of the other communities profiled in this book, the conflicts it has experienced are familiar. Its recent population growth has been fueled by an influx of immigrants, including refugees, and the dramatic expansion of James Madison University. The city has also invested in rehabilitating its downtown with the aim of drawing economic activity to the community. Employing the lens of human geography, Way takes note of the tensions arising in areas such as infrastructure improvements, public transportation, and education. City leaders and university officials have at times clashed over development priorities. Likewise, the arrival of immigrants has expanded the city's labor force and bolstered local spending power, yet efforts to lure people to the city's refurbished center have largely ignored these newcomers. Despite positive population trends, income figures remain low, inequality persists, and decisive, coherent planning seems elusive.

Way points to two key factors that contribute to Harrisonburg's difficulties, both of which are characteristic of many small cities. The first is the city's "in-between status." Neither a metropolitan center nor a rural outpost, it does not slot comfortably into the categories that govern Virginia's community development efforts, which focus on larger cities or struggling small towns and rural districts. Yet, as a modest-sized place, it lacks the resources to fund vital initiatives on its own. The city's self-definition also wavers between small town and regional urban center as it adjusts to rapid demographic and economic change, impeding efforts to develop an integrated approach to managing its growth. Way also emphasizes a second factor inhibiting improvement, the lack of coordination among the interests spearheading the city's three growth-inducing trends: James Madison University's expansion, downtown redevelopment work, and efforts to attract and welcome immigrants. Each trend seems to proceed without consideration of the other. The result is uncoordinated, incoherent planning that has not adequately addressed issues such as housing and inequality.

Harrisonburg appears to lack the civic infrastructure that the Boston Fed is seeking to cultivate in New England, leaving it ill prepared to capitalize on its advantages in an equitable way. Colleen Dawicki reports on the Boston Federal Reserve's Working Cities Challenge, an initiative designed to help economically struggling cities across New England pursue redevelopment opportunities. The initiative stresses the development of civic infrastructure in cities, which Dawicki defines as "high capacity leaders, organizations, and networks that mobilized residents and resources" to pursue a shared vision of community redevelopment. The most striking aspect of the program's approach is its foundational assumption; it recognizes that the sorts of divisions that Way finds in Harrisonburg are common to many small cities. Instead of seeking to incentivize communities to compete to attract new businesses, treating them as single-minded actors prepared to act in a coherent way, the Working Cities Challenge recognizes that they each have particular internal dynamics that can help or hinder redevelopment. It stresses the need to strengthen the civic infrastructure in these places so that cooperative action that acknowledges the needs and desires of the various segments of the community is possible.

Five years in, indications are that the Working Cities Challenge has helped bolster capacity for action in participating cities. Examples from the Massachusetts cities that were part of its initial cohort demonstrate ways in which a stronger civic infrastructure fosters effective approaches to economic and community development. Dawicki also describes development tools made available to cities seeking to assess and build their own civic infrastructures in the service of promoting economic growth and opportunity. Some of these tools have been piloted in the winning cities, including an independent evaluation framework, a self-assessment, and a city leader survey, all of which provide communities with important insights into their own civic infrastructures and how best to improve them as vehicles for economic growth.

One of the most significant opportunities for growth available to small cities stems from the country's high levels of immigration, as Harrisonburg's experience suggests. In places with less than robust economies, which are less likely to attract significant numbers of voluntary migrants, refugees represent one of the few viable options for boosting population levels. Jennifer Erickson examines the benefits and the challenges resulting from refugee resettlement in Sioux Falls, South Dakota, and Fargo, North Dakota. Before the region began to prosper from a natural gas boom, both communities became refugee resettlement destinations during the 1990s.

Using long-term ethnographic research with an emphasis on everyday practices, Erickson reports on the tensions arising in largely white, native-born cities that experience a significant influx of international migrants. She argues that developing a framework for intercultural policy benefits cities both economically and socially, and she provides best practices for small cities in accommodating and welcoming international migrants. Specifically, rather than associate diversity and cultural differences with conflict and social disorders, Erickson contends that even seemingly homogeneous small cities should embrace their urban—and therefore diverse—identities, resulting in a competitive advantage in an age of intensified global economic exchange and international migration. Such a step is especially relevant as refugee attraction becomes an increasingly important development tool.

William Holt's discussion of revitalization efforts in Bessemer, Alabama, reminds us that industrial decline is not limited to the Rust Belt. His chapter helps understand the circumstances shaping redevelopment work in Bessemer, a deeply impoverished small city lying just southwest of Birmingham that was once the home to US Steel's southern headquarters and a major Pullman Standard railcar facility. These industries flourished until the 1960s when the violent backlash against the Civil Rights Movement in the South created racial unrest and the steel industry's globalization decimated the region. The city's majority-black population peaked in 1970 and has declined considerably since as its industrial base withered. These changes prompted Bessemer leaders to adopt a variety of familiar strategies, beginning during the 1980s, including a push to refurbish downtown, luring big-box retailers with tax incentives, and more recently the creation of recreational amenities. The city has also attracted several distribution operations, capitalizing on the city's access to two interstate highways. The most notable of these was an Amazon fulfillment center that employed 6,000 people by early 2021 and became the site of labor organizing drive that drew national attention (Weise and Corkery 2021).

Whether these measures can turn Bessemer's fortunes around remains an open question. It remains unclear how many of the new jobs at Amazon and elsewhere have gone to local residents or have brought new residents, although the city is striving to offer reasonably priced housing to attract them. Perhaps the city's biggest advantage is its proximity to Birmingham, but it seems that even that locational advantage has been a mixed blessing at best. Holt's survey research also demonstrates that the needs and desires of local residents have not matched up perfectly with local economic development agendas, although they may now be starting to align. By offering us a snapshot of a southern, suburban city attempting to revive its fortunes, Holt provides a good sense of what is required to achieve inclusive economic redevelopment.

The second half of the book turns its attention from the internal dynamics of individual cities to discussion of broader patterns and strategies. It begins with Allan Mallach's chapter describing how many smaller, geographically isolated cities are increasingly dependent on public spending. Using several small Midwestern cities as examples, he illustrates the extent of this "urban transfer payment economy" in those cities that rely heavily on money derived from federal programs such as SNAP, TANF, and Social Security. The substitute economic sectors to which many of these communities are turning are equally dependent on federal funds. Even supposedly productive substitute economic sectors, like "eds and meds," depend heavily on public dollars. An economic strategy employed by many formerly industrial cities, *eds and meds* count on universities (*eds*) and hospitals (*meds*) as anchor institutions, which in turn rely on transfer payments via Pell Grants and federally guaranteed student loans for higher education and Medicare and Medicaid payments for health care. Expressing doubts about the durability of such arrangements, as well as about the value of tax incentives aimed at luring new business, Mallach cites refugee attraction, human capital development, quality of life improvements that attract educated residents, and strategies to capture more of the revenue produced by transfer payments as potentially useful. But even these measures are likely to fall short of producing the substantial investments necessary to turn these legacy cities around. Only a "major infusion of public resources" in education, infrastructure, social welfare, and other areas will rescue these communities, he argues, although he admits that such a step is unlikely in the contemporary political climate.

Mallach's analysis highlights the structural weaknesses that impede small city revival in the United States. Many such places well beyond the Rust Belt have lost their *raison d'être* as industrial centers and have become heavily dependent on the constant injection of federal and state funds into their economy. Such support is constricted by ideological and political factors and, at best, can only keep these places afloat without hope for improvement. Only a fortunate few possess the necessary internal resources or a locational advantage—Mallach calls it "place luck," citing Reese and Ye (2011). Absent substantial intervention, the best that the unlucky many can expect is to limp along, relying on the willingness of the rest of the country to sustain them.

In their discussion of the vagaries of the federal government's regional classifications, J. Matthew Fannin and Vikash Dangal further underscore the dependent status of smaller cities and towns. Citing examples from Louisiana, they trace shifting official Micropolitan Statistical Area definitions and consider the people- and place-based development challenges that small cities and other intermediate population density regions face when this definition is so unstable. These categorizations are far more than a technical matter. They are key to setting federal funding distributions to hospitals and local governments for programs such as Medicare and Community Development Block Grants, among others. A community in an area that shifts from metropolitan to micropolitan status stands to lose both resources and autonomy. Fannin and Dangal propose reforms to federal statistical organizations and agencies implementing place- and people-based programs, as well as strategies for small cities that are not close to metropolitan centers to use as they navigate vulnerabilities that arise from the volatility in policy-leveraged regional definitions.

Smaller urban communities located within metropolitan regions face their own challenges, especially in the Rust Belt. Hannah Lebovits highlights the degree to which residents and governmental actors in fourteen inner-ring suburbs in Cuyahoga County, Ohio, perceive their suburban municipalities as self-governed, independent small cities and the ways in which they concern themselves with small-city governance practices. Cuyahoga County, which encompasses Cleveland, resides in a region of the United States where, during the golden age of manufacturing, cities were local economic drivers and metropolitan regions expanded rapidly. Today, Cuyahoga County is a shrinking region in which the economy is unstable, a large number of residents are leaving, and measures of social equity are troubling. The suburbs in this case study are distinguished from others in the county by their aging housing stock and their proximity to the central city, as well as their economic and demographic trends. While noting the need for further research, Lebovits makes the provocative point that these communities increasingly see themselves as separate from Cleveland and are striving to create distinctive, independent urban identities. No doubt Cleveland's weak economic position and negative image feeds this tendency, but the pattern Lebovits detects prompts us to rethink our understanding of governance, community building, and civic life in older Rust Belt suburbs, which may feel compelled to reorient themselves when the adjacent central city is economically weak.

It is also possible that Cleveland's inner-ring suburbs have begun acting more independently because of a broader policy regime that incentivizes communities to compete with each other to attract economic development. No state has been more aggressive in this regard than Ohio's western neighbor, Indiana. Among the Hoosier State's major reforms was the implementation of property tax caps, which dramatically reduced revenue for some local governments while having little effect on others. The legacy cities of Anderson, Gary, and Muncie, for example, experienced property tax revenue losses of greater than 30 percent of the certified levy, while Bloomington (a college town) and Carmel (a prosperous suburb near Indianapolis) experienced reductions of less than 3 percent. Using 2007–2014 data on twenty-eight municipal governments in Indiana, Dagney Faulk, Charles Taylor, and Pam Schaal examine two policy options available for managing declining revenues: (1) reducing spending and employment, or (2) raising additional revenue through local income taxes and annexation. They find that revenue losses from property tax caps are a significant determinant of decreases in municipal budgets and spending and in a reduction in local government employment over this period. These cuts appear to have a particularly negative effect on highway department and parks and recreation employment. Fire and police services were also hit, though not as severely. There was no apparent reduction in other administrative employment. Perhaps most surprising, there is little indication that smaller cities sought to use the tools that the state provided to offset revenue losses. Annexation, a means of expanding the local tax base, did not increase, nor did local income tax rates. Faulk, Taylor, and Schaal admit that they offer only a short-term picture and that an examination of a longer period is in order, but their findings, if sustained, raise interesting questions about why these communities do not, or cannot, take advantage of the tools at their disposal to address severe budgetary difficulties.

Michael Hicks digs into a different body of data to consider the utility of employment multipliers, a key measure of the impact of business attraction efforts by local economic development leaders. Traditional economic development thinking has assumed that the value of luring a new business to town or adding a new product line to a local factory extended beyond the new positions it opened up. The added jobs presumably had a multiplier effect, as new employees increased spending on local goods and services, thus generating economic growth across the community. Likewise, job losses resulting from business closures or departures supposedly had a negative ripple effect.

Although focused on technical questions, Hicks's effort to refine our understanding of multiplier effects over the last forty years has striking implications. His analysis indicates that the benefits from landing a new plant or from the substantial expansion of an existing operation have diminished over time but that the negative impact of losing employment has increased. There are important variations in the general pattern of a declining multiplier effect. Most significant, the negative employment consequences that come from a factory closure or the loss of a business have been proportionally larger than the effects of luring a new firm to town. Such a finding suggests that replacing the loss of one plant with another is ultimately a losing proposition. Also relevant to understanding revival efforts in legacy cities is evidence that positive multiplier effects are more substantial in bigger communities than in smaller ones. Each of these claims points us away from the customary business-attraction model that has dominated small-city economic development thinking, and each claim raises vital questions about the sources of these trends that warrant further investigation.

The book closes with an afterword from Greg Goodnight, the mayor of Kokomo, Indiana, from 2008 to 2019. Originally presented as the keynote address at the 2018 Vulnerable Communities conference at Ball State University, it offers a hands-on perspective of the revitalization of a Rust Belt legacy city. Kokomo lost more than half its factory jobs during the first decade of the twenty-first century. With assistance from the federal government's Troubled Asset Relief Program (TARP), the city's manufacturing employment levels stabilized and later increased. Goodnight has earned praise for his leadership of the city, not only for spearheading municipal efforts to sustain its industrial base, but also for helping create a more attractive, livable community. Detailing the practical political and social challenges encountered as a small city attempts to implement the kinds of urban redevelopment plans promoted by scholars and activists, it reminds us to pay special attention to both the internal dynamics and the external obstacles that influence actual redevelopment work.

Vulnerable Communities aims to help scholars and policy analysts think more carefully about how to help struggling small cities. It is customary in writing about revival efforts in such places to acknowledge that there is no "silver bullet" and no "one-size-fits-all" solution. Such demurrals are appropriate in dealing with a diverse array of long-established communities. They are multifaceted places, not only in terms of their internal dynamics but with regard to the particular economic and political circumstances that have shaped their development and will continue to shape their prospects. Those seeking to understand them and to help them must recognize this complexity.

The original gathering that produced these and other examinations of smaller cities and towns included both scholars who write about them and practitioners who manage them.[1] The idea was for each group to learn from the other, an approach that encouraged the participating academics to write for a broad, nonspecialist audience without watering down their arguments. The contributions collected here represent some of the best research presented at the gathering. They are offered in the same spirit, with the belief that they will be useful for those seeking to better understand how so many of these places came to be so vulnerable, as well for those struggling to enact practical, effective, and inclusive redevelopment policies at the local, state, and federal level to change the course of America's small cities.

Notes

1. The gathering was the "Vulnerable Communities: Research, Policy, and Practice" conference, held in May 2018 at Ball State University.

References

Arnosti, Nathan, and Amy Liu. 2018. *Why Rural America Needs Cities*. Washington, DC: Brookings Institution. https://www.brookings.edu/research/why-rural-america-needs-cities/.

Bell, David, and Mark Jayne. 2009. "Small Cities? Towards a Research Agenda." *International Journal of Urban and Regional Research* 33, no. 3 (September): 683–699. https://doi.org/10.1111/j.1468-2427.2009.00886.x.

Badger, Emily. 2017. "What Happens When the Richest US Cities Turn to the World?" *New York Times*, December 22, 2017. https://www.nytimes.com/2017/12/22/upshot/the-great-disconnect-megacities-go-global-but-lose-local-links.html?rref=collection/byline/emily-badger&action=click&contentCollection=undefined%C2%AEion&module=stream_unit&version=latest&contentP.

Berube, Alan. 2019. *Why Midsize Metro Areas Deserve Our Attention*. Washington, DC: Brookings Institution. https://www.brookings.edu/research/why-midsized-metro-areas-deserve-our-attention/.

Berube, Alan, and Cecile Murray. 2018. *Renewing America's Economic Promise Through Older Industrial Cities*. Washington, DC: Brookings Institution. https://www.brookings.edu/research/older-industrial-cities/#01073.

Bowen, William M. 2014. *The Road Through the Rust Belt: From Preeminence to Decline to Prosperity*. Kalamazoo, MI: W.E. Upjohn Institute for Employment Research.

Breitbart, Myrna M. 2016. *Creative Economies in Post-Industrial Cities: Manufacturing a (Different) Scene*. Abingdon, UK: Routledge.

Burayidi, Michael A. 2001. *Downtowns: Strategies for Revitalizing Small Urban Communities*. New York: Routledge.

Burayidi, Michael A. 2013. *Resilient Downtowns: A New Approach to Revitalizing Small and Medium City Downtowns*. New York: Routledge.

Connolly, James J., ed. 2010. *After the Factory: Reinventing America's Industrial Small Cities*. Lanham, MD: Lexington Books.

Erickcek, George A., and Hannah McKinney. 2004. "Small Cities Blues: Looking for Growth Factors in Small and Medium-Sized Cities." *SSRN Electronic Journal.* https://doi.org/10.2139/ssrn.558183.

Fox, Radhika, and Miriam Axel-Lute. 2008. *To Be Strong Again: Renewing the Promise in Smaller Industrial Cities.* Oakland, CA: PolicyLink. https://www.policylink .org/sites/default/files/ToBeStrongAgain_final.pdf.

Florida, Richard. 2002. *The Rise of the Creative Class: And How It's Transforming Work, Leisure, Community and Everyday Life.* New York: Basic Books.

Garrett-Petts, W. F. 2005. *The Small Cities Book: On the Cultural Future of Small Cities.* Vancouver, BC: New Star Books.

Hoyt, Lorlene, and Andre Leroux. 2007. *Voices from Forgotten Cities: Innovative Revitalization Coalitions in America's Older Small Cities.* Oakland, CA: PolicyLink. https:// community-wealth.org/content/voices-forgotten-cities-innovative-revitalization -coalitions-america-s-older-small-cities.

Krugman, Paul. 2017. "The Gambler's Ruin of Small Cities (Wonkish)." *New York Times,* December 30, 2017. https://www.nytimes.com/2017/12/30/opinion/the-gamblers -ruin-of-small-cities-wonkish.html.

Longworth, Richard. n.d. "Blue Dots in a Red Sea: America's Urban-Rural Divide." Chicago: Chicago Council on Global Affairs. Accessed October 21, 2020. http://digital .thechicagocouncil.org/American-Urban-Rural-Divide/landing-9836-17212S.html.

Mahoney, Timothy R. 2003. "The Small City in American History." *Indiana Magazine of History* 99, no. 4 (December): 211–30. https://www.jstor.org/stable/277 92510.

Mallach, Alan. 2018. *The Divided City: Poverty and Prosperity in Urban America.* Washington, DC: Island Press.

Miraftab, Faranak. 2016. *Global Heartland: Displaced Labor, Transnational Lives, and Local Placemaking.* Bloomington: Indiana University Press.

Moretti, Enrico. 2013. *The New Geography of Jobs.* Boston: Mariner Books.

Norman, Jon R. 2013. *Small Cities USA: Growth, Diversity, and Inequality.* New Brunswick, NJ: Rutgers University Press.

Ofori-Amoah, Benjamin, ed. 2006. *Beyond the Metropolis: Urban Geography as if Small Cities Mattered.* Lanham, MD: University Press of America.

Reese, Laura A., and Minting Ye. 2011. "Policy Versus Place Luck: Achieving Local Economic Prosperity." *Economic Development Quarterly,* 25 (3): 221–236. https://doi .org/10.1177/0891242411408292.

Rich, Meghan A. 2013. "'From Coal to Cool': The Creative Class, Social Capital, and the Revitalization of Scranton." *Journal of Urban Affairs,* 35 (3): 365–384. https://doi .org/10.1111/j.1467-9906.2012.00639.x.

Robertson, Kent A. 1999. "Can Small-City Downtowns Remain Viable?" *Journal of the American Planning Association,* 65(3): 270–283. https://doi.org/10.1080/0194436990 8976057.

Rodden, Johnathan. 2019. *Why Cities Lose: The Deep Roots of the Urban-Rural Political Divide.* New York: Basic Books.

Safford, Sean. 2009. *Why the Garden Club Couldn't Save Youngstown: The Transformation of the Rust Belt.* Cambridge, MA: Harvard University Press.

Schragger, Richard, 2016. *City Power: Urban Governance in a Global Age.* New York: Oxford University Press.

Smith, Noah. 2017. "A Road Map for Reviving the Midwest: Universities and Immigration are Vital. Unfortunately, Both are Under Attack." *Bloomberg Opinion,* December 26, 2017. https://www.bloomberg.com/opinion/articles/2017-12-26/a-road-map -for-reviving-the-midwest.

Tumber, Catherine. 2012. *Small, Gritty, and Green: The Promise of America's Smaller Industrial Cities in a Low-Carbon World*. Cambridge, MA: MIT Press.

US Census Bureau, Population Division. 2019. *Annual Estimates of the Resident Population for Incorporated Places of 50,000 or More, Ranked by July 1, 2018 Population: April 1, 2010 to July 1,2018*. Washington, DC: US Census Bureau.

Vey, Jennifer S. 2007. *Restoring Prosperity: The State Role in Revitalizing America's Older Industrial Cities*. Washington, DC: Brookings Institution. https://www.brookings.edu/research/restoring-prosperity-the-state-role-in-revitalizing-americas-older-industrial-cities/.

Vey, Jennifer A., and Richard M. McGahey. 2008. *Retooling for Growth: Building a Twenty-First Century Economy in Older Industrial Areas*. Washington, DC: Brookings Institution Press.

Weise, Karen, and Michael Corkery. 2021. "Amazon Workers Vote Down Union Drive at Alabama Warehouse." *New York Times*, April 9, 2021. https://www.nytimes.com/2021/04/09/technology/amazon-defeats-union.html.

Wilkinson, Will. 2018. *The Density Divide: Urbanization, Polarization, and Populist Backlash*. Washington, DC: Niskanen Center. https://www.niskanencenter.org/the-density-divide-urbanization-polarization-and-populist-backlash/.

Part I

INTERNAL DYNAMICS

1

THE PERILS OF "IN-BETWEENNESS"

Fragmented Growth in a Virginia Small City

Henry Way

In the 1970s, Harrisonburg, a small city in the central Shenandoah Valley of Virginia, contained a population of a little over 15,000, of whom almost all were white and fewer than 1.5 percent were of Latino origin. In the 1980s, the former State Normal School for Women (a teachers' college), now James Madison University, maintained an enrollment of around 10,000 students. In the 1990s, downtown Harrisonburg experienced the severe economic and cultural contraction common to many smaller towns and cities. It was moribund enough for the downtown booster organization to describe it as "a place to avoid . . . filled with crumbling sidewalks, worn buildings, vacant storefronts, and faded pride" (HDR, n.d.; Harrisonburg Economic Development, n.d.).

Today, with consistent growth since the 1970s, Harrisonburg is a city with middle-sized pretentions, boasting a more diverse population of around 55,000, of whom nearly 20 percent are of Latino origin. James Madison University is a thriving, masters-level comprehensive university with almost 22,000 students, nearly 4,000 faculty and staff, and a budget of over half a billion dollars (Rephann 2016). Downtown Harrisonburg has seen a striking turnaround, winning a Great American Main Street award in 2014, becoming home to Virginia's first Culinary District with around forty restaurants across forty blocks, experiencing a four-fold growth in the number of residential units downtown, and receiving at least $35 million in building renovation investment since 2006 (Accordino and Fasulo 2014), among other superlatives.

To most observers, this trajectory would seem enviable. Harrisonburg appears by most measures a success story. It has seemingly benefited enormously from the twin boosts of immigration and higher education, identified as important to the success of smaller cities away from larger metropolitan areas (Smith 2017). It has nurtured a revived downtown, a consistent characteristic of more successful small and midsized cities. Harrisonburg does indeed offer a positive and distinctive case study of the advantages of such a three-pronged basis for growth. This analysis explores the characteristics of these factors supporting the city's growth—immigration, education, and downtown—with a particular focus on the strategies developed (or stumbled upon) to assist the revival of downtown, and it offers some useful comparative information for other communities.

However, the chapter also takes an analytic step back to examine the more challenging reality behind these positive top-line figures and data points. In particular, it considers how the context of the city's size shapes this three-way supported growth. A picture emerges of a city benefiting from higher education, immigration, and downtown growth, but in a somewhat complicated way. In many ways, significant—and new—challenges are evident. Harrisonburg's perilous status as an "in-between" kind of place is explored, and the problems of the lack of connection—both conceptually and in the material urban geography of the city—between the three key factors in the city's growth are emphasized. Although each city's experience is mediated by its own distinct circumstances and geographical contexts, this exploration offers other communities a more nuanced perspective on the experience of growth. Even robustly supported "truths" about what stimulates economic and demographic growth—in this case the traditionally prominent forces of education, immigration, and downtown investment—might not be unalloyed panaceas, and it is worth considering ways to make the most of the benefits they bring, especially when they exist in some combination as is the case in Harrisonburg. On a more hopeful note, the chapter ends by suggesting that the vulnerabilities manifested with the growth that this small city has experienced can be addressed by the distinctive characteristics of that particular small city's size.

A quick note about the approach that this account and the research take: the analysis is a hybrid perspective drawn from academic human geography (the home discipline of the author), and from the practical experience of city planning and green infrastructure work in Harrisonburg itself—the latter developed, for instance, through the author's work as chair of the city's Planning Commission, among other activities. This brings a distinctive disciplinary take on the vulnerability of smaller cities as well as some real-world research and implementation experience. The geographical, spatial lens is emphasized in a more theoretical way in the first part of the chapter with a brief discussion of the ways that geographers have engaged with smaller cities (and urban areas more generally), but the spatial perspective permeates the analysis throughout, offering a distinctive way to understand the conundrums of growth faced in this case study. Pertinent planning literature also helps to establish the issues here and provides a valuable frame through which to evaluate the approach taken in the city—especially with regard to downtown regrowth. The latter part of this narrative both sets out the patterns and strategies for growth found in Harrisonburg and develops a wider analytical framework for understanding the positive and problematic trajectories observed. This fusion of the theoretical/conceptual and the empirical offers useful case-study information and a deeper understanding of the processes at work, with more general applicability.

Academic Setting and Literature

Contemporary human geography is a diverse and theoretically fertile academic field. In the economic realm, geographers emphasize the ways economic mechanisms not only exhibit spatial patterns but are in many ways determined by the contexts of space and place (Martin 1999, 83). There is a strong critical and historical materialist streak in the economic geography literature that emphasizes questions of uneven development and justice at a global and local scale (Smith 1984; Harvey 1982). Cultural geographers have similarly adopted a theoretically informed and diverse set of approaches to the world, incorporating a critical lens, postcolonial theory, humanistic approaches, or postmodern social theories; for example, Jackson (1989), Soja (1989), Anderson (2015), and Cresswell (2013, 2015) present accessible introductions. Urban geography is similarly diverse, including critical questions of justice (Mitchell 2003; Merrifield 2014), comparative approaches to cities across the world (see Peck 2015 for a critical assessment of this field and Ward 2008 for an overview), interpretations and critiques of "global" cities (see Amin and Graham 1997 or Robinson 2005, for example), cities in particular regions (see Myers 2011 on African cities, for instance), and a broad range of considerations of the challenges and opportunities of urban sustainability, among other directions.

   In general, the geographical perspective can emphasize the way broader processes are profoundly shaped by—and in many ways emerge from—the contexts of specific places and the variegated spaces across which they operate. It is a diverse approach that draws out the specificity of particular locations, the ways space configures human relations at all scales, and the distinctive ways a range of factors (cultural, political, economic, and environmental) combine to make places the way they are. As a key framing context for the processes seen in Harrisonburg, the literature concerning geographical questions of city size is highlighted and reviewed here, but a broad geographical lens informs this entire analysis.

As a broad motivation, this focus on a smaller city heeds Robinson's call for a more expansive engagement with the urban world: "the spatial imagination adequate to capturing cityness—in its diverse forms—must necessarily be multiple and sophisticated" (Robinson 2005, 763). Much urban geography focuses on larger metropolises or "world cities" (inspired by Sassen 1991 and others), and has left undertheorized the question of city size. Part of the blindness to size in geography results from confusion about the question of scale—a matter explored with some sophistication by Marston, Jones, and Woodward (2005). The differentiation of size from scale is important because the former is concerned first with *intrinsic* qualities of a place—area, population, and so on—whereas scale emerges relationally (the local is positioned in relation to the global and so on). The explicit focus on small cities—emphasizing size as an analytical lens—has been more limited partly because of this undertheorization of the value of this potentially ontological category. Size captures something usually very material (such as the number of people, volume of objects, or territorial extent), and that material nature can be considered a fundamental shaping context for economic or social processes in a place. Size is not an abstract conception helping to organize the understanding of the human world in the way that scale might be seen to be (Way 2016, 139).

Clarifying *size* as distinct from *scale* in the geographic context should add a richer understanding of how cities work. Historically in geography, the work of modelers such as Christaller informed an integrated economic structuring of urban hierarchies (Christaller 1966). An array of more recent studies explores the applicability of Zipf's law in the urban context (Gonzales-Val 2011; Holmes and Lee 2010, for example). With more global reach, the call for attention to be given to "ordinary cities" has started a momentum to consider cities that rank beneath the global megalopolis in size (Amin and Graham 1997; Robinson 2002).

The literature that focuses more specifically on smaller cities is growing. The works of Bell and Jayne offer a wide-ranging examination of the experiences of small cities in recent years (Bell and Jayne 2006, 2009; Jayne, Gibson, Wait, and Bell 2010, for example). European case studies examine the role of governance in a small-city context (Weck and Beisswenger 2014). More US-focused collections and studies also draw out the variegated and often challenging experience of small cities (Norman 2013; Ofori-Amoah 2007; Markusen, Lee, and Di-Giovanni 1999, for example). Others have considered especially the implications for environmental progress and sustainability in small cities (Tumber 2011; Mayer and Knox 2010; Pitt and Bassett 2013; Friedman 2014). Recent studies have taken a more regional approach, revealing the different pathways smaller cities have taken (for the Rust Belt, see Hollingsworth and Goebel 2017, for instance).

Of particular relevance to this study is the literature that examines downtowns within the category of smaller cities. The particular emphasis here is on downtown revitalization, with much of the scholarship coming from the fields of planning and economics. Seeking to go beyond the focus on large cities and to avoid a simply descriptive, single-case-study approach, a number of authors have developed an analysis of several small-city downtown experiences and drawn out the common features of effective downtown revival (Robertson 1999; Burayidi 2001; Faulk 2006, for example). Faulk (2006, 631) proposed a conceptual development process model for downtowns to broaden the analysis from the specific to the general. In an attempt to identify the key characteristics of successful downtowns, surveying city policy makers and key stakeholders has offered a fertile approach (Bias, Leyden, and Zimmerman 2015; Filion et al. 2004).

The value of historic preservation tax credits in the context of downtown (and neighborhood) revitalization has also been identified (Ryberg-Webster 2013). In particular, as in Virginia, the combination of federal and state rehabilitation tax credits can be particularly beneficial for redevelopment projects (Tapp 2019). As the value of older buildings for communities becomes clearer both socially and economically (Powe et al. 2016), the impact of preservation and rehabilitation tax credits in declining and "legacy" cities has been more widely studied (Ryberg-Webster and Kinahan 2017; Kinahan 2019). However, as Ryberg-Webster and Kinahan (2014, 131) have suggested, a broader investigation of the economics of historic preservation and more analysis of the relative impact of different variables on urban revitalization need to take place to more fully understand the benefits of historic preservation. Further research into the mechanisms of quality-of-life enhancement brought by rehabilitated historic downtowns and neighborhoods is needed, the authors have suggested. To this we should add the variable of city size: work still needs to be done on identifying the costs and value of historic preservation and related tax credits in smaller cities in particular.

All the literature emphasizes the range of practices undertaken across a diverse collection of smaller cities—there is no one-size-fits-all approach—but some common themes for successful small and middle-sized city downtowns can be identified. The efficacy of the Main Street approach (with its four-point program) is noted by some (Robertson 2004; Bias, Leyden, and Zimmerman 2015), but it has also been suggested that many cities have gone beyond this program, and the strategy leaves out critical areas of emphasis beyond the promotion of the retail environment, such as supporting immigration and downtown housing (Burayidi 2013). Beyond the Main Street approach, immigration, and housing (the last often supported through the use of mixed-use zoning), analyses of case studies and surveys of policymakers commonly flag a concern for place making or the nurturing of a *sense of place* (the quality or distinctiveness of a place's identity and how people perceive it: a prominent theme within the field of humanistic geography also—see Tuan 1974). Small cities and their downtowns should emphasize their distinctive characteristics, build on their assets, and look for niche features to promote, as well as invest in creating a pleasant, accessible urban environment. A primary broader inspiration is the work of global practitioners such as Jan Gehl (2011), for example, and the United States–based Project for Public Spaces, a development of William H. Whyte's studies (Whyte 1980). The support for historic features, preservation, and adaptive reuse are commonly cited ways of maintaining a downtown's identity and attractiveness. In addition to investing in the built environment, the development of strong public-private partnerships in projects and planning and in delivering meaningful civic engagement has also been noted across many of the studies. Focusing and spearheading efforts through a downtown-focused organization and developing a clear vision (and way of monitoring the progress of a city's core) are also identified. Across all studies, a clear emphasis on deepening partnerships, playing to a place's strengths, developing its distinctive assets, and differentiating the downtown from the suburban environment is evident.

The Need for a Focus on Small and Midsized Cities

Before a closer examination of the Harrisonburg case, the value and relevance of focusing on smaller cities are considered. Building on Robertson's (2001) identification of distinctions between large-city and small-city downtowns—such as pedestrian-scale development, perceptions of less crime, and less district function segmentation in smaller communities—Burayidi (2013) highlighted the social differences of smaller cities, often including less international immigration. Also in distinction from larger cities, the same author highlights that small-city downtowns may have more affordable land prices (relative to their suburbs) by dint of their size, be more accessible from more of their surrounding city, and generate a greater sense of pride because of that intimacy or the more singular focus. A few prominent families may also have a larger role to play in smaller-city downtowns, whereas larger cities are dominated by corporate presence (Burayidi 2013, 2–4). Hollingsworth and Goebel (2017, 13) pointed to additional opportunities for smaller cities—the manageable scale, lower cost of living, quality of life, accessibility, and potential to be laboratories for urban initiatives. The same authors also pointed, however, toward the distinct challenges smaller cities face because of their size—more limited resources to cope with changing economic or demographic circumstances, fewer civic staff to assist in economic growth initiatives, and the outsize challenge vacant land or nonprofit land owner-ship can have on tax revenue (Hollingsworth and Goebel 2017, 12).

These discussions point to broader issues concerning small and middle-sized cities, and the opportunities and challenges of what we might term *in-betweenness*—that is, occupying a position between largeness and smallness, both in size and in cultural or economic outcomes. Although each community is shaped by geographically specific forces, it is interesting to consider whether small cities have the "best of both worlds." They may possess features people value, mixed with the greater opportunities of an urban environment, or they may fall perilously in between, suffering from the worst elements of rural and metropoli-tan systems. This *betweenness* dilemma and the balance between these size-oriented poles clearly present a tension with which many smaller cities grapple and that is clearly evident in Harrisonburg. Many of those examining small cities point to the relative absence of this type of settlement in the planning (or economics or geography) literature. Small cities are a somewhat overlooked category despite the excellent scholarship that has emerged in the last two decades. This lacuna warrants filling with well-informed, critical, and analytical scholarship.

A few statistically informed reasons might illustrate how these places are over-looked and why that may be a problem. Although metropolitan growth or de-cline does not always equate with individual city growth or decline, figures of this population change can be suggestive; figure 1.1 shows population percent-age changes in different population categories of metropolitan and micropolitan areas between 2010 and 2017 (at the time of writing, the most recent figures avail-able from the US Census).

Academic and policy attention is naturally drawn to the challenges of those places at the two extremes: the smaller communities that are losing population and the larger communities that are gaining significantly. Are the places in the lower end of the middle (the smaller cities in these metropolitan area ranges) experiencing manageable levels of population change, or is the typical level chal-lenging for these places because of their relatively less diversified economies and populations? Being in the middle hides all manner of interesting questions and contexts.

The experience of international migration also reveals some distinct patterns (and potential challenges) worth considering in the context of smaller cities. While much of the international migration to urban areas is found in the larg-est metropolises, some smaller cities have witnessed enormous—and dispropor-tionately significant—growth in their foreign-born population. Again, the impact of a large international migration on a smaller community is larger than that in a much greater (and likely already diverse) population center. An analysis

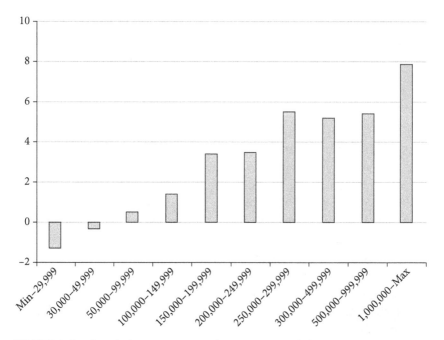

FIGURE 1.1.   Population percentage change in metro/micropolitan-area size groups, 2010–2017

Source: Data drawn from US Census.

of some of the patterns of this international diversification in small cities reveals some common characteristics of places that have received large number of international migrants. Figure 1.2 illustrates that around 85 percent of the smaller metropolitan/micropolitan areas with high levels of international migration are characterized as college towns (labeled Education), house a military establishment (often an army base), or have a significant food processing facility (such as a meatpacking or poultry processing plant).[1]

Analysis such as this illustrates the oversize influence a particular economic factor can have on the demographic and cultural character of a smaller city, in contrast to the more diversified economies of larger cities. It also reveals that many small cities are indeed experiencing high levels of international migration, perhaps at odds with the more typical idea of a demographically stable or homogeneous small city.

Indeed, a compelling reason to develop analyses of the smaller/midsized city experience is that such cities are numerous and consequently have a wide range of distinct experiences. Figure 1.3 illustrates this graphically.

Although a greater population lives in the largest metropolises in the United States, over 60 million people—roughly a fifth of the US population—are found

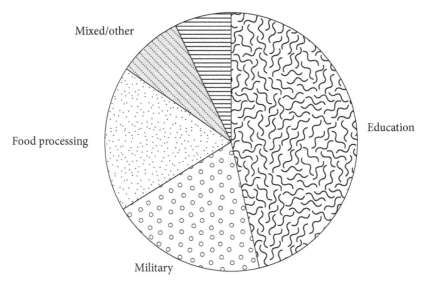

FIGURE 1.2. Primary characteristics of high international immigrant small and midsized cities

Sources: Data drawn from US Census and individual city research.

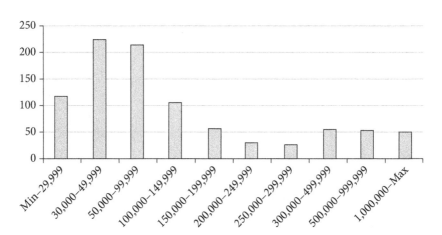

FIGURE 1.3. Number of metropolitan and micropolitan areas by population range, 2017

Source: Data drawn from US Census.

in metropolitan (and micropolitan) areas of 30 thousand to 300 thousand people. This in itself is a not insignificant number, but as figure 1.3 indicates, the *number* of cities in this smaller size range is much greater than the number of larger cities. There are 658 different metropolitan and micropolitan areas in that 30 thousand to 300 thousand range. Hence in terms of academic and policy-oriented study, they are a fascinatingly numerous and broad collection of entities with which to engage and of which to make some sense.

The Place: Harrisonburg, Virginia

Some facts and trends for Harrisonburg are useful for setting the scene for this analysis. As indicated in the introduction, Harrisonburg has grown quite significantly in recent decades. Figure 1.4 shows its population growth from less than 20,000 in 1980 to nearly 55,000 today.

Harrisonburg city (in the context of Virginia, an *independent city*, which functions as a county) is surrounded by the more rural Rockingham County. Rockingham County is the leading agricultural producer of the Commonwealth of Virginia and is also seeing more suburban overspill growth from Harrisonburg, which sits at its center. The overall population of the Harrisonburg metropolitan area—which includes the city of Harrisonburg and Rockingham County—is

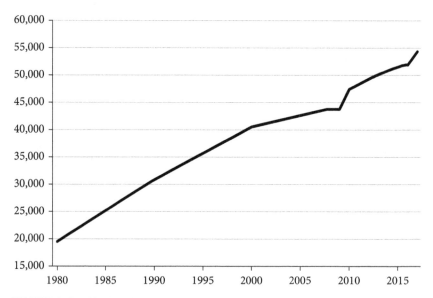

FIGURE 1.4. Harrisonburg population, 1980–2016

Source: Data drawn from US Census.

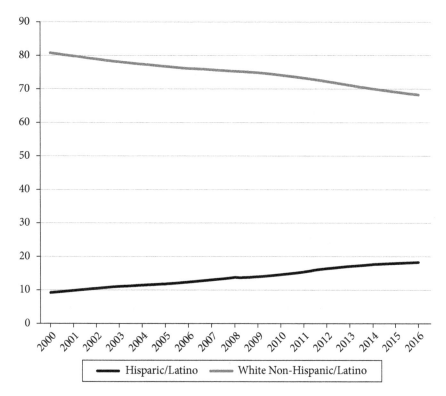

FIGURE 1.5. Percentage white non-Hispanic/Latino and percentage Hispanic/Latino, 2000–2016

Source: Data drawn from US Census.

around 135 thousand people (all population figures are from the US Census). These topline population figures conceal some interesting transitions in the city. For instance, Harrisonburg has witnessed a significant increase in the Latino population to around 20 percent of the total population today, as shown in figure 1.5.

Although the city is still mostly white, the proportion of non-Hispanic white residents in the city has declined to around 68 percent (from around 95 percent in the 1970s). The foreign-born population, from Latin America and a range of other countries, stands at about 17 percent of the overall population. Other important geographical aspects of the city include its location at the center of the Shenandoah Valley, around 120 miles from Washington, D.C., and Richmond, surrounded on two sides by mountains—the Alleghenies to the west and the Blue Ridge to the east, home to Shenandoah National Park. Although Harrisonburg is somewhat remote from larger metropolitan areas, it is well connected by interstate highways—I-81 runs through the city and is part of a major trucking route for the East Coast. It has always been (from pre-European settlement times) a crossroads—a meeting point between north-south routes through the Shenandoah Valley and east-west trails. Its heritage is as this connecting point, which allowed it to grow as an agricultural market town through much of its history, serving the productive agricultural economy of that part of the valley. The legacy of this agricultural role is still prominent—grain elevators still rise above the northern part of the downtown, for example—and today a poultry processing center in the city and its environs reflects a new form of agricultural industry. As well as being a smaller-sized regional retail and service center, the economy today is supported by the city's institutions of higher education, most notably James Madison University.

Analyzing the Issues
Becoming a College Town

The presence of a university in a community has long been heralded as an economic, cultural, and demographic boon—and this is especially the case for attracting businesses and new residents to smaller cities (Liu 2015; Andersson, Quigley, and Wilhelmsson 2009). In the case of Harrisonburg, the presence of both a smaller college (Eastern Mennonite University, with about 1,200 students) and a growing, large comprehensive university (James Madison University) has brought an influx of people and spending. James Madison University (JMU) is located about a mile south of downtown, extends over a mile and a half of the city, crossing Interstate-81, and incorporates an expansive and growing footprint of nearly 750 acres. The university has relatively few graduate students (around 2,000, mostly at the master's level) but a large number of undergraduates (about 20,000). The student population is mostly nonminority, about three-quarters from Virginia, with the largest significant portion coming from the mostly suburban Northern Virginia area around Washington, DC, and suburban Richmond and Virginia Beach (James Madison University 2018). As mentioned, the head count of the university has increased markedly over the past two decades, and the faculty and staff employment has similarly expanded to around 3,745 in full-time or part-time jobs (James Madison University, n.d.). A recent study estimates that James Madison University has a significant local economic impact—to the tune of around $516 million. It is estimated that almost 8,500 local jobs are supported by the presence of the university (Rephann 2016). Beyond the immediate numbers of people and their spending, the university has helped bring more attention to the city through its arts and cultural activities and its modest sporting success.

The growth of JMU—in student numbers and physical form—has its roots in strategic decisions made by the university leadership, especially under the tenure of long-serving president Ronald Carrier (Jones 2004, 169). Responding to the growth in demand for higher education in Virginia and especially for greater diversity in the student body and opportunities for a more comprehensive curriculum, a close and productive relationship developed between the university and its governing board, and the Virginia legislature and the state higher education agency (SCHEV). Beyond the raw expansion in numbers, JMU has in recent years responded to particular demands for technology-oriented and health and human services–focused career preparation for undergraduates, with new campus developments for each (Jones 2004, 218). So, although bolstered by mostly favorable state demographics and a growing demand for higher education generally, the university has seen robust expansion by its own particular choices to focus on a comprehensive undergraduate education, nurture a supportive student experience on campus, and take advantage of strategic opportunities as they arise.

The vigorous institutional leadership and collegial relationship with state government have supported James Madison University's growth. But that growth has not been without local tensions and seems to have happened almost independently of its immediate community. Even in the 1970s, local residents were squeamish about the university's expansion: "Many local citizens abhorred the growth and opposed Madison's quest for university status" (Jones 2004, 170). Expansion nevertheless continued with increased energy. Such sentiments point to the often marginal role local cities and communities play in the development of their sometimes-dominant educational institutions and the potential for breakdown in town-gown relations: actual problems with traffic, noise, land development, and so on, exacerbated by a perception that external forces are shaping local affairs.

Immigration Boom

Immigration to Harrisonburg is augmented to some extent by the university, but two other drivers have propelled international and especially Latino immigrant growth. As outlined previously, the foreign-born population has risen to around 17 percent of the population, and ethnic diversity has grown significantly, to the extent that the city is less than 70 percent white (very low for the Shenandoah Valley). One driver has been the role Harrisonburg has played as a refugee resettlement center. The Church World Service has been active in the resettling of refugees in Harrisonburg from places of conflict for thirty years, averaging between one hundred and 250 per year, and offering a focus for immigration of others from these refugees' countries of origin (Zarrugh 2008; Community Land Use & Economics Group 2017). The other principal driver of immigration, especially Latino, is the agricultural industry, particularly the various poultry processing plants in the area (Zarrugh 2008). The Latino population is estimated to be around 20 percent of the city total (US Census, n.d.).

Agriculturally, the Shenandoah Valley has long been distinct from much of the rest of Virginia. Smaller family farms predominated, in contrast to the larger plantation and slave-dominated history of rural areas east of the Blue Ridge mountains. European settlement came from the north, by German (including Mennonite) and Scotch-Irish immigrants; mixed with the distinctive physical geography, agricultural development has taken a different direction from elsewhere in the state. In the twentieth century, agriculture also took the form of a focused investment in intensive chicken and turkey raising, precipitating the rapid growth in poultry processing in the central Shenandoah Valley, clustered around Harrisonburg. As early as the 1930s, Harrisonburg proclaimed itself the "turkey capital of the East," and Rockingham County has long been a leading county nationwide for turkey production (Zarrugh 2007, 241). Latino immigration to the area is directly tied to this industry. Generally starting in the 1970s with Mexicans, the industry accelerated and diversified in the 1980s with Salvadorans and Guatemalans escaping strife in their home countries, and it continued in the 2000s with Uruguayans and Hondurans; "the poultry plants have functioned as the main port of entry to local employment for most non-English-speaking immigrants" (Zarrugh 2007, 242). Associated Latino entrepreneurial activities have augmented this rapid expansion in population.

In addition to these particular draws for an international (and recent immigrant) population, many nonimmigrant and non-Latino residents have been active in living up to the city's fitting motto, the Friendly City. This largely welcoming attitude toward immigrants is reflected in a popular yard sign, originating in Harrisonburg (initially as a response to perceived national uncertainties) and commonly seen around the city, now spreading throughout the state, and beyond (see figure 1.6 and Domonoske 2016). For the most part, the city has been supportive of the diverse newcomers. Schools have developed extensive second-language and now dual-language programs. Religious communities and places of worship—Muslim and Latino-oriented Christian—have flourished. The city's ethnic culinary landscape is notably popular and diverse. A highly successful International Festival celebrating this international presence with performances, food, drink, art, and games has become a prime occasion on the community calendar.

Downtown Re-emergence

The trajectory of Harrisonburg's downtown has been not only a revival but also a refocusing. Similar to many other small city downtowns (illustrated by the case

FIGURE 1.6.   Twin community priorities

studies in literature discussed previously), the CBD has transitioned from serving primarily as a business/professional and retail center to offering a much greater focus on recreational and "lifestyle" amenities such as restaurants, coffee shops, and a recent blossoming of microbreweries (four of these downtown in 2018, from none five years earlier). The retail offerings have become more niche and particularly oriented toward artistic endeavors and outdoor activities. Beyond refocusing the types of economic activities in the center of the city, in the last ten to fifteen years the downtown has become more iconic to the identity of Harrisonburg as a whole and more clearly branded, incorporating heritage and architectural iconography and drawing on a clear sense of the place (figure 1.7). These are hallmarks of the Main Street approach (with which Harrisonburg has been active and successfully recognized) and the results of effective messaging and promotion by a dedicated downtown organization, Harrisonburg Downtown Renaissance.

The actions taken downtown (and in some ways repeated in planning across the city) follow many of the precepts laid out in the small city and downtown revitalization literature, with some particular local approaches, present here. As a way of distinguishing the downtown from the suburbs and helping put Harrisonburg distinctly on the map, icons of downtown architecture—such as an historic well, and the courthouse—are used assertively across promotional material and city maps. Harrisonburg Downtown Renaissance has been instrumental in this messaging. Further, the fusion of a downtown sense of place or iconography and the leisure and lifestyle urbanism that has become a larger cultural and economic draw has been notable. The downtown has been officially

FIGURE 1.7. Court Square, Harrisonburg

designated Virginia's first Arts and Cultural District, for instance. Revealing this fusion between place icons and cultural/economic identity, recent promotional materials superimpose modern lifestyle-type activities on to the historic shape of the iconic downtown courthouse (see figure 1.8). Echoing the recommendations of Burayidi (2001) and others, the city has been purposeful about emphasizing distinctive, heritage-oriented, and walkable street design through instruments such as the *Downtown Streetscape Plan* (City of Harrisonburg 2014).

Historic preservation and adaptive reuse of older structures have similarly been emphasized in the downtown core. Such preservation helps maintain the aesthetics and distinctive *place* of downtown. Indeed, historic resources and their economic and cultural value are given a prominent place in the city's *Comprehensive Plan*, reflecting this concern for maintaining and drawing value from the distinctive elements of the city's built environment (City of Harrisonburg 2011). A further dedication can be seen in the robust use of tax credits to support some of the costs of older building rehabilitation. Virginia generally has been a leader in preserving and supporting the preservation of historic structures (Accordino and Fasulo 2014, 1). Offering a further 25 percent tax credit for qualified rehabilitation expenditures through the Virginia Historic Rehabilitation Tax Credit Program, on top of the Federal Historic Tax Credit program, many cities in the state have seen substantial preservation efforts. Over the ten years between 2006 and 2016, Harrisonburg has seen almost $36 million spent

HARRISONBURG
VIRGINIA

FIGURE 1.8. "Sweet Harrisonburg" by local artists Jeff Guinn and Matt Leech, 2015, for Harrisonburg Downtown Renaissance. Reproduced by permission of the artists and Harrisonburg Downtown Renaissance

in the downtown area on historic structures, all supported by these tax credits. Over the life of Harrisonburg Downtown Renaissance (since 2003) there have been 250 historic preservation projects of various sizes downtown. This aggressive use of these rehabilitation tax credits have been of particular value to a small city such as Harrisonburg, where older properties make up much of the distinctive downtown building stock and where other financial resources are limited.

This rehabilitation of buildings has also generated a small boom in adaptive reuse projects that bring new lifestyle amenities and housing to the city's core. A recent $14 million project to rehabilitate an unsightly ice plant downtown has turned it into a complex of apartments, restaurants, a microbrewery, yoga studio, jewelry workshop, coffee shop, and offices. This is the largest of such efforts, of which there have also been a number of smaller-scale projects that have transformed older buildings to house restaurants, coffee shops, retail, or galleries on the first floor and residential units above. Supported by the city's Planning Commission and *Comprehensive Plan*, there is a growing downtown area zoned for mixed use, and developers have been supported in their initiatives to bring new life to these older buildings and to bring more residents downtown. There are now almost 600 residential units downtown, from just 150 in 2003.

In developing the cultural and lifestyle focus of downtown, a notable growth in the number of restaurants has been supported and is evident the economic landscape. Reflecting growth initiated in part by the Downtown Dining Alliance—an organization formed by downtown restaurant owners to cooperate in supporting establishments downtown—the city is home to Virginia's first Culinary District (designated by City Council resolution in 2014). There are now 40 mostly locally owned restaurants in this downtown district, and the city is marketing and promoting this very sellable strength. The rise of craft breweries and the successful development of large events downtown—such as the annual Beer and Music Festival—add to this sense of its recreational purpose and role as a gathering place. Local food and agriculture have been further emphasized (noting the city's historic place as an agricultural market center), with well-supported features such as an active farmers' market downtown.

The recreational and leisure-oriented draw extends to the recognition of the city's geographical location near a national park and national forests. Successful stores include outdoor gear and, especially, bicycle retailers. The city has been recognized as a Top 10 Mountain Biking Town by *National Geographic* magazine for the various efforts to support bicycling. The city has been purposeful about this in terms of internal infrastructure with an official *Bicycle and Pedestrian Plan* (City of Harrisonburg 2017). New multiuse trails recently completed or in planning have helped offer alternative routes within the city. Securing designation as an Appalachian Trail Community and developing the idea of a

FIGURE 1.9.   City of Harrisonburg Comprehensive Plan community planning meeting

Mountains 2 Main Street connection with other local cities have reinforced this connection with outdoor recreation. The city's new branding scheme uses the tagline *by nature* as a further emphasis on its geographical situation and opportunities outdoors.

It is clear that the city—especially downtown—is focusing on its distinctive strengths and assets to build economic resiliency using this cultural and recreational lens. Beyond building on these strengths, the city government has been supportive of developing public-private partnerships (such as a hotel (Hotel Madison) and conference center and a potential downtown park), and it has been especially proactive in developing meaningful engagement with city residents in the development of plans and initiatives. The most recent *Comprehensive Plan* revision has included numerous workshops and genuinely focused and productive community engagement sessions (see figure 1.9). A very active Bicycle and Pedestrian committee made up of interested community members and relevant city staff has been especially effective and prominent in supporting the biking and walking infrastructure and activities of the city. Public design charrettes for the development of a new downtown park were very well attended and drew much local interest, for example. Perhaps drawing on one of the advantages that smaller cities might boast, it reflects a greater civic accessibility for the citizenry with their government.

Underlying Strains

On the surface, things are looking good for Harrisonburg. Many cities in the United States would be thrilled to experience the three-pronged growth Harrisonburg is experiencing, with momentum coming from the university, immigration, and a revived downtown. Of course, most people in Harrisonburg itself have welcomed this growth and the opportunities it brings. However, this analysis must also evaluate these forces thoroughly and consider the challenges or inconsistencies found beneath the encouraging numbers. Such analysis illustrates the sorts of issues that growth can generate—even growth spurred by things (education, immigration, downtowns) considered central to smaller-city success in the twenty-first century. It also deepens the understanding and analysis of how the spurs to growth and the challenges that they prompt can be tied to the smaller size of these cities. Finally, it suggests how the nature of the interaction of these phenomena might exacerbate some of the limits to resiliency in a small city.

First examined are the challenges posed by the growth of the university. The most obvious challenge here is the rapid expansion of James Madison University, which has left the city sometimes scrambling to catch up with regard to transportation services and infrastructure and the sensible planning of off-campus housing. The spatial extent of the university and its continued attention to providing parking for as many student and faculty/staff commuters as possible have exacerbated the suburban sprawl–type growth that is predominant on much of the city's southern and eastern sides. Student housing is isolated in homogeneous areas that are spread across the city, seemingly apart from its fabric, partly because of the rapid, ill-planned growth and the focus on automobile transportation.

Some tension has arisen around particular university projects perceived as the university's absorbing city space, such as a new performing arts center that took over a city block, the purchase and razing of a cooperative farm supply and store, and the university's ongoing purchases of individual properties on the campus margins. Occasional flashpoints reveal the problematic isolation of the student presence in the city around cheap clustered apartment buildings that are somewhat removed from the older fabric of the city—perhaps the most notable example is a student party that got out of hand and became an eight-thousand-student street "riot" in 2010. These individual instances of development pressure or student-community conflict reveal the historic problem of planning that is relatively uncoordinated between the university and the city (which is improving, as subsequently discussed), and consequently the city's sense that in its approach to development and expansion, the university and its population are to some degree an "outsider" force. (The view is complicated, of course, by a recognition of the economic and cultural benefits that the institution brings.)

James Madison University has developed into a significantly sized institution, but it remains a predominantly undergraduate-focused university—it has few doctoral programs and limited major research funding. Therefore it plays a valuable role in the state's higher education landscape, but because of its modest postgraduate programs there are fewer of the research/business-oriented spillovers and spin-offs associated with more comprehensive research-focused universities. This constraint—combined with the internal urban geography of the college presence, the isolation of the younger, undergraduate population, and a strong ebb and flow of the student population as the undergraduates depart for the summer—means that even though JMU is a large force in the city, Harrisonburg is not quite a *college town* in a cultural sense. Indeed, the university is a formidable presence—its budget is twice that of the municipal government, and its student population is around 40 percent of the total city figure—which has sometimes led to some griping from the noncollegiate population, and some tension with the city, especially with regard to property and transportation development. One anxiety is that as the university purchases real estate, that property is no longer subject to city zoning ordinances (potentially undermining planning efforts) and is removed from taxation. As the university displaces more commercial and residential activities (perhaps over the city line into Rockingham County), this may become a greater financial concern. It is perhaps more difficult for the city (government or populace) to embrace the university when it is such a large force and when the city is not yet culturally a college town in the way that nearby cities such as Charlottesville (University of Virginia) and Blacksburg (Virginia Tech) are.

Immigration brings people, spending, and diversity to a place, and Harrisonburg has undoubtedly been stimulated by the infusion of life and income that the large immigrant communities have brought over the last twenty or so years. Again, however, although the headline numbers are enviable, they have also brought challenges. The very rapid growth in international migrants (especially the Latino population) has not brought too much in the way of cultural tension, but it has put significant pressure on the city's budget, especially regarding the city's public schools. The latest Harrisonburg city public schools figures indicate that fifty-six different languages are spoken in the schools, in which students come from fifty-two different countries; 46 percent of school students have "limited English proficiency" and are English language learners; and 71 percent of the school population come from an economically disadvantaged background. This is a challenge for any school system and especially for one that just two decades earlier was much smaller, predominantly US-born, and relatively stable.

It is a special challenge for a small city like Harrisonburg with limited financial resources. A recent study reported that the Harrisonburg school division had the fastest growing enrollment in the state between 2010 and 2016 (all school data from HCPS, n.d.). This enrollment growth has to be accommodated; a new elementary school has recently opened, and the school board and City Council have been engaged in an intensive debate over the potential of building a second high school. The perceived lack of resources (or rather, the impact on the city's borrowing limits) has meant a delay for the approximately $80 million plan—but the community was highly energized over the issue and it was the biggest political story of the late 2010s (figure 1.6).

One of the financial challenges is that despite the burgeoning population numbers, driven largely by students and new immigrants, these groups have not brought vast wealth. The city's per capita income (skewed by the student population in particular at just over $18,000) and household income (just under $40,000) are on the low side because these are not high-income employed populations. The poverty rate is around 28 percent. This situation has also put an upper cap on property prices in the city, with the changes in the public schools also anticipated to dampen demand for city housing, especially vis-à-vis the more suburban surrounding Rockingham County. Another marker that does not help is the low owner-occupied housing proportion of around 37 percent. With many of the new immigrants to the city taking up less-desirable former student rentals, the fragmented urban geography of this distribution has also undermined more coherent city planning.

Finally, the renaissance of the downtown has been an economic and iconic boost to Harrisonburg. Here again the situation is complicated. There are still many physical gaps in the built environment, some of them self-inflicted from an earlier phase of urban renewal (Ehrenpreis 2017, 165), some a result of the sprawl-producing development and economic transitions common to most American cities in the twentieth century (see Duany, Plater-Zyberk, and Speck 2000, for example). Harrisonburg Downtown Renaissance—the downtown-supporting organization that helps to promote the redevelopment of the core—has been highly energetic and has successfully helped to brand the downtown and support the growth of the restaurant and lifestyle focus so clearly evident today. However, that organization and other initiatives have also been slowed by the limited resources available because of the small size of the city and the relatively less well-off population within the city. Needs such as the new high school meant that other initiatives, such as a proposed new downtown park, come up as an either/or proposition against that more pressing need. There is still a view of the modest role of government that means that sometimes it can take some time to see downtown-supportive ideas turned into practice. One of the main challenges for the revival of downtown is the in-between state in which the city in many ways finds itself.

Understanding the Challenges: In-Betweenness and Disconnection

In trying to make sense of the underlying challenges that these three dimensions of growth have brought to Harrisonburg, two analytic observations might be offered: the perils of being a smaller city with the *in-between* status that might imply and the lack of integration between the three poles of growth.

There is a small/mid-sized city paradox and a perilous state of in-betweenness that has emerged in Harrisonburg's experience. These tensions are manifested in different ways and can be seen to emerge from—or lie behind—some of the challenges outlined in the preceding section. Conversations in policy-making circles in the city have focused on how Harrisonburg currently inhabits a middling economic status—between burgeoning wealth and a challenging plight—which has had a tendency to disincentivize significant governmental support for downtown projects. Part of the lack of urgency from the city in regard to a plan for a downtown park that has been around since 2011 is that there is not a pressing need for it—this is not a decrepit Rust Belt scenario—but neither are there the diversified and extensive resources to support such a modest (around four to five million dollars) proposal that might be available in a larger metropolitan area. Harrisonburg finds itself in a position in which things are "OK," which undermines any urgency or significant creativity in downtown or wider city projects; it is not spurred into action because of imminent or existential crises, but it is not able to throw abundant city funds at projects. Hollingsworth and Goebel have pointed to a similar picture in Lowell, Massachusetts, in which the city had to be confronted with a crisis before it was prompted into meaningful action; "this shows that in smaller cities conditions often do get really bad before successful revitalization efforts can take hold" (2017, 38).

This *in-betweenness* or state of being in transition that small cities may find themselves—especially as being neither truly *rural* nor perhaps fully *urban* or *metropolitan* in the qualitative sense of those terms—is exhibited in additional ways in Harrisonburg. Conversations in the Planning Commission and *Comprehensive Plan* work sessions have grappled with how the city can balance appealing to outsiders and visitors as part of an economic strategy while at the same time ensuring a keen focus on developing the community and quality-of-life features for its residents. In a small city like Harrisonburg, with some energy behind the downtown as a destination, it might be tempting to overlook the need for addressing the less glamorous issues within the city limits. The cultural and heritage-oriented focus for downtown might be a sensible approach, but it does reveal another tension between the almost backward-looking appeal to the past identity of the city as a smaller, agricultural "authentic" local center and the more global reach of both the current population and its economic orientation.

While overall the smaller size and more limited resources that that brings to the city have exacerbated some of the problems of growth described previously (in many ways this is the essential paradox—growth, but with a struggle to support that expansion at this size), the transitional nature of the city's culture and politics adds a material context. Although the city's politics have moved more in a pro-government direction and real estate tax rates have increased somewhat, there is still a distinctly careful attitude in the city with regard to fiscal matters. The city council is relatively balanced in a political sense, and there is a hesitancy about increasing taxes or being aggressive with things like business improvement districts (BIDs) or tax increment financing (TIF) (or even architectural review boards) which stems from the more rural, small-town age of the city's heritage. The city has some of the challenges of larger urban areas but is still, at heart, more a small, conservative polity. There is an interesting bifurcation within the municipal government of more progressive and more traditional city workers and leaders. This discussion has described the difficulties that come with not quite being a college town and the challenges that come with receiving a large immigrant population without the diversified economy to fully support opportunities for these groups. Both these things have meant some more significant turnover in population, with students not staying in the city after they graduate and less stable immigrant family presence in the public schools, for instance.

Harrisonburg is the beneficiary of these three areas of growth—the university, immigration, and the downtown. However, the characteristics of growth in one of these areas may have problematic ramifications for the other areas under some circumstances, as discussed previously: the relatively low incomes of the immigrant and student communities, for instance, result in less money available for downtown revival projects. These three growth factors are in some ways interrelated, but to a striking degree, in Harrisonburg these three things are significantly disconnected conceptually, in terms of many processes and in the physical space of the city.

There is very little immigrant presence either demographically or in the cultural presentation of the downtown. The promotion, while not excluding the large Latino population, or other groups, emphasizes recreational and lifestyle urban amenities that are probably beyond affordability for the typical local incomes of these groups. Again, there is not any explicit exclusion, and in many ways the city is thoughtful about being as open as possible in its promotion; there is simply little recognition of the Latino (or other diverse group) cultural presence in the way it is presented, relative to the contemporary demographic significance of these groups. As indicated previously with the notion of the transitional status many growing smaller cities experience, perhaps the culture and promotion of downtown will in time catch up with this demographic shift. Similarly, there appears to be room to develop the interaction between James Madison University and the immigrant communities. The "bubble" of the somewhat nondiverse university appears to preclude much widespread meaningful engagement, especially on the part of the students, despite some notably active individual examples of connection and learning. Furthermore, the student population of the university seems little engaged in the life of the downtown, and this may partly be a product of the undergraduate focus of the university.

This conceptual disconnection is mirrored and perhaps propelled by a set of physical disconnections in the space of the city. The urban geography may undermine efforts to integrate these growth factors. For instance, James Madison University is a large physical presence, but it is almost a mile remote from the downtown core, across barriers such as recently widened roadways that undermine much interaction between the two. If the college were more physically integrated into the central city fabric, the city would likely be more quickly recognized as a college town. Exacerbating this tendency toward locational diffusion is the fragmentation of student off-campus living and its separation from downtown toward more peripheral sections. This also serves to undermine the vitality of downtown. Along with similar fragmentation of much of the immigrant community (and the dispersal of many neighborhoods away from downtown), this means that downtown is forced to focus on enticing people to it (rather than simply being a natural part of the urban day-to-day spatial existence) and to provide extensive parking—which has the effect of *suburbanizing* the downtown and undermining its walkability and distinctiveness.

Reconnecting the Growth

This is clearly a more qualitative and subjective assessment, but there is the sense that Harrisonburg is somehow less than the sum of these three parts, that it is still an *emergent* city, and that there remains a good deal of fragmentation between these things, in concept and in space, that undermines how much that the city is getting from these forces. The three-way disconnections are also hampering the management of the inconsistencies and challenges the growth in these areas brings, and exacerbating some of the pressures wrought simply by facing these things as a small city. Attempts should be made, therefore, to develop better connections between these growth poles. Again, these should be both in terms of processes and the physical space of the city. Already, projects such as a new 231-bed hotel and conference center—Hotel Madison—are showing the potential way forward. This project is the product of a partnership between the city government, JMU, and a private developer, and is located on a prime site in the area between downtown and the campus. This fusion of city-university action, and the fusion of these two hitherto separated spaces illustrates how meaningful connections have the potential to be transformative. Greater efforts have been made more recently to connect city planning with university planning. The latest revision of the city's *Comprehensive Plan* considered not only the plans of JMU, but asserted some broader questions that the city should proactively consider in its growth in light of the growth of the university and its future role.

On the academic side, the university has recently supported efforts to connect more with diverse neighborhoods in the city. A recent gallery, book, and set of events have recognized and celebrated the diverse heritage of one of the city's historically more marginalized neighborhoods (Ehrenpreis 2017). The refugee and Latino populations were very consciously considered and invited to the city's *Comprehensive Plan* revision work groups and discussions, incorporating a much more diverse set of perspectives than the previous iteration. Connecting three worlds, students at JMU have been investigating as part of their academic work the opportunities for marginalized neighborhood development that might come from a new multiuse greenway trail connecting the north part of the city with the downtown. Members of the university and the immigrant community have been important partners in the planning for the Northend Greenway, which should help connect more people to the downtown.

A number of good projects and efforts such as these are underway, and they certainly help. However, it is essential to focus on tying together these three important assets in order for the city to mobilize the advantages that they bring and to ensure broader, more resilient growth for the city. Currently, these three assets are divided in space, and more should be done with the city's land-use planning and transportation infrastructure to bring them together geographically. This must be carried out if the city is to realize a key quality-of-life benefit of a smaller city—greater spatial proximity and (walkable) accessibility. Infill developments should be encouraged, and a deeper focus on residential neighborhoods proximate to downtown would also help to develop this spatial connection.

Another advantageous aspect of a small city, the deeper civic government accessibility and closer social and professional networks, can be mobilized and refined to ensure not only better communication between the university and other parts of the city but especially between immigrant and minority communities and their city government. Relative smallness, quality of life, and accessibility are key advantages of small cities that can serve to help connect these fragmented forces in Harrisonburg.

Harrisonburg has witnessed three important boosts—immigration, university education, and downtown development—in concurrence but perhaps not in significant combination. There is significant disconnection between these three elements of growth, in concept and in space, which has perhaps hindered the ability to manage some of the more challenging features of change. Harrisonburg, it is evident, is a community *in-between* in many ways. As it continues to develop it can use some of the distinctive things about itself and its size and tie together these fragmented elements to fully realize the opportunities that growth brings.

For other smaller and midsized cities, a principal lesson to be drawn from Harrisonburg's challenges and opportunities is the need to work with and use what is characteristic and distinguishing of smaller communities, geographies, polities, and economies. Use these opportunities of size to chart a path that is not an attempt to be a smaller-scale "big city" but instead a city that is qualitatively different and more appropriate to local conditions. Ultimately, a city will be more successful and attractive if the benefits of smallness can be fully realized. Embrace your smaller size—the opportunities of being neither a small town or a big city—not only as an end point, and also as the means through which you reach that destination.

Notes

1. Defined as those in the top 100 ranked nationwide for international migrants as a percentage of their total population; n = 71. Large metropolitan areas (ranked in the top 100 by total size in the United States) and two cities on the United States–Mexico border are excluded from this analysis.

References

Accordino, John, and Fabrizio Fasulo. 2014. *Economic Impact of Historic Rehabilitation Tax Credit Programs in Virginia.* Richmond, VA: VCU Center for Urban and Regional Development. https://www.dhr.virginia.gov/pdf_files/VCU_Historic%20Tax%20Credit%20Report_FINAL_21-1-2014.pdf.

Amin, Ash, and Stephen Graham. 1997. "The Ordinary City." *Transactions of the Institute of British Geographers* 22, no. 4 (December): 411–29. https://doi.org/10.1111/j.0020-2754.1997.00411.x.

Anderson, Jon. 2015. *Understanding Cultural Geography: Places and Traces.* New York: Routledge.

Andersson, Roland, John M. Quigley, and Mats Wilhelmsson. 2009. "Urbanization, Productivity, and Innovation: Evidence from Investment in Higher Education."

Journal of Urban Economics 66, no. 1 (July): 2–15. https://doi.org/10.1016/j.jue
.2009.02.004.

Bell, David, and Mark Jayne, eds. 2006. *Small Cities: Urban Experience Beyond the Metropolis.* New York: Routledge.

Bell, David, and Mark Jayne. 2009. "Small Cities? Towards a Research Agenda." *International Journal of Urban and Regional Research* 33, no. 3 (September): 683–99.
https://doi.org/10.1111/j.1468-2427.2009.00886.x.

Bias, Thomas, Kevin Leyden, and Jeremy Zimmerman. 2015. "Exploring Policy-Maker
Perceptions of Small City Downtowns in the USA." *Planning Practice & Research*
30 (5): 497–513. https://doi.org/10.1080/02697459.2015.1023074.

Burayidi, Michael A., ed. 2001. *Downtowns: Revitalizing the Centers of Small Urban
Communities.* New York: Routledge.

Burayidi, Michael A. 2013. *Resilient Downtowns: A New Approach to Revitalizing Small-
and Medium-City Downtowns.* New York: Routledge.

Christaller, Walter. 1966. *Central Places in Southern Germany.* Translated by C. W.
Baskin. Englewood Cliffs, NJ: Prentice Hall.

City of Harrisonburg, VA. 2011. *Comprehensive Plan for Harrisonburg, VA.*

City of Harrisonburg, VA. 2014. *Downtown Streetscape Plan for Harrisonburg, VA.*

City of Harrisonburg, VA. 2017. *Bicycle and Pedestrian Plan.*

Community Land Use and Economics Group. 2017. *Retail Market Analysis for City of Harrisonburg and Rockingham County, Virginia.* http://harrisonburgdevelopment.com
/wp-content/uploads/2018/01/Harrisonburg-Rockingham-Co-Market-Study
-FINAL-1-7-2018.pdf.

Cresswell, Tim. 2013. *Geographic Thought: A Critical Introduction.* Oxford: Wiley-
Blackwell.

Cresswell, Tim. 2015. *Place: An Introduction.* Oxford: Wiley-Blackwell.

Domonoske, Camila. 2016. "A Message of Tolerance and Welcome, Spreading from
Yard to Yard." *National Public Radio (NPR),* December 9, 2016. https://www.npr
.org/sections/thetwo-way/2016/12/09/504969049/a-message-of-tolerance-and
-welcome-spreading-from-yard-to-yard.

Duany, Andres, Elizabeth Plater-Zyberk, and Jeff Speck. 2000. *Suburban Nation: The
Rise of Sprawl and the Decline of the American Dream.* New York: North Point
Press.

Ehrenpreis, David, ed. 2017. *Picturing Harrisonburg: Visions of a Shenandoah Valley
City since 1828.* Staunton and Charlottesville, VA: George F. Thompson Press and
University of Virginia Press.

Faulk, Dagney. 2006. "The Process and Practice of Downtown Revitalization." *Review of
Policy Research* 23, no. 2 (March): 625–45. https://doi.org/10.1111/j.1541-1338.2006
.00219.x.

Filion, Pierre, Heidi Hoernig, Trudi Bunting, and Gary Sands. 2004. "The Successful Few:
Healthy Downtowns of Small Metropolitan Regions." *Journal of the American Planning Association* 70 (3): 328–43. https://doi.org/10.1080/01944360408976382.

Friedman, Avi. 2014. *Planning Small and Mid-Sized Towns: Designing and Retrofitting
for Sustainability.* New York: Routledge.

Gehl, Jan. 2011. *Life Between Buildings: Using Public Space.* Washington, DC: Island Press.

Gonzales-Val, Rafael. 2011. "Deviations from Zipf's Law for American Cities: An Empirical Examination." *Urban Studies* 48 (5): 1017–35. https://doi.org/10.1177/00420
98010371394.

Harrisonburg City Public Schools (HCPS). n.d. Website. Accessed March 2018. http://
harrisonburg.k12.va.us.

Harrisonburg Downtown Renaissance (HDR). n.d. Downtown Harrisonburg. Accessed January 2018. http://downtownharrisonburg.org.

Harrisonburg Economic Development. n.d. Downtown Harrisonburg Infographic. Accessed February, 2018. http://harrisonburgdevelopment.com/downtown-harrisonburg-infographic/.

Harvey, David. 1982. *The Limits to Capital*. Oxford: Basil Blackwell.

Hollingsworth, Torey, and Alison Goebel. 2017. *Revitalizing America's Smaller Legacy Cities: Strategies for Postindustrial Success from Gary to Lowell*. Cambridge, MA: Lincoln Institute of Land Policy.

Holmes Thomas J., and Sanghoon Lee. 2010. "Cities as Six-by-Six-Mile Squares: Zipf's Law?" In *Agglomeration Economics*, edited by Edward Glaeser, 105–31. Chicago: University of Chicago Press.

Jackson, Peter. 1989. *Maps of Meaning*. London: Routledge.

James Madison University. n.d. Faculty and Staff Data (website). Accessed March 2018. http://www.jmu.edu/oir/faculty-staff.shtml.

James Madison University. 2018. "2017–18 Statistical Summary." http://www.jmu.edu/oir/oir-research/statsum/2017-18/2017-18toc.shtml#STUDENT.

Jayne, Mark, C. Gibson, G. Wait, and D. Bell. 2010. "The Cultural Economy of Small Cities." *Geography Compass* 4, no. 9 (September): 1408–17. https://doi.org/10.1111/j.1749-8198.2010.00380.x.

Jones, Nancy Bondurant. 2004. *Rooted on Blue Stone Hill: A History of James Madison University*. Santa Fe, NM: Center for American Places.

Kinahan, Kelly L. 2019. "Historic Preservation as a Community Development Tool in Legacy City Neighbourhoods." *Community Development Journal* 54, no. 4 (October): 581–604. https://doi.org/10.1093/cdj/bsy035.

Liu, Shimeng. 2015. "Spillovers from Universities: Evidence from the Land-Grant Program." *Journal of Urban Economics* 87 (May): 25–41. https://papers.ssrn.com/sol3/papers.cfm?abstract_id=2586870.

Markusen, Ann, Yong-Sook Lee, and Sean DiGiovanni, eds. 1999. *Second Tier Cities: Rapid Growth Beyond the Metropolis*. Minneapolis: University of Minnesota Press.

Marston, Sallie, John Paul Jones III, and Keith Woodward. 2005. "Human Geography without Scale." *Transactions of the Institute of British Geographers* 30, no. 4 (December): 416–32. https://doi.org/10.1111/j.1475-5661.2005.00180.x.

Martin, Ron. 1999. "The New 'Geographical Turn' in Economics: Some Critical Reflections." *Cambridge Journal of Economics* 23, no 1 (January): 65–91. https://www.jstor.org/stable/23600667.

Mayer, Heike, and Paul Knox. 2010. "Small-Town Sustainability: Prospects in the Second Modernity." *European Planning Studies* 18 (10):1545–65. https://doi.org/10.1080/09654313.2010.504336.

Merrifield, Andrew. 2014. *The New Urban Question*. London: Pluto Press.

Mitchell, Don. 2003. *The Right to the City: Social Justice and the Fight for Public Space*. New York: Guilford Press.

Myers, Garth. 2011. *African Cities: Alternative Visions of Urban Theory and Practice*. London: Zed Books.

Norman, John R. 2013. *Small Cities USA: Growth, Diversity, and Inequality*. New Brunswick, NJ: Rutgers University Press.

Ofori-Amoah, Benjamin, ed. 2007. *Beyond the Metropolis: Urban Geography as if Small Cities Mattered*. Lanham, MD: University Press of America.

Peck, Jamie. 2015. "Cities beyond Compare?" *Regional Studies* 49 (1): 160–82. https://doi.org/10.1080/00343404.2014.980801.

Pitt, Damien, and Ellen Bassett. 2013. "Collaborative Planning for Clean Energy Initiatives in Small to Mid-sized Cities." *Journal of the American Planning Association* 79 (4): 280–94. https://doi.org/10.1080/01944363.2014.914846.

Powe, Michael, Jonathan Mabry, Emily Talen, and Dillon Mahmoudi. 2016. "Jane Jacobs and the Value of Older, Smaller Buildings." *Journal of the American Planning Association* 82 (2): 167–80. https://doi.org/10.1080/01944363.2015.1135072.

Rephann, Terance J. 2016. *The Economic Impact of James Madison University on the Harrisonburg Metropolitan Area and Commonwealth of Virginia.* Charlottesville, VA: Weldon Cooper Center for Public Service.

Robertson, Kent A. 1999. "Can Small-City Downtowns Remain Viable?" *Journal of the American Planning Association* 65 (3): 270–83. https://doi.org/10.1080/0194436 9908976057.

Robertson, Kent A. (2001). "Downtown Development Principles for Small Cities." In *Downtowns: Revitalizing the Centers of Small Urban Communities,* edited by Burayidi, M. A. New York: Routledge, pp. 9–22.

Robertson, Kent A. 2004. "The Main Street Approach to Downtown Development: An Examination of The Four-Point Program." *Journal of Architectural and Planning Research* 21, no. 1 (Spring): 55–73. https://japr.homestead.com/files/ROBERTSO.pdf.

Robinson, Jennifer. 2002. "Global and World Cities: A View from off the Map." *International Journal of Urban and Regional Research* 26, no. 3 (September): 531–54. https://doi.org/10.1111/1468-2427.00397.

Robinson Jennifer. 2005. "Urban Geography: World Cities, or a World of Cities. *Progress in Human Geography* 29 (6): 757–65. https://doi.org/10.1191/0309132505ph582pr.

Ryberg-Webster, Stephanie. 2013. "Preserving Downtown America: Federal Rehabilitation Tax Credits and the Transformation of US Cities." *Journal of the American Planning Association* 79 (4): 266–79. https://doi.org/10.1080/01944363.2014.903749.

Ryberg-Webster, Stephanie, and Kelly L. Kinahan. 2014. "Historic Preservation and Urban Revitalization in the Twenty-First Century." *Journal of Planning Literature* 29 (2): 119–39. https://doi.org/10.1177/0885412213510524.

Ryberg-Webster, Stephanie, and Kelly L. Kinahan. 2017. Historic Preservation in Declining City Neighbourhoods: Analysing Rehabilitation Tax Credit Investments in Six US Cities." *Urban Studies* 54 (7): 1673–91. https://doi.org/10.1177/00420 98016629313.

Sassen, Saskia. 1991. *The Global City: New York, London, Tokyo.* Princeton: Princeton University Press.

Smith, Neil. 1984. *Uneven Development: Nature, Capital, and the Production of Space.* Athens: University of Georgia Press.

Smith, Noah. 2017. "A Road Map for Reviving the Midwest." *Bloomberg,* December 26, 2017. https://www.bloomberg.com/view/articles/2017-12-26/a-road-map-for-reviving-the-midwest.

Soja, Edward W. 1989. *Postmodern Geographies: The Reassertion of Space in Critical Social Theory.* London: Verso.

Tapp, Renee. 2019. "Layers of Finance: Historic Tax Credits and the Fiscal Geographies of Urban Redevelopment." *Geoforum* 105 (October): 13–22. https://doi.org/10.1016/j.geoforum.2019.06.016.

Tuan, Yi-Fu. 1974. *Topophilia: A Study of Environmental Perception, Attitudes, and Values.* New York: Columbia University Press.

Tumber, Catherine. 2011. *Small, Gritty, and Green: The Promise of America's Smaller Industrial Cities in a Low Carbon World.* Cambridge, MA: MIT Press.

United States Census Bureau. n.d. Website. Accessed February 2018. https://www.census.gov/data.html.

Ward, Kevin. 2008. "Editorial—Toward a Comparative (Re)turn in Urban Studies? Some Reflections." *Urban Geography* 29 (5): 405–10. https://doi.org/10.2747/0272 -3638.29.5.405.

Way, Henry. 2016. "Beyond the Big City: The Question of Size in Planning for Urban Sustainability." *Procedia Environmental Sciences* 36:138–45. https://doi.org/10 .1016/j.proenv.2016.09.024.

Weck, Sabine, and Sabine Beisswenger. 2014. "Coping with Peripheralization: Governance Response in Two German Cities." *European Planning Studies* 22 (10): 2156–71. https://doi.org/10.1080/09654313.2013.819839.

Whyte, William H. 1980. *The Social Life of Small Urban Spaces*. New York: Project for Public Spaces.

Zarrugh, Laura. 2007. "From Workers to Owners: Latino Entrepreneurs in Harrisonburg, Virginia." *Human Organization* 66, no. 3 (Fall): 240–8. https://www.jstor .org/stable/44127373.

Zarrugh, Laura. 2008. "The Latinization of the Central Shenandoah Valley." *International Migration* 46, no. 1 (March):19–58. https://doi.org/10.1111/j.1468-2435.2008.00435.x.

2

BUILDING CIVIC INFRASTRUCTURE IN SMALLER CITIES

Lessons from the Boston Fed's Working Cities Challenge on Paving the Way for Economic Opportunity

Colleen Dawicki

A graduation rate that rose from 52 to 72 percent in six years.[1] A 10.5 percent increase in the labor force participation rate. Population growth of 10.1 percent.[2] Lawrence has too often served as the "poster city" for decline in Massachusetts's smaller industrial cities, but its story is much more complex—and as these statistics demonstrate, hopeful—than headlines suggest. Although the "hopeless smaller city" narrative still persists in the media, it is increasingly clear that there is much that these communities can do to rewrite their stories. Smaller cities will never be insulated from the kinds of economic shocks that decimated manufacturing industries and then populations, but local leaders and their institutions can make a real difference for their cities and residents through their approaches to economic development, human capital development, and quality of life.

The playbook on effective strategies in these domains is growing ever thicker: reinvesting in historic downtowns, focusing on business retention as well as recruitment, leveraging historic and cultural assets, building the capacity of small businesses, strengthening neighborhoods, and developing regional approaches to economic development are among the pathways smaller cities are encouraged to pursue.[3] But as the Boston Fed's research on revitalizing smaller industrial cities illustrates, it's not only what you do—it's how you do it. Implementing technical solutions like these requires both capacity and infrastructure: capacity to implement effectively and adaptively, and the infrastructure with which this capacity is housed, resourced, and sustained.

Indeed, in a study of what it takes for smaller industrial cities to achieve resurgence, the key factor identified by Boston Fed researchers was effectively a strong civic infrastructure—high-capacity leaders, organizations, and networks that mobilized residents and resources—that allowed the community to pursue a shared vision and implement technical strategies to achieve it (Kodrzycki and Munoz 2009).

This finding was important for the Boston Fed, where our community development efforts seek to advance economic opportunity in smaller industrial cities across New England. This inspired a question: what would it take for the Boston Fed to support smaller industrial cities in strengthening their civic infrastructures and thereby advance economic opportunity for low-income residents? Our hypothesis was that if we provided financial and technical support to cross-sector teams pursuing a shared result that benefits their low-income residents, then those teams would build capacity and make lasting improvements to their cities' civic infrastructures.

This hypothesis was named the Working Cities Challenge (WCC), and five years after its 2013 launch in Massachusetts, we have early but promising evidence that this hypothesis was correct.[4] The four cities that won the initial round of the competition showed meaningful gains in capacity over the course of the three-year competition. Their teams have deployed systems-level strategies that will sustain change beyond the grant period. They have empowered new voices through resident engagement and improved their practices as a result of introducing new perspectives to their leadership tables. Learning has been prioritized, and data is increasingly used to shape, improve, and adapt approaches in ways that were not happening earlier. Most importantly, the capacity to lead collaboratively across sectors and silos has fundamentally changed the way business is done in these places, resulting in a stronger civic infrastructure that will enhance these cities' responses to new challenges or opportunities far beyond the life of their Working Cities Challenge grants.

These places have already begun to leverage their more powerful civic infrastructures to achieve better results for their low-income residents. The Lawrence Working Families Initiative has connected over 200 parents to new or better jobs, resulting in an average wage increase of 25 percent. Holyoke's SPARK initiative has generated thirty-three new businesses that employ eighty-two people. Large parcels of vacant real estate in downtown Fitchburg are being developed to re-energize the neighborhood. Chelsea Thrives is gaining traction in reducing its crime rate by fundamentally shifting the way the city of Chelsea identifies and supports high-risk people and families.

Begun three years ago, these efforts will take years longer to bear the kind of fruit that sustains lasting, population-level change. But the work of these teams provides important lessons not only for their Working Cities Challenge peers in subsequent rounds in Massachusetts, Rhode Island, and Connecticut, but also

for smaller industrial cities throughout New England and beyond that are seeking lessons in making and sustaining change in complex, underresourced environments. Those lessons include the following:

1. Collaboration is given the highest priority. To do this effectively and
   leverage collaboration for results, teams benefited from structured
   incentives, flexible funding, and focused capacity-building to support
   working in new and different ways.
2. The Working Cities Challenge emphasizes and practices an ethos of
   learning and adaptation, which gives teams the flexibility to reassess
   and shift in ways that unlock important progress.
3. The role of dedicated leadership in the form of full-time Initiative Directors
   has been invaluable to keeping the collaboration moving forward. It also
   pushes leaders and organizations to think more intentionally about
   leadership development: in addition to how the work will be sustained,
   who will be poised to lead it?
4. The pursuit of systems change requires teams to informally assess and
   influence each dimension of civic infrastructure. At the same time, a
   city's civic infrastructure itself—the way resources are allocated or the
   process of engaging residents in decision making—can be an important
   target for systems change.
5. The branding of this initiative and the spotlight it shines on often
   neglected smaller industrial cities has paid off tremendously for winning
   teams, both through their ability to leverage their initial awards and
   through their ability to collectively attract investments from national
   philanthropy that recognizes the promise of investing in smaller—and
   often more nimble—systems and cities.

In an effort to model the learning orientation we ask our teams to demonstrate,
the Boston Fed readily acknowledges that we have much more to learn when it
comes to strengthening civic infrastructure in smaller cities. Since we last reflected
on lessons and adaptations, there is a new and growing set of learning questions
we are pursuing in order to understand and respond to the level of readiness that
cities need in order to compete in the WCC; the influence of city size on a team's
ability to succeed in the WCC; the degree to which progress on a shared result is
linked to progress strengthening civic infrastructure; the influence a sharper focus on racial equity will have on teams' initiatives; the role that leadership development can play in bolstering and sustaining civic infrastructure gains; and what
it takes to sustain these initiatives beyond the three-year grant period.

In addition to key lessons and examples emerging from the Working Cities
Challenge on what it takes—and what it looks like—to strengthen civic infra-

structure, this chapter also shares some tools that the Boston Fed has prototyped to help cities better understand, talk about, and improve their civic infrastructures in order to enhance their long-term prospects for resurgence.

Working Cities Challenge Background
History

The Boston Fed's Regional and Community Outreach division is concerned with advancing economic opportunity for New England's low-income and moderate-income communities, and the majority of those communities are smaller cities that reached peak population and productivity through manufacturing. Springfield, Massachusetts, is one of our biggest, and its barriers to revitalization—steep declines in population, manufacturing, and workforce participation coupled with insufficient growth in educational attainment—became the focus of our research and outreach staff from 2008 to 2010. In the process of looking at specific issues like low labor-force participation, and small business development, a broader question was pursued: can cities that have lost as much ground as Springfield achieve economic resurgence, and if that is possible, what does it take to achieve?

This question was answered through an investigation into the trajectories of twenty-five of Springfield's peer cities across the country, ten of which recorded substantial gains for their residents.[5] While strategies varied, the importance of a strong civic infrastructure remained constant: sustained collaboration across individuals, institutions, and sectors underpinned each community's turn-around narrative (Kodrzycki and Munoz 2009). This unexpected finding led the Boston Fed to another question. If a strong civic infrastructure is what it will take for Springfield and other struggling, smaller cities in New England to achieve better outcomes for their residents, then what does it take to strengthen civic infrastructure?

Our pursuit of that question led us to an exploration of models that advance cross-sector collaboration and systems change, including models that pursue *collective impact*. It also introduced us to the idea of a competition for funding and the benefits that such an approach could have on building the capacity of communities seeking resources in new and different ways. And as we looked at approaches for building civic infrastructure, we also realized the importance of building a cross-sector, collaborative infrastructure of our own. This became our Steering Committee, populated by public, private, nonprofit, and philanthropic leaders from Massachusetts, through which we decided that a pilot would be most feasible given an established, state-level commitment to supporting the places branded as Gateway Cities.[6]

With the support of our Steering Committee, the Working Cities Challenge was piloted with a competitive grant opportunity made available to twenty Massachusetts cities with high poverty and low educational attainment, with populations between thirty-five thousand and 250 thousand. In Round 1, four cities—Chelsea, Fitchburg, Holyoke, and Lawrence—were awarded three-year grants by an independent, cross-sector jury. Thanks to the early success of that round, in 2015 a second Massachusetts round was introduced for the initially nonwinning cities, and the WCC has subsequently introduced the model to Rhode Island and Connecticut.

Model

While the model has evolved considerably on the basis of lessons from the pilot round of the WCC, the overarching theory of change of the Working Cities Challenge is that teams will translate their short-term efforts to build capacity and pursue a shared result into a stronger civic infrastructure (Benderskaya and Dawicki 2017). This stronger civic infrastructure will then be leveraged to improve economic and quality-of-life outcomes for their cities' residents, much like the "resurgent cities" cited in the Boston Fed's research have done.

This theory is put into practice through the key features that comprise our approach:

- A state-level steering committee informs the development and implementation of the competition to ensure that the WCC is adapted for the context of each state and their cities.
- Funding is provided by state government, the private sector, and philanthropy (local and national); no funding is provided by the Boston Fed.[7]
- Staffing is provided by the Boston Fed to manage the competition and support the winning teams during implementation.
- A set of core elements guides how teams approach their work, to ensure that teams make progress toward their shared result while strengthening civic infrastructure:

    Collaborative leadership: the ability to work together across the nonprofit, private, and public sectors to achieve a shared, long-term vision;
    Community engagement: authentic involvement of residents that empowers them to participate in the development and implementa-

tion of your initiative, with an intentionality around race, equity, and inclusion;

Learning orientation: the willingness to tackle hard questions, use evidence to inform your decisions about strategies and priorities, and change course when needed; and

Systems change: altering activities, priorities, resources, capital flows, and/or decision-making structures within a larger system in order to better solve a problem or deliver services.

- Design grants of $15,000 were awarded by an independent jury to a large subset of eligible teams (ten each in Connecticut and Massachusetts, and seven in Rhode Island) that demonstrated readiness. Grants supported six months of planning, during which the Boston Fed convened team capacity-building workshops.
- Implementation grants of $400,000 to $475,000 were awarded by an independent jury to teams that made progress in the design phase and developed compelling initiatives to achieve an ambitious, ten-year shared result. Grants were for three years and were matched locally to ensure that teams had sufficient resources to hire Initiative Directors and implement strategies.
- Coaching and technical assistance were provided by the Boston Fed staff and external consultants over the course of implementation.
- A learning community brought teams together several times a year to build collective capacity and exchange ideas.
- Independent evaluations of each round were performed to advance the Boston Fed's understanding of how to support teams in the short term and how to improve our model across rounds.

WCC Implementation Illustrated

What does this model look like in practice? In Connecticut our most recent round reflects our best learning from previous rounds. It began with an effort to secure commitments from state-level, cross-sector stakeholders to fund and champion a round of the competition. Many of those funding partners joined the Steering Committee to help the Boston Fed shape the competition process, which kicked off with an announcement in October 2016 that sixteen cities would be eligible to compete for $15,000, six-month design grants. All sixteen applied, and ten were selected by a jury composed of steering committee members who scored applications and conducted interviews to assess which teams were design ready.

Those ten teams embarked on a six-month process of growing and building relationships within their teams, engaging residents, learning more about the challenges they intended to address, and building capacity in the core elements through four day-long sessions facilitated by the Boston Fed. Those sessions featured practitioners sharing lessons from their own cross-sector, collaborative work, including Initiative Directors from Round 2 teams in Massachusetts. They concluded with homework assignments that helped the Boston Fed gauge progress and ensure that the design phase was on track to produce competitive, implementation-ready applications.

Nine teams emerged from the design phase with applications for $450,000 implementation grants (one team decided not to proceed). The steering committee again served as the jury, reviewing teams' submissions and conducting interviews to assess teams across a set of criteria that assessed progress during the design phase, capacity and alignment across the core elements, and the strength of teams' approach to understanding and pursuing a feasible pathway to their shared result. Five teams prevailed in that process, yielding the cohort of WCC winners in Connecticut who will receive not only three years of implementation funding but also coaching and technical assistance from the Boston Fed, opportunities to work together across cities to advance learning, support and advice from the steering committee, and independent feedback on their progress through the evaluation.

While the competition processes across rounds have yielded important lessons for our model, it is the work of the winning teams themselves that has contributed most significantly to our understanding of what it takes to support cities as they undertake the complex work demanded of them by the WCC. As of February 2018, we had sixteen unique cities, teams, and initiatives from which to draw lessons. Because each round is at a different stage of the work, they all stand both to inform and to benefit from adaptations along the way. Appendix A features details on winning cities and their initiatives.

Measuring Civic Infrastructure

Before shifting to sharing evidence that—and reasons why—the WCC is positively impacting civic infrastructure, it's important to address how we are gathering that evidence in the first place. Moreover, some of our emerging lessons about impacting civic infrastructure relate to measuring it. As the saying goes, "What gets measured gets done." So, what impact might it have on teams and cities if we put a more intentional focus on addressing and tracking progress on civic infrastructure during the WCC, rather than wait to put together an assessment until the end of the grant period?

Current Approach to Measuring Civic Infrastructure

A key feature of our model is that an independent evaluation assesses the impact of the WCC for each round at key intervals: the end of the design phase, the start of implementation, the midpoint of the grant period, and the conclusion of year three. These assessments offer key insights on how teams are progressing, the degree to which that progress reflects or demands something more than or different from our model, and whether that progress is putting teams on a path toward lasting civic infrastructure gains.

Our most recent insights on the WCC's impact come from the final evaluation of Round 1, which concluded in September 2017. Unlike the midpoint evaluation for this round, which assessed teams' progress implementing their strategies and integrating the core elements, this review looked at how teams translated those things into broader civic infrastructure gains.[8] Through surveying and interviewing key stakeholders in each city, observing the teams at work, and reviewing teams' grant reports and other documentation of their work, the final evaluation assessed civic infrastructure using the following outcomes that reflect the WCC theory of change: (1) expanded and sustained collaborative leadership; (2) the value of core elements in advancing shared result, and the diffusion of core elements within partner organizations; (3) resident engagement; and (4) external recognition and resources. See appendix B for the detailed rubric Mt. Auburn Associates used to inform their assessment of teams' progress toward the WCC's overarching civic infrastructure goals.

Exploring Additional Tools

While the analysis conducted at the close of Round 1 offers important insights about the WCC and civic infrastructure, it also leaves us with some important questions around cities' baseline levels of civic infrastructure. To what extent does a team's starting point affect or reflect their ability to make progress? Further, because "what gets measured gets done," we'd like to know whether measuring civic infrastructure at the city level—even for smaller cities without a resource-intensive intervention like the WCC—could help cities target scarce resources toward areas in which progress will make the most difference. While there are secondary measures that may have utility as indicators for some key dimensions of civic infrastructure, including nonprofit density, voter turnout, resource attraction, and individual philanthropy, factors such as leadership and collaboration prove much harder to gauge (Dawicki 2013).

Working with the Lawrence Partnership, a cross-sector group of leaders in Lawrence advancing inclusive economic development, we piloted a survey of nearly one hundred city leaders to assess their perceptions of civic infrastructure across its dimensions with questions like, "To what extent do citizens, government, private companies, and nonprofits work together to solve community problems?" (Examples of survey questions are included in appendix C.) In partnership with graduate students from Northeastern University, we used similar questions to measure civic infrastructure through the perceptions of leaders with a statewide perspective (working in state or federal government as well as philanthropy) to determine whether this target group could provide insights across multiple cities. (See appendix D for sample questions.) Both these tools show promise, and we hope to test them on a larger scale and across more cities and states to find ways to simplify the methodology or even to identify proxy indicators that can be measured through secondary data alone.

How Is the WCC Impacting Civic Infrastructure?

The independent evaluation of Round 1, completed in early 2018, objectively validated the story that our winning teams were telling us: that their capacity had grown significantly as a result of the WCC and that this had translated into strengthened civic infrastructures. Mt. Auburn Associates found "substantial evidence that the WCC teams have generated outcomes for their respective communities that extend well beyond progress toward their shared result but ultimately affect the communities' capacity to tackle any challenges in the future, regardless of the specific goal" (Mt. Auburn Associates 2018). What does that substantial evidence include? The Round 1 evaluation found the following effects on leaders, organizations, networks, resident engagement, and resources.

Impact on Leaders

Foundational to the progress made by teams was the degree to which participating leaders strengthened their connections and collaborative capacity. In a survey of WCC team members across the four cities, 92 percent agreed that their WCC initiatives yielded new or deeper relationships and/or catalyzed changes in perspectives among local leaders. Team members expect that this will have a lasting influence on how their cities approach challenges or opportunities. One participant shared, "The relationships that have been formed are not going to go away. When there's a new grant, everyone's already thinking about how we can collaborate" (Mt. Auburn Associates 2018).

Winning teams from future rounds have observed how even the six-month design phase meaningfully changed leaders' connections with each other. In a survey of design phase participants, one respondent noted, "The design phase brought greater visibility to stakeholders that are less well known than the major institutional players. We were able to recognize the value those stakeholders brought to the process and will bring to the initiative."

In some cases, teams are already moving beyond strengthening leadership capacity among the team and toward putting systems in place to sustain a strong—and more diverse—bench of leaders. This has included identifying and adding members to their teams, but it is also extending to influence civic life. Chelsea's Board Leadership Boot Camp has prepared over fifty residents for positions on municipal boards and commissions, and a majority of participants now serve their communities in this capacity. The Round 2 teams of Pittsfield and Lowell are also pursuing inclusive leadership development strategies aimed at diversifying the voices of appointed and elected leaders through candidate nights and efforts to make their City Council meetings more accessible.

Impact on Organizations

Each team experienced leadership turnover in the course of the WCC, and that fact of life makes it particularly important that the capacity changes at the individual leadership level spill over to affect those leaders' organizations, too. The evaluation found strong progress in the area of collaboration—a majority of organizations reported an increased level of engagement within and across sectors, with 75 percent reporting increased engagement with nonprofits and businesses since the WCC began.

Public sector turnover presented a significant threat to teams in both Fitchburg and Chelsea, where the now-departed mayor and city manager, respectively, played important roles in winning the WCC. These initiatives proved resilient in part because teams took quick action to engage those leaders' successors. However, the teams had also developed other relationships in city government to deepen public sector engagement before those transitions happened, and that engagement would have proven difficult to undo.

Almost every team included a higher education partner, and in the case of Fitchburg State University (FSU), the WCC significantly enhanced the way that anchor institution contributes to the city's civic infrastructure. Beyond making investments in the team's target neighborhood, FSU took over the backbone role in the initiative, leveraging its institutional capacity to ensure that the initiative was housed and staffed beyond the WCC grant period—a significant investment that will be critical for the sustainability of this work.

In addition to new and deeper collaboration among organizations, the WCC catalyzed shifts in policies and practices in ways that enhanced organizational efficacy as well as the impact of cities' initiatives. Organizations embedded the core elements in their practices to become more learning- and systems-oriented and improved the ways that they engage residents. For example, Lawrence CommunityWorks, the city initiative's backbone agency, was disinclined to use and analyze data at the start of the WCC. When surveyed at the end of the initiative, staffers reported an increased value and use of data within the organization—a lasting change that will likely enhance the organization's efficacy beyond the WCC.

The increased level of organizational collaboration is also likely to spread and sustain beyond the WCC: 83 percent of participants saw an increased importance in sharing decision making and responsibility across organizations. Perhaps most importantly, 69 percent of Round 1 team members reported that their organizations had changed policies, practices, and/or resource allocations to facilitate stronger collaborations with other entities in their cities.

Impact on Networks

The WCC itself catalyzed a new network in each city by asking each team to develop a formal, cross-sector table to guide the initiative. Because teams committed to pursuing their result for a full ten years, these new networks represent critical elements of cities' current and future civic infrastructures. The impact of the WCC on catalyzing and strengthening networks goes beyond the initiative level. The Round 1 evaluation found new collaborative networks emerging from the WCC, along with new efforts to align existing networks in service of a broader vision for improvement in these cities. The Fitchburg team aligned with the nascent Fitchburg Plan, which resembles the Lawrence Partnership. The business leaders driving this new entity began engaging with the WCC team on capital investment opportunities downtown, and they are also exploring ways to collaborate more deeply on developing a pathway for sustaining the WCC initiative's work beyond the grant period.

Another way that WCC teams are influencing networks reflects the nature of these places and the degree to which they are more tightly knit than their large-city counterparts. Smaller-city leaders often wear multiple hats in their communities, which allow teams to link to more networks and influence more systems. In Lowell, one team member represented a nonprofit and served on the

School Committee, bridging two sectors and issue areas at once. The Waterbury team had two members who represented organizations and also sit on their city's Board of Alderman. These overlapping networks reflected and enhanced teams' power to influence local systems in service of their shared result, and they also reinforced the value of formal and informal networks in helping cities operate more effectively.

Impact on Resident Engagement

The influence of the WCC on resident engagement has bolstered leaders' and organizations' value of and practice with this dimension of civic infrastructure: 72 percent of survey respondents expressed that they now place more importance on seeking diverse resident perspectives to inform their work as a result of the WCC, and 83 percent reported an increase in how they value resident empowerment and leadership.

At the same time, it's difficult to determine how much teams' progress in this area reflected their starting place. The backbone agencies for the Chelsea and Lawrence teams began the WCC with strong practices in place to ensure that resident voices informed and contributed to their work, and this capacity helped ensure not only that their initiatives embedded engagement, but also that organizational partners—including the community colleges in Lawrence and the City of Chelsea—began changing practices to enhance their own work.

The Boston Fed adapted our model for subsequent rounds to provide more targeted technical support in this area when we learned how Round 1 teams' gains in this area were largely reflective of their baseline capacity. We thus expected—and have already seen evidence among Round 2 teams—that this dimension of civic infrastructure will produce stronger gains going forward. In Lowell, where elected officials do not reflect the city's racial and ethnic diversity, the WCC team introduced a new model for resident engagement that promotes inclusivity and accessibility. Groups in the city, including the municipality, have begun using the Working Cities model to design public processes that yield a deeper and more representative level of engagement.

Impact on Resources

The easiest influence to measure with regard to enhanced civic infrastructure is a city's ability to align and generate new resources. To date, the Round 1 teams have used the WCC's investment of $1.8 million to attract another $8.4 million to support their collective work. Importantly, all these investments—from regional and state-level foundations, state and federal grants, and national philanthropy—represented new funding that these cities would have been un-likely to attract without using a cross-sector, collaborative initiative as the hook.

Beyond leveraging the innovative nature of their work, these teams have also made the most of their relationship with the Boston Fed and its funding part-ners to heighten the profile of their cities. For example, the Fitchburg team se-cured an opportunity to bring a team of leaders to an out-of-state workshop hosted by The Kresge Foundation on laying the groundwork for capital invest-ments. Not only did this new resource bolster capacity and connections to out-side resources but it also bolstered relationships among key leaders through the amount of time they spent together on the trip. Meanwhile, both Chelsea and Lawrence were recognized by the Robert Wood Johnson Foundation's Culture of Health Prize, thanks in part to their collaborative work undertaken through the WCC.

Of significant importance is the shift in perceptions among Massachusetts leaders interviewed for the Round 1 evaluation, who expressed hope that the WCC cities emerged from the grant period with stronger prospects for future funding. Indeed, the state's Urban Agenda grant program, explicitly modeled after the WCC, has awarded over one-third of its most recent competitive dol-lars to cities from Rounds 1 and 2 in support of projects that align with WCC initiatives.

Leveraging Civic Infrastructure for Better Results

As some of the aforementioned examples demonstrate, teams have already used their strengthened capacities and infrastructures to pursue new and promising strategies around economic opportunity and quality of life. In a sense, they are applying the adaptive skills developed through the WCC to technical challenges and opportunities—many of which are straight out of the "smaller and/or post-industrial city revitalization" playbook. It is encouraging to see the critical link between civic infrastructure and population-level change resulting in outcomes for low-income residents at this early stage. Though we expect that measurable impacts will take several more years to reach scale, a Boston Fed analysis of key indicators comparing Round 1 cities to their peer cities in Massachusetts sends promising signals: between 2011 and 2016, Chelsea, Holyoke, and Lawrence were among just five of twenty-one Working Cities–eligible places that actually ex-perienced declines in poverty rates.

The Fitchburg team is taking two interconnected strategies out of the estab-lished playbook to mobilize two key assets: its walkable, historic downtown and its public university. Through their engagement with the WCC, FSU has made downtown redevelopment its own strategic priority and followed through with investments in real estate. These investments make revitalization efforts much more likely to succeed, and they may not have happened without the strong relationships that were built through FSU's deep and sustained engagement with a network committed to improving this neighborhood.

Inclusive economic growth is another solution for which cities are encouraged to strive, but pathways for doing so, particularly in places with limited growth, are less clear. Nevertheless, WCC teams have made real headway in ensuring that those most disconnected from their cities' economies are not only targeted beneficiaries but also receive seats at the decision-making table so that local leaders can better understand what it takes to be inclusive in both process and outcomes. The Lawrence Working Families Initiative is on the leading edge of this work. In alignment with the Lawrence Partnership, the team is bridging the language and cultural gaps between parents needing work and employers needing workers. Through strategies such as mock interviews, employer engagement and resident engagement have begun to intersect, and learning proceeds in both directions: prospective workers gain a better sense of what it will take to get hired, while employers learn about the needs and assets of entire sections of the community with which they may not have engaged in the past.

A third area representing significant potential for growth is these cities' approaches to workforce development. Although best practices in this area abound, the Springfield team can attest that the changes that needed to be made in the area of data sharing and tracking alone depended on a foundation of trust. After trusting relationships are built, partners still need to agree on how to use data for learning and not for judgement—or worse, for resource reductions. Though they are still honing their data strategy, the early progress that the Springfield team has made in developing one signaled that they were ripe for more investment. This signal yielded $75,000 from the state's Urban Agenda program that helped the team augment its programming to support even more low-income residents during the second half of their WCC implementation grant.

What Aspects of WCC Make a Difference for Civic Infrastructure?

It was necessary to verify that the WCC is a model that can demonstrate meaningful gains in civic infrastructure, but for most audiences—leaders in smaller cities in particular—the key question concerns the application of these findings. What interventions seem to have the most influence on strengthening the capacity of leaders, organizations, and networks and on mobilizing human and financial capital?

Focus on Collaboration

As the evaluation shows, the WCC had the strongest impact on collaboration among leaders and organizations. This was no mistake: teams had to demonstrate a commitment to collaboration in their applications and jury interviews, write about progress in this area for grant reports, and be subject to an external evaluation on it at the beginning, middle, and end of the grant period. However, collaboration was more than a refrain sung at key intervals across three years; most importantly, it was tied directly to resources.

Simply completing the WCC application provided Round 1 teams and their competitors with their first incentive to collaborate. Although eligible cities had many ideas that might fit the parameters of the WCC, each city was allowed to submit just one application, forcing some early and hard conversations about how local leaders would work together to put forth a single proposal that represented their best opportunity. This requirement has continued across each subsequent round because of its impact in challenging and ultimately strengthening the teams.

The structure of the competition not only incentivized collaboration with dollars but through the incorporation of the design phase it also created a defined space and structure within which a collection of organizations could become a team. Across the evaluations of each design phase, teams referenced the design sessions and the Boston Fed as forcing agents that required them to tackle the hard questions and conversations that broke new ground for building relationships. One Massachusetts design phase participant called this structure "a sturdy enough container to 'hold' some rather uncomfortable conversations." Even two years after the planning period, Round 2 teams reflected on how they had informally tackled thorny issues like competition, power, and race during the long car rides that they shared to attend these sessions. They also talked about how those opportunities helped them know each other as people and not just professionals, which built a foundation of trust on which this work necessarily depends.

The WCC also represents an intentional investment in collaboration. Working in this way often represents a new way of doing business in smaller cities and requires sufficient flexible dollars to make it possible. Even the highest-functioning collaboratives need to be staffed, so the WCC directs dollars to the cost of initiative directors who work full-time in service of their teams' work.

Backbone agencies need funding to cover the cost of initiative director support and supervision, space, and fiscal oversight—more complex than a typical grant because teams often distribute dollars across multiple partners. Effectively, the WCC provided collaborative teams with general operating funds that gave initiatives the security they needed to test new ideas, take risks, and adapt when strategies did not bear fruit—an approach that is otherwise difficult to adopt in resource-limited environments in which dollars are often tied to delivering on specific programmatic commitments.

In addition to the competition structure and resourcing, collaboration was bolstered through coaching and technical support. Perhaps the most meaningful intervention on this level has been training on adaptive leadership. This framework and the supporting tools to which teams have been introduced have helped them make important progress on the complex, human-centered challenges of their work.

Learning and Adaptation

Providing training on adaptive leadership was just one way the WCC encouraged teams to embrace the iterative nature of this work. We also revised our core elements to move away from a sharp focus on data and toward a broader emphasis on learning orientation, which still includes but is not limited to technical capacity to measure progress.

This shift was prompted by a few factors. First, teams were struggling to clear what they perceived to be a too-high bar when it came to the ability to gather, track, and respond to data that reflected their outcomes. What the Boston Fed wanted was not data for data's sake; instead we wanted teams to adopt an ethos that ensured that their strategies evolved in response to and generated the information needed to decide what to shift, scale, or even stop in order to achieve their shared result. This shift was felt by participants in the Round 2 design phase, one of whom appreciated "the use of data as a navigational tool, not a club."

The second thing that pushed us toward learning orientation was that Round 1 teams were making the biggest leaps after they significantly reassessed and adapted their work. In Chelsea, that looked like changing the ten-year shared result upon which their initiative was founded. In Fitchburg, the team reduced the number of their focus areas from six to three, which made the work feel more feasible to a thinly stretched team. Instead of waiting for teams to ask permission to dramatically alter the course of their work as would a traditional grant maker, we decided to encourage and celebrate this kind of adaptation more explicitly in our model.

The final factor that elevated the concept of learning orientation was the observation from our inaugural design phase that learning-oriented teams made the most progress in this six-month span. Teams in Round 2 and in Rhode Island that participated actively and thoughtfully, spoke openly about their challenges, sought data from new and different sources to better understand their challenges, and emerged with new insights about their teams and communities not only made strong progress during the design phase but also appeared to be best poised to put their plans into action at the start of implementation. As a result of this finding in particular, learning orientation was not only cemented as a core element but it also became the leading criterion for selecting implementation grantees in Connecticut.

Value of Initiative Directors

In this complex and adaptive work the role of initiative directors cannot be understated nor can the importance of finding—and supporting and retaining—the right person for this position. Initiative Directors hold a challenging role: in many cases, they are the only individuals whose sole responsibility is to move their initiatives forward, and so a major task is to ensure that the high-level leaders who comprise their teams remain engaged and accountable despite the many demands on their time. In addition to the challenges that come with leading the leaders, which draws heavily on the adaptive skills needed to build trust, communicate effectively, and anticipate (and manage) conflict, initiative directors must also develop and draw upon technical capacities in order to support the team's efforts to use data, engage residents, communicate to stakeholders, and manage resources (including the WCC grant itself). Because each WCC team is responsible for hiring its own initiative director, the backgrounds of people in this role vary considerably on the basis of each team's needs. Accordingly, initiative directors range from younger professionals with five to ten years of experience stepping into a leadership role for the first time to seasoned leaders who can draw on relevant experience and relationships to advance the work of their teams.

An important finding from the Round 1 evaluation was that developing the leadership of initiative directors represented a major step toward strengthening this dimension of civic infrastructure. Two Round 1 initiative directors have translated their success into new public sector leadership roles in their respective cities, which extends the reach of their WCC work into new spheres while making room for two new leaders to build their skills in this role. We look forward to watching how the career paths of the WCC initiative directors spread and sustain the influence of this model in their cities and beyond.

Pursuit of Changes to Systems

The WCC has strongly influenced the degree to which each team's work left a mark on its city's civic infrastructures, because changes to systems require understanding and influencing multiple dimensions of civic infrastructure itself. For any systems change that a team is targeting, they must ask: which leaders need to be engaged and influenced? Which organizations affect the system now, and how might their internal policies and practices need to align with this effort? To what extent can networks be mobilized as contributors or advocates? How do resource flows obstruct or facilitate the changes needed to advance a team's shared result? And how can strengthening resident engagement bolster a systems-change effort or even represent a systemic change by itself?

Some systems changes target civic infrastructure directly. In cities like Pittsfield, several WCC initiatives are changing the way residents are engaged in planning, decision making, and leadership. One change that this team is making across the city is ensuring that residents are compensated for their time, because they are often asked to volunteer their time while working alongside paid professionals in planning and decision-making processes. This first required demonstrating the value of this new way of operating to leaders within the WCC network. Once bought in, those leaders have adapted their own organizational practices to ensure that residents are compensated for participation in efforts beyond the WCC. This systems change has even affected resource flows: a large grant recently awarded to support engagement in the region's cultural sector intentionally allocates resources for stipends to pay residents for their time.

In this case and in the experience of many other teams, systems changes that can be seen and felt at the policy, practice, and resource level often start with a significant amount of unseen work to influence the perceptions and beliefs of systems leaders themselves. Demonstrating the value of paying residents for their time, for example, necessitates understanding how leaders currently value the time of residents. Do they recognize the opportunity cost incurred to attend a public meeting? Have they ever experienced the barriers many residents, especially those living in poverty, must overcome in order to simply attend, including transportation, child care, and language? The Pittsfield team invested a significant amount of time talking about mental models that leaders might hold about low-income residents and how learning about the lived experience of these residents can shift those narratives—a necessary precursor to shifting the policies and practices that make engagement more engaging.

If WCC teams were working in a strictly programmatic space, they may have achieved measurable results sooner by deploying dollars exclusively to scale up existing interventions or fill voids that served low-income residents directly.

Instead the push to change systems has led teams outside of their boundaries and comfort zones. Although changing systems is slower and messier, this is the work that not only makes a lasting difference for community members but also directly pushes a city's civic infrastructure to work differently and better on behalf of its low-income populations.

Elevating Profile of Smaller Cities

An early and enthusiastic advocate for the potential of smaller cities was Living Cities, whose Integration Initiative informed the early design of the WCC. Our partnership provided a valuable comparison between opportunities and possibilities in smaller cities—in which the close connections among high-level leaders help them assemble quickly in response to a challenge or opportunity—and larger cities in which relationship building can take much longer (starting with getting everyone in the same room). This comparison helped Living Cities and other national funders such as The Kresge Foundation and Doris Duke Charitable Trust recognize the value of investing in and learning from more nimble and tightly woven places that have historically struggled to attract their dollars, becoming key investors and partners.

Influential private actors now see smaller cities in a different light as well. The Massachusetts Competitive Partnership, which comprises the state's largest employers, invested heavily in both of this state's rounds because they valued the way that civic infrastructure improves the business climate in these places. In Connecticut, a tremendous number of private sector partners, such as Stanley Black & Decker and Travelers Insurance, not only have invested in smaller cities by contributing to the funding pool but have become highly involved in shaping the competition through participation on the steering and advisory committees. Their level of financial and even personal investment represents a significant shift for Connecticut's smaller cities.

State governments have also strengthened their support for smaller cities. Governors committed significant new dollars to facilitate each state's participation in the WCC despite challenging budgetary environments. Key state officials hold seats on each state's Steering Committee, and their offices have taken steps to align their economic development approaches with the WCC. In Massachusetts, the Office of Housing and Economic Development created the Urban Agenda grant program that explicitly references the WCC in its call for proposals and has borrowed elements of the WCC application review process to guide their own. In Connecticut, the Department of Economic and Community Development integrated the WCC in its Opportunity Zones application process, a promising step to ensure that smaller cities attain a greater level of recognition in that state.

What Comes Next for the WCC: Emerging Lessons and Adaptations

Thanks to the learning orientation of our winning cities, the Boston Fed gained new—and sometimes unexpected—insights about what it will take to better support current and future teams on their paths to achieving results and strengthening civic infrastructure. As we better understand and interpret the questions the teams and evaluators have helped us raise, we expect to continue shifting or augmenting our model as needed to accelerate progress. Questions on our current learning agenda include the following:

What does it take to be ready to engage in collaborative, systems-changing work? The WCC is designed to reward sufficiently ready places that have capacity, momentum, and a foundation of civic infrastructure to build on. The design phase represented a significant adaptation that bolstered capacity for implementation grantees and nonwinning teams alike. And while the sustained progress of nonwinning cities concerns us, so too do the fortunes of cities that lacked the capacity and readiness to even participate in the design phase. What does it take then to prepare lower-capacity, less-ready cities to engage in something like the WCC? Learning more about this question will help us understand the key levers of civic infrastructure building and assess how our model might need to adapt to support even smaller cities in northern New England where we hope to expand.

How does city size affect—or reflect—a WCC team's ability to have an impact on their shared result and on civic infrastructure more broadly? The WCC's definition of *smaller* is rather broad. While the population size is capped to disqualify only one New England city (Boston), winning cities are as small as Newport (population 24,570) and as large as Providence (population 178,851). The core group of leaders on any WCC team typically—and for governance purposes, almost necessarily—hovers around eight to ten members. So, depending on city size, this group may overlap significantly or minimally with the leaders, institutions, and networks that comprise a city's civic infrastructure, affecting the degree to which a WCC initiative achieves meaningful spillover impacts. The Springfield (population 153,991) team is showing signs of promise with regard to influence beyond their team, but we will be interested to learn whether city size requires teams to work harder and/or more intentionally to ensure that their initiatives make a lasting impression.

How much progress do teams need to make on their shared result in order to achieve civic infrastructure gains? The WCC model hypothesizes that if teams pursue a shared result in a way that integrates the core elements, then they will make lasting improvements to their cities' civic infrastructures. Our Round 1 evaluation found this hypothesis to be correct, stating, ". . . improvements to civic infrastructure can be produced as a spillover, a positive externality of the work toward the team's shared result" (Mt. Auburn Associates 2018). But how much progress is enough for that to occur?

A threshold level of progress is likely necessary to ensure that team members value the hard work of collaboration. We hope to learn more about what this threshold looks like and whether it takes the form of better outcomes for low-income residents, the implementation of meaningful systems changes that will logically translate to better long-term outcomes, or something else entirely. Although this question is almost impossible to measure among four Round 1 cities, we should be able to better understand the relationship between the shared result and civic infrastructure across sixteen teams in three states.

How will a sharper focus on racial equity influence the work and impact of the teams? The WCC model has shifted to become increasingly explicit about how considerations of racial equity should be reflected in teams' leadership teams, strategies, and approaches to community engagement, among other aspects of their initiatives. This reflects not only teams' lessons about how racial and ethnic divides in their cities affect the problems that they are trying to solve but also the support that WCC teams have asked for as they have proactively sought to make progress in this area. Responding to teams' needs and ambitions has started with updating the language in our model, but it also requires working with teams to understand the level of progress cities hope to make on this front and the support they need to achieve it. Depending on how our intervention changes, it will also be important to work with our evaluator to learn whether and, if so, how advancing racial equity has a spillover effect on the dimensions of civic infrastructure.

How do we help teams build and sustain the leadership capacity to advance their initiatives and strengthen civic infrastructure over the long term? Although the emphasis of the WCC is on collaborative leadership, doing this well requires strong individual leadership at multiple levels. Capable, collaborative, and adaptive leadership is required of Initiative Directors and of team members themselves. But if these initiatives are to sustain, a pipeline of leaders must be developed to ensure that turnover does not hinder progress and to keep the lessons and values of the WCC alive beyond the grant period. These pipelines must be inclusive across age, race, ethnicity, and gender, particularly in the many smaller cities where leaders do not reflect the growing diversity in their populations. Smaller places in which the leadership bench is shallow from the start can ill afford to ignore the talent that has historically gone untapped if they are to achieve resurgence that is felt by the whole community.

So, what will it take to help cities ensure that they are developing a representative, high-quality pool of leaders who can sustain the capacity built through initiatives like the WCC and the pursuit of better outcomes for low-income residents? The Boston Fed is tackling this question as we consider how to sustain our support of New England's smaller cities beyond the WCC. We expect that this exploration will build on promising practices demonstrated by our teams, including efforts to elevate residents to leadership positions and the professional development gains made by Initiative Directors themselves.

What will it take for teams to sustain their efforts beyond year three? The WCC represents a three-year catalytic investment intended to accelerate teams on a pathway toward a ten-year result. And although we now know more about the ability of the WCC to have a catalyzing effect, we do not yet know what it will take for teams to persist. Will the team stay together? Will they continue to focus on the same shared result? Will they be able to sustain the work at its current level?

In preparation for the end of Round 1, our team conducted a literature review to better understand what sustainability has looked like for similar investments and initiatives. We found an empirical link between long-term sustainability and the following factors:

- Flexible funding for operations and capacity building. In many cases, these funds came from multiple sectors, including team-member organizations themselves.
- A formal plan for sustaining the initiative that goes beyond funding to address governance structures and functions as well as how to respond to emerging needs or challenges. As with any plan, success depended upon teams' ability to carry them out.
- Depth of leadership experience, particularly in the areas of collaborative management and living and working in the community, influenced sustainability regardless of funding level or collaboration structure.
- Distributed leadership among partners, which is essential to keep staff and organizations motivated during times of struggle or turnover.
- Buy-in among community members who can advocate for continued investment, particularly when initiatives are threatened by community shocks or leadership turnover.

The Boston Fed and our Round 1 teams put these lessons into practice through a one-year sustainability planning phase that provided teams with the resources and technical support needed to develop sustainability plans and transition toward new sources of support. This, too, was independently evaluated in 2018 to inform how we approach sustainability with teams in subsequent rounds. Key lessons from that evaluation included ensuring that the work could speak for itself by delivering results in the third year; pushing team members to clearly define their roles and responsibilities, with an emphasis on how individuals will step up when resources go down; determining whether and how to let go of aspects of the work to reduce demands on time and resources; and focusing on communicating the impact and value proposition of the work to ensure sustained support from key stakeholders, including but not limited to future funding partners. A particularly important lesson was that teams need to tackle these topics before the moment of transition is upon them, and in response we now integrate sustainability-planning tools and conversations in the third and final year of our approach to learning and technical assistance.

Takeaways for Smaller-City Leaders and Advocates

More learning questions and responsive adaptations will necessarily emerge as the Boston Fed and the winning teams progress through each round of the WCC. While we expect to have some fascinating insights on what it takes to build civic infrastructure across sixteen smaller industrial cities when the Connecticut round wraps in 2021, leaders in these places cannot afford to wait for a third-party evaluation to guide the way. So, what are some key steps leaders can take now to strengthen their cities' civic infrastructures in ways that allow them to more effectively pursue the strategies that promise progress?

Assess Your Civic Infrastructure

What needs shoring up, and where does your city have strengths it can leverage? The Lawrence Partnership is taking this step to understand not only where progress is needed; these leaders also recognize that naming civic infrastructure as priority and having regular conversations about it are essential to strengthening and leveraging this critical asset.

Invest in People, Not Just Projects and Programs

Developing the capacity of leaders to implement technical strategies effectively will ensure that scarce resources yield the greatest benefits. And unlike specific interventions, capacity has staying power. In cities where leaders tend to play multiple roles at once, these abilities will make a difference across multiple domains of civic life.

Leverage the Power of Size to Change Systems

Smaller cities have smaller systems, so that you can often fit key system leaders in a single room—and they likely already know each other. Changing relationships, policies, and practices is invariably challenging, but when leaders in smaller cities are committed to this, change can be put into motion more quickly.

Build Coalitions for Shared Learning and Advocacy

WCC teams have come together formally and informally throughout the competition, and the ability to exchange lessons, ideas, and challenges has been invaluable for growth and persistence through the shared struggle. Increasingly, those relationships are also turning into coalitions of communities with shared interests in state-level policy. Given their collective legislative influence, there is significant power in working across smaller cities to advance a common agenda, particularly when this leverages the capacity strengthened through the WCC.

Smaller cities benefit from assets and opportunities that larger cities struggle to muster. By building capacity and leveraging their civic infrastructures, these places have a real opportunity to rewrite their stories—and more importantly, change the stories of the low-income families who have shared the long struggle to get ahead.

Notes

1. The views expressed in this chapter are those of the author and do not necessarily represent those of the Federal Reserve Bank of Boston (the author's employer) or the Federal Reserve System.

2. From 2000 to 2016, via the Federal Reserve Bank of Chicago's Peer City Identification Tool (https://www.chicagofed.org/region/community-development/data/pcit).

3. Examples of playbooks include Hollingsworth and Goebel 2017; Lambe, Longworth, and Stauber 2017; Kresge Foundation, Initiative for Responsible Investment, and the Federal Reserve Bank of Boston 2016.

4. This chapter provides an evaluation of the 2014–17 progress and lessons learned from cities receiving Working Cities Challenge grants.

5. The ten resurgent cities included Evansville, Indiana, Fort Wayne, Indiana, Grand Rapids, Michigan, Greensboro, North Carolina, Jersey City, New Jersey, New Haven, Connecticut, Peoria, Illinois, Providence, Rhode Island, Winston-Salem, North Carolina, and Worcester, Massachusetts.

6. More about this designation and its history is available via MassINC: https://massinc.org/our-work/policy-center/gateway-cities/about-the-gateway-cities/.

7. Cross-round funders supporting the WCC in Massachusetts, Rhode Island, and Connecticut include the Doris Duke Charitable Foundation, The Kresge Foundation, Living Cities, and NeighborWorks of America.

8. Evaluation reports can be found at https://www.bostonfed.org/workingplaces.aspx.

References

Benderskaya, Kseniya, and Colleen Dawicki. 2017. "Sparking Change in New England's Smaller Cities: Lessons from Early Rounds of the Working Cities Challenge." *Communities & Banking,* Spring 2017. https://www.bostonfed.org/publications /communities-and-banking/2017/spring/sparking-change-new-englands-smaller -cities-lessons-from-early-rounds-of-working-cities-challenge.aspx.

Dawicki, Colleen. 2013. "Civic Infrastructure in Gateway Cities." *MassBenchmarks,* 15, no. 1 (August): 20–31. https://donahue.umass.edu/documents/vol15i1a.pdf.

Hollingsworth, Torey, and Alison Goebel. 2017. *Revitalizing America's Smaller Legacy Cities.* Cambridge, MA: Lincoln Institute of Land Policy. https://www.lincolninst.edu /publications/policy-focus-reports/revitalizing-americas-smaller-legacy-cities.

Kodrzycki, Yolanda K., and Ana Patricia Munoz. 2009. *Reinvigorating Springfield's Economy: Lessons for Resurgent Cities.* Community Affairs Discussion Paper 2009–03. Boston, MA: Federal Reserve Bank of Boston.

Kresge Foundation, Initiative for Responsible Investment, and Federal Reserve Bank of Boston. 2016. *Capital & Collaboration: An In-Depth Look at the Community Investment System in Massachusetts Working Cities.* https://www.bostonfed.org /publications/one-time-pubs/capital-and-collaboration.aspx.

Lambe, Will, Susan Longworth, and Karl Stauber, eds. 2017. *Looking for Progress in America's Smaller Legacy Cities: A Report for Place-Based Funders.* A joint publication of the Funders' Network for Smart Growth and Livable Communities, and the Federal Reserve Banks of Atlanta, Boston, Chicago, and New York. https:// www.chicagofed.org/Home/region/community-development/community -economic-development/Looking%20for%20Progress%20Report.

Mt. Auburn Associates. 2018. *Working Cities Challenge: Final Assessment of Round 1 Progress.* https://www.bostonfed.org/workingplaces.aspx.

3

DIVERSITY IN THE DAKOTAS

Lessons on Intercultural Policies

Jennifer Erickson

Increasingly, globalized capitalism has resulted in unprecedented quantities of goods, services, ideas, and people circulating throughout the planet, which has provoked a variety of responses at the local level. These responses range from excitement and acceptance of new forms of diversity, to fear, aversion, and panic, depending on the responder's experiences and point of view. Wars, violence, poverty, and climate change are forcing ever more people to flee their homes and seek refuge and opportunity in urban centers. As a result, diversity has become a key concern for cities (Vertovec 2007). The need to address diversity as part of urban policy emerged in Fargo, North Dakota, and Sioux Falls, South Dakota, in the 1990s and 2000s when thousands of refugees from Asia, Africa, and Europe—more than ever before then—were resettled to these small cities, bringing new and different languages, (dis)abilities, religious practices, family structures, and skin tones. North Dakota and South Dakota, along with Idaho, Nebraska, and Vermont, have resettled more refugees relative to their populations than any other states (Guo 2015). These states share several features, including low population density, low unemployment rates, and the lowest rates of racial and religious diversity in the country.

This chapter analyzes a range of responses by the overwhelmingly white, Christian, English-speaking dominant population to the influx of refugees and makes the case that attracting and promoting diversity and embracing intercultural policy frameworks provide a competitive advantage for small and midsized American cities. North Dakota and South Dakota have some of the strongest economies and lowest unemployment rates in the country, due in part to the oil boom in the western part of North Dakota, software and biomedical fields in the eastern part of the state, and biomedical and banking industries in South Dakota. Due to strong economies and to their refugee resettlement programs, the cities of Sioux Falls and Fargo have become more diverse and intercultural and, therefore, more resilient. As a result of refugee resettlement, the two cities have instituted policies and ethical practices that acknowledge diversity, actively combat discrimination, and foster dialogue. These steps have helped them prosper, promoting economic growth, social cohesion, and civic health. This chapter argues that while the specific socioeconomic and cultural characteristics and everyday practices outlined here are unique to Fargo and Sioux Falls, the lessons learned about refugee resettlement have broader implications for other small and midsized cities, especially those eager to attract and promote diversity and to develop intercultural policy frameworks.

Background and Overview of Methods

This study is based on long-term ethnographic research as well as professional experiences. From 2001 to 2002, I worked for Lutheran Social Services Center for New Americans, the refugee resettlement agency in Sioux Falls. I provided case management to single mothers, families, and individuals experiencing difficulties achieving self-sufficiency in the allotted eight-month period, and to secondary migrants, refugees who were resettled elsewhere in the United States, but migrated to Sioux Falls in search of economic opportunities or to reunite with family.

Ethnography is a qualitative research method that uses long-term everyday engagement in a community. Ethnography is also a product of research presented in a medium such as a nonfiction book or film. The primary method for ethnographers is participant observation, which means observing everyday practices that are recorded in field notes and then coded and analyzed for patterns. Ethnographic methods also include interviews, discourse analysis, mapping, theory, and primary and secondary historical sources to contextualize a given place or group of people, among other possible methods. Ethnographers triangulate or cross-check their data from field notes, interviews, historical patterns, and multiple theoretical perspectives.

In 2005, as a doctoral student I conducted three months of ethnographic research in Sioux Falls on the relationship between refugee resettlement and the city. Methodologies included dozens of hours of participant observation recorded daily in field notes, analysis of news and social media about refugee resettlement, and forty-five semistructured interviews with people who worked with refugees, including staff at human service agencies, healthcare clinics, schools, employers, and nonprofit organizations; volunteers; housing managers; police officers; and staff of elected officials. I also conducted participant observation and interviews with Southern Sudanese refugees, one of the largest groups of New Americans in the city. I returned to Sioux Falls in 2012 to conduct two months of additional research to observe changes in this city's socioeconomic and cultural landscape and the ways in which Southern Sudanese experienced and contributed to the city. Since 2012, I have visited the city annually, as my parents live about thirty miles away, where I grew up. These visits are not primarily for research, but I visit friends, former colleagues, and research collaborators who informally update me on the situation for refugees and changes to the city.

In 2007 and 2008, I conducted one year of dissertation fieldwork on the ways in which refugee resettlement transformed the city of Fargo from the 1980s to 2010s, focusing on the relationship between the refugee resettlement agency, county welfare agency, and volunteers to better understand relationships between public and private sectors with regard to refugee resettlement and diversity. I also compared the ways in which white Bosnian Muslims, Bosnian Roma, and Black Southern Sudanese Christians adjusted and contributed to the city (Erickson 2020). Methodologies included participant observation at meetings, at cultural and political events, and in the homes of Bosnians and Southern Sudanese; sixty semistructured interviews with social service providers and New Americans; and discourse analysis of demographic and economic data, news, and social media. I returned to Fargo in 2010, 2011, 2016, and 2019 to research and observe changes over time.

Key Socioeconomic Characteristics of Fargo and Sioux Falls

Fargo and Sioux Falls are located 240 miles apart on Interstate 29, both across the border from Minnesota, on the eastern edge of the Great Plains. In 2016, the cities had populations of roughly 120,000 and 170,000, respectively. Both are the largest cities in their states and within a nearly 200 mile radius. They are growing steadily at a 2 percent annual rate (Data USA 2016). Downtown Sioux Falls and Fargo share common features, including historic districts that experienced long-term degradation followed by a process of urban renewal, rehabilitation, and gentrification. They feature breweries, hotels, locally owned shops and restaurants, and riverside bike paths. Downtown Sioux Falls is located near the banks of the Big Sioux River. Nearby is Falls Park, a 123 acre park featuring a historic mill and water falls after which the city is named. Downtown Fargo is located on the banks of the Red River, which forms the border with its sister city, Moorhead, Minnesota. Sioux Falls and Fargo serve as tourist destinations and art and cultural centers. They also have areas dominated by national chain box stores, malls, and strip malls, where new homes and apartment complexes seem to clone themselves on the prairie landscape and resemble other retail landscapes across the country.

Over the last fifty years, Fargo and Sioux Falls have transformed from cities centered on manufacturing and agriculture to more diversified economies that include finance and insurance, healthcare and social assistance, wholesale and retail trade, and food service. They have some of the lowest unemployment rates in the country, hovering around 4 percent, and the Great Recession barely registered in either city. The 14.6 poverty rate in Fargo is slightly higher than the national average of 14 percent but is lower in Sioux Falls at 11.7 percent. However, there are significant differences in poverty rates based on race. According to the Henry J. Kaiser Family Foundation (2017), poverty rates among Black, Hispanic, New Americans, and Native Americans are between 30 and 40 percent, compared with 10 percent of whites. Before 1990, the population of both cities was 99 percent white and the largest minorities in the states were Native Americans, most of whom lived on tribal land. In 2016, around 85 percent of the cities' populations were white (table 3.1). Refugee resettlement is a notable cause for this shift in racial demographics and religious and linguistic differences. The primary reason refugees are resettled to Fargo and Sioux Falls is the availability of jobs.

The largest industry in both cities is the biomedical field. Denny Sanford, an entrepreneur, venture capitalist, and multimillionaire, accumulated most of his wealth by using South Dakota's anti-usury laws to attract Citibank's credit card division and then offered cards to people with poor credit scores while monitoring them to avoid delinquencies. Sanford has distributed his wealth to hospitals and clinics, among other organizations, across the region and nationally. After his $400 million donation in 2007, Sioux Valley Health System changed its name to Sanford Health. In 2009, Sanford Health bought out Meritcare in Fargo. Headquartered in Sioux Falls, it is one of the largest healthcare systems

TABLE 3.1.   Racial demographics of Fargo and Sioux Falls

	WHITE ONLY	HISPANIC	BLACK	AMERICAN INDIAN	ASIAN	MULTIRACIAL	NON-ENGLISH LANGUAGE SPEAKERS
Fargo	85.5	3.	4.54	1.1	3.33	2.5	9.4
Sioux Falls	82.5	5.03	4.84	2.6	2.3	2.5	10.3

Source: Table created from Data USA 2016.

in the country. It employs more people in both cities than any other employer. Other key employers are in the education, manufacturing, hospitality, and retail industries, in addition to local government. In Sioux Falls, finance and banking employ a large fraction of residents, and in Fargo, Microsoft and North Dakota State University are two key employers. The cities also differ in that Sioux Falls has benefited and suffered from South Dakota's notoriously low tax rates, whereas Fargo has alternately benefited and suffered from North Dakota's oil boom in the western part of the state.

Compared with other small cities, Sioux Falls has an unusually high number of finance and insurance, healthcare, social assistance, and wholesale trade industries (Data USA 2015). Favorable tax laws, including a lack of state income tax, personal-property tax, inventory tax, inheritance tax, and corporate income tax, lure businesses to the city. The state created laws conducive to massive exploitation of a federal tax loophole. Simply by renting an address in Sioux Falls, out-of-state families take advantage of South Dakota's tax-friendly trust laws to shelter their investments from income taxes in their home states through dynasty trusts, which are designed to avoid the federal estate tax (Mider 2014). As such, South Dakota is considered a low tax state and has become a tax haven for the super-rich (Scannell and Houlder 2016). South Dakota ranks fifty-first nationally in taxes collected as a share of personal income. Compared with other states, it has an outsized reliance on sales taxes (4.5 percent) to fund government, which are 16 percent higher than the national average (even food is taxed), and it has the highest average in the country when measured relative to personal income (ITEP 2015). The poorest 20 percent of taxpayers, who are disproportionately racial and ethnic minorities, pay nearly 11 percent of their income in taxes compared with the wealthiest 1 percent, who pay 5.4 percent (ITEP 2015).

In 2006, dozens of companies began drilling in the Bakken formation in western North Dakota. The region instantly transformed sleepy farm towns into magnets for transient workers from all over the United States. Poor farmers turned into millionaires overnight. Employment increased by more than 35 percent and wages more than doubled between 2007 and 2011 (Ferree and Smith 2013). North Dakota quickly surpassed Alaska to become the second-largest producer of oil in the country, after Texas. North Dakota ranks forty-eighth in terms of total state population, but during the oil boom it was the fastest-growing state in the union (Hargreaves 2013). The biggest effects from the boom were seen in western North Dakota, but businesses in the eastern part of the state also experienced some success in the oil industry. As oil production in the western part of the state increased, business leaders in Bismarck called the director of refugee resettlement in Fargo to inquire about recruiting refugees to work in the oil fields. The director told me that he explained to them that for such a program to be successful, schools and medical clinics must be prepared for New American families, not just individual workers. Also, interpreter services would be necessary to communicate with those who do not speak English, as well as social services for those who fall through the employment cracks. Refugees are more than simply laborers, although their economic contributions can be substantial (New American Economy 2017a; *New York Times* 2017), a point I address in more detail below. First, I provide a brief history of refugee resettlement to the Dakotas, and then I make the case for incorporating intercultural policy frameworks into city structures.

A Brief History of Refugee Resettlement to the Dakotas

From the 1940s to the 1980s, churches served as sponsors for refugees in North and South Dakota. Sponsors volunteered to help refugees navigate their new life in the United States, and they did so with minimal guidance or oversight. Southeast Asian refugees were among the largest groups of refugees resettled at this time, and many of those who were resettled to the Dakotas eventually left in search of cities with more support for refugees, such as a sufficient number of interpreters, more diverse schools, and more people from their home countries.

As a result of the Refugee Act of 1980, nationwide, refugee resettlement shifted from a loosely organized, primarily church-based sponsorship to sponsorship by refugee resettlement agencies with paid staff, case management, employment services, standardized guidelines, and more accountability. At this time, the Department of State also began placing more refugees in more cities across the country in addition to the traditional gateway cities such as Chicago, New York, and Los Angeles. The Department of State and Office of Refugee Resettlement determine where refugees will be resettled on the basis of housing and employment availability, levels of community support, and family reunification cases. The Office of Refugee Resettlement partners with state refugee offices and national voluntary agencies involved in the refugee resettlement program. About half these agencies are religious organizations that include resettling refugees as part of their core mission. *Preferred communities* for refugee resettlement allow ample opportunities for early employment and sustained economic independence (ORR 2016). This includes small cities, such as Sioux Falls and Fargo, that have strong economies and a history of resettlement, including networks of volunteers, who help paid staff in the resettlement process (Erickson 2012). To be considered in good standing for refugee reception and placement, local resettlement agencies must meet an employment standard of 75 percent within

180 days of refugees' arrival. That is, 75 percent of employable adults must find work within 180 days.

The Department of State and the Department of Health and Human Services fund resettlement agencies through federal programs like the Reception and Placement Grant. The distribution of funds is contingent on the number of refugees supported during a given time period. In return for federal funds, local affiliates provide sponsorship, pre-arrival resettlement planning, and placement. They find newly arrived refugees apartments, receive them at the airport, and provide basic needs support for at least thirty days (food, clothing, and furnishings). They also provide community orientation, referral to other providers (healthcare, employment, and education), and case management and tracking for 90–180 days. The goal of these services is to aid in the achievement of economic self-sufficiency, which is defined as employment, regardless of salary or benefits.

In the 1990s, Lutheran Social Services agreed to resettle thousands of refugees to Sioux Falls and Fargo (figure 3.1). The largest groups of New Americans in Fargo and Sioux Falls are Karen(ni) from Burma, Iraqis, Somalis, Bhutanese, Eritreans, Congolese, Afghans, Southern Sudanese, Ethiopians, Somalis, former Yugoslavs, and Liberians. Unlike earlier waves of Southeast Asian refugees in the 1970s and 1980s, more of these groups stayed in the region. Resettlement alleviated some of the labor shortages and counterbalanced the outmigration of young people occurring in the 1990s (*Forum of Fargo-Moorhead* 2001). It also brought unprecedented racial and cultural diversity to predominantly white, Christian cities, and resulted in strains on schools, police departments, and social services.

Generally speaking, caseworkers and employment specialists receive little training in refugee resettlement. In interviews with resettlement staff in 2005 and 2008, they told me that expectations from clients, the resettlement agency, and the city—especially during the biggest influx in the late 1990s and early 2000s—were untenable with the training and resources they received. As more refugees were resettled, staff struggled to keep up with the demands of so many arrivals and relied heavily on volunteers to maintain caseloads. Welfare agencies, police departments, schools, and other social service organizations argued that resettlement agencies were dumping refugees into unprepared cities and disregarded pleas to slow down the number of cases. There was little consensus among stakeholders as to whose responsibility refugees should be. Despite ongoing criticism and lack of support from many city institutions, Lutheran Social Services continued to resettle refugees, and they had some support in these efforts. Schools, police departments, medical centers, and social service agencies felt as though they were being forced to serve the needs of refugees, and they

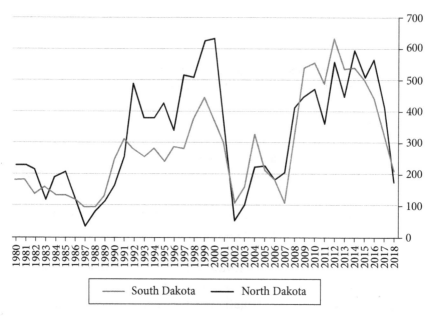

FIGURE 3.1. Refugee arrivals to South Dakota and North Dakota, 1980–2018

Source: Data drawn from ORR 1983, 1996, 1999, 2006, 2009, 2018.

did so reluctantly and haphazardly for many years. After 9/11, however, refugee resettlement came to a standstill (figure 3.1), even though none of the 9/11 attackers had come to the United States as a refugee. With the slowdown in resettlement numbers, agencies had a chance to recoup, evaluate their practices, and increase their public/private partnerships; however, I witnessed few significant changes. Nevertheless resettlement continued, and with more refugees in the cities, public and private institutions needed to accommodate them.

Rather than train all staff to accommodate new forms of diversity, schools, police departments, medical clinics, and social service agencies designated one or two staff members to deal with New Americans. However, as the number of New Americans in the cities grew, designating a few people to work with New Americans became increasingly challenging. The relentless support of refugee advocates, the contributions of New Americans to the cities, and strong, diverse economies that attracted high-skill workers from other parts of the world forced Fargo and Sioux Falls to recognize that they would need to implement policies to integrate diversity more strategically into their cities. In the remainder of this chapter, I highlight some of the ways in which these cities developed intercultural policy frameworks that have made the cities more resilient, inclusive, and economically secure.

Establishing and Maintaining an Intercultural Policy Framework

Becoming an intercultural city means using policy to "raise awareness about the advantages of diversity but also seek to reduce the negative impact of discrimination at the same time as it encourages positive interactions between people of different ethnic and racial backgrounds" (White 2018, 2). Promoting diversity and working across a range of social differences takes time and requires new communication strategies, practices, dialogue, and ways of thinking (27). Rather than wait for refugees or immigrants to come to a city or be unprepared as Sioux Falls and Fargo were initially, cities can get ahead of the curve by adopting intercultural policies and practices as soon as possible. In the process, they will attract immigrants and become more welcoming and resilient. White (2018, 28–39) recommends three key intercultural strategies to help cities welcome diversity and inclusion: (1) recognize diversity, (2) fight against discrimination, and (3) promote dialogue. These steps can help create a better quality of life for all urban residents. I subsequently explain each of them to demonstrate how Fargo and Sioux Falls addressed increased racial, ethnic, religious, and linguistic diversity and learned to incorporate difference into city structures over time.

Municipalities are especially well positioned for intercultural policy work because they have more flexibility than state or federal governments. Cultural diversity has proven to be an advantage for cities because it leads to economic development and entrepreneurial innovation, but tensions in attitudes about refugees and immigrants (as well as other minorities) play out at the local level, which is why policies must be decidedly intercultural. In conclusion, I extend White et al.'s (2018) recommendations to include a plan for partnering with other cities to design and promote intercultural policy frameworks. By working with other cities on attracting and increasing diversity in all its forms (cultural, national, racial, geographically regional, (dis)ability, religious, gendered, sexual orientation), cities put themselves and one another in advantageous positions, both socially and economically.

Recognize Diversity

People are different. Differences must be named, especially in contexts where they can be identified as barriers to entry or as a source of discrimination (White 2018, 27–28). The dominant population of white Euro-Americans are not a homogeneous group, and neither are New Americans. They come from different cultural, socioeconomic, and historical backgrounds that include not only war but also socialism, colonialism, and mixed economies, all of which influence how they adapt to life in the United States. Even within national borders, in places like South Sudan and Bosnia-Herzegovina, there are remarkable differences in languages, ethnicities, religious practices, abilities, and educational and professional backgrounds. Understanding differences across and within dominant and minority populations can allow for the recognition of similarities, mitigation of differences, and more intercultural solidarity. For example, in my work with Southern Sudanese, I have found that Christianity has served to soften (but not eliminate) racism leveled against them in Sioux Falls and Fargo and provide opportunities to connect across differences with white Christians, even to the point of garnering monetary support for projects in South Sudan (Erickson 2020). Host societies are transformed by the process of migration just as refugees and immigrants are, which is why cities should not limit their attention to *either* the dominant population *or* to migrants; "it must always take into consideration both" (White 2018, 38–39). All cities have diversity and most cities have foreign-born populations and can therefore benefit from this approach. By recognizing present forms of diversity, whether this includes foreign-born populations or not, and preparing for new forms of diversity, including but not limited to cultural diversity, cities can more readily adjust to shifts in populations over time.

Some stakeholders in Fargo and Sioux Falls recognize diversity but seek to ignore or avoid it, which results in diminishing opportunities for, if not outright discrimination against, New Americans. For example, some staff at human service agencies in both cities told me that they "treat everyone the same." The goal was likely to preemptively challenge assertions that refugee populations are being treated differently and hence unfairly. However, to claim that individuals from such different backgrounds as Ukraine, Ethiopia, or Haiti should be treated "the same" does not acknowledge that different groups of people have been and continue to be treated differently by societal institutions from schools to police and from housing programs to welfare. Different groups of people need different resources and services. For some, interpreters matter most; for others the key factor might be education or childcare.

Sam Brown, a white man in his sixties in 2005, was a Sioux Falls welfare caseworker. He told me that many of his coworkers were "afraid of [refugees]." According to Brown, when these colleagues were assigned to work with refugees, they sometimes closed the case as soon as possible to avoid confronting differences that made them uncomfortable (e.g., race, language, and different approaches to parenting). They preferred to send refugee clients to Brown, who was not hired to work specifically with refugees, but due to his willingness to do so he became a default refugee case worker. After his retirement, the agency hired a New American caseworker. Oscar Chol, Brown's successor, told me in

2005 that he felt like a token, hired for his New American status and race (he was Black), and to help white caseworkers avoid working with refugees. Rather than integrate refugee clients into their everyday practices and facilitate dialogue and understanding, the agency preferred to direct all refugee clients to one caseworker. Similarly, the only foreign-born staff member at a social service agency in Fargo told me she overheard coworkers telling clients, "I can't understand a word you're saying!" She regularly translated from accented or imperfect English among foreign-born clients into more standard English that her coworkers could understand. She felt that her coworkers disliked New Americans but would never say so because they had to be "politically correct." Still others, like Brown, enjoyed working with New Americans.

Dave Pinder, a plant manager at a glass-making plant in Fargo whose staff was composed of more than 50 percent New Americans, learned the first and last names of every single employee, which he demonstrated to me on a tour of the plant. Pinder understood the economic and social value of New American employees and boasted of his employees' work ethic and their diversity. Greg Johnson, a human resource manager at a cabinet-making factory in Sioux Falls, told me that because many of his employees were refugees he began to follow world news more closely. After thirty-two employees missed work when the newly inaugurated first President of South Sudan and Vice President of Sudan, John Garang de Mabior, died in a helicopter crash in 2005, Johnson said the absences were "hard on the business side of things, but on the people side of things, they [employers] have to understand the situation." Some workers received warning slips, but no one was fired. Johnson told me he could understand that, "what's going on in Sudan's a lot more important than some slip of paper." Generally speaking, businesses were welcoming of New American workers, but there were a range of responses by human resource managers to cultural differences at the work place. Some employers, for example, allowed breaks for prayer time and even provided prayer rooms for practicing Muslims, while others did not.

"Thirty years ago, when I started this job," Dan Olson, a white police officer in Sioux Falls told me in 2005, "you would stop in the street if you saw a Black man." At a routine traffic stop he noticed Sioux Falls was changing when the people in the car didn't speak English, leading him to think, "You've got people from all over the world now that are making Sioux Falls home." Before the influx of refugees in the 1990s, Olson said, a routine traffic accident required about 20 minutes, but the need for interpreters increased this exponentially. The police departments quickly recognized that New Americans came to Fargo and Sioux Falls with different experiences with law and policing. Despite myths to the contrary, New Americans have not committed more crimes than other populations (Bernat 2019;

New American Economy 2017b; Ousey and Kubrin 2009). However, without addressing misunderstandings due to language barriers, culture, and fear of law enforcement, the job of police officers and experiences of New Americans in the cities would be more challenging. The police departments created refugee liaison officers to work on building trust and educating New Americans about law enforcement. They gave presentations about US laws at new refugee arrival orientation sessions, established relationships with elders and other leaders in New American communities, and trained new police recruits in best practices in working with New Americans. Southern Sudanese men in particular mentioned police profiling as a problem. Nevertheless, creating these positions and working to develop trust among New Americans was an important step in establishing and maintaining intercultural policies by recognizing difference.

In the 1990s, there were few English language learning (ELL) teachers or students, but seemingly overnight three hundred new students per year were arriving. It was tough on teachers, who had performance goals to meet but received scant support to accommodate the changes taking place in their classrooms. The school district needed to hire more teachers, aides, and social workers, and the change was, according to Constance Larson, an ELL teacher in Fargo, "slow in coming," but the schools adapted. In 2000, the Sioux Falls school district opened an entire school devoted to teaching ELL and offered training classes to teachers who were not certified in ELL to work with ELL students. The Sioux Falls School District recognized difference and trained others how to adapt to this influx of diversity. By the 2010s, ELL teachers and ELL training were dispersed in schools throughout the district. In 2014, residents of Sioux Falls spoke at least 137 different languages and dialects, and schools reported sixty different languages among students (Walker 2014). Similarly, Fargo schools reported seventy-one different languages spoken in the school district and sixty nations represented in the district (Schmidt 2016).

In these examples, difference was ignored, embraced, or accommodated. To avoid discrimination, hiring diverse staff is important, but so too is training *all* staff in best practices for equity and inclusion. These include using interpreters with New American clients who do not speak English, speaking more slowly, and learning to explain what may seem obvious to people born in the United States. For many refugees, language is one of the biggest barriers for full participation in society. Both cities recognized this and developed interpreter services and adult ELL classes. In 1994, the Metro Interpreter Center opened to provide training and administrative support for a decentralized network of interpreters that operated in the Fargo metro area. The city concurrently developed the Cultural Diversity Resource Center to embrace its ethnic diversity, including both Native and New Americans, and to assist diverse populations in overcoming barriers to community participation. The Center for New Americans coordinates interpreter services out of their resettlement office in Sioux Falls, but in the mid 1990s, the city worked to establish the Multicultural Center, which offers interpreter services, diversity trainings to businesses, and an affordable space to gather for cultural celebrations. Both cities have a range of public, private, faith-based, and secular programs and organizations that feature, for example, after-school programs for New American children, housing assistance, and disability services. Table 3.2 summarizes some of the key organizations, businesses, and programs that provide support for New Americans in Sioux Falls and Fargo at the time of this article. It is by no means comprehensive but gives the reader an idea of the work that the cities have done to support New Americans. Understanding that people are different and adapting to differences does not necessarily result in discrimination. To ensure that it does not, cities must fight discrimination when it occurs.

Fight against Discrimination

To avoid disruptive conflicts, cities should send a clear message that discrimination will not be tolerated. Racist violence is part and parcel of United States history and culture, and racialized violence, including physical assault and intimidation, has been and continues to be targeted specifically at New Americans in addition to Native American, Latinx, Asian, and Black populations in the United States. If cities want the benefits of diversity, then they must also stand up to discrimination and violence. Fargo and Sioux Fall are no exception to this pattern. In May 2001, a white father and son were convicted of assault after beating a twenty-one-year-old Sudanese man with a club. Soon after 9/11, a group of white men beat up one of my clients as they called him a terrorist. White supremacists have used flyers and confederate flags to intimidate and scare minority populations (Ferguson 2017, Hagen 2017). From 2012 to 2017, the Fargo Police department reported forty-eight hate crimes. Between 2010 and 2015, North Dakota was one of the top five states for the number of reported hate crimes and actions per capita (Majumder 2017). From 2013 to 2018, 102 hate crimes were reported in South Dakota. Nearly 60 percent of the crimes were race related.

In 2003, violence between Southern Sudanese and US-born students (white and Native American) broke out on school grounds. Soon after, 30 white students brought knives and crowbars to an apartment building where Southern Sudanese lived, looking for a fight, and painted *KKK* on the side of an apartment building. The school's principal, Bill Morgan, told me in 2005 that he believed that the

TABLE 3.2. Summary of programs for refugees in Fargo and Sioux Falls

FARGO	SIOUX FALLS
Lutheran Social Services of North Dakota, New American Services, the refugee resettlement agency	Lutheran Social Services of South Dakota, Center for New Americans, the refugee resettlement agency
· Unaccompanied Refugee Minor Program (not present in SD)	· Onsite English language learning classes (not present in ND)
· Immigration lawyer	· Interpreter services
· Case management for refugees	· Immigration lawyer
· Employment specialists	· Case management for refugees
	· Employment specialists
Cultural Diversity Resource Center, including Metro Interpreter Services, a city- and grant-funded nonprofit to help manage diversity and promote diversity awareness in the city; it works with Native and New American populations and other ethnic minorities	Multicultural Center, a city- and grant-funded nonprofit to help manage diversity and promote diversity awareness in the city; also includes case management and interpreter services, driver's education classes, adult education; it works with Native and New American populations, and other minorities
ESL programs in K-12 schools and the Adult Learning Center, which offers English learning classes for New American adults	Whittier School, a school for ESL students Separate organizations for adult learning
Nonprofit organizations with programs for New Americans and others (Charism, Giving+Learning Program, WE Center, Peoples Diversity Program)	Nonprofit organizations with programs for New Americans and others (Inter-lakes Community Action Partnership), Children's Inn
State eligibility programs (TANF, SNAP, SSI, WIC, federal housing, Medicaid, JOBS)	State eligibility programs (TANF, SNAP, SSI, WIC, federal housing, Medicaid, JOBS)
Cultural Liaison Officer works with New Americans and Native Americans in the Fargo-Moorhead region, trains new recruits on cultural diversity, and conducts outreach	New Immigrant Citizen Education (NICE), a program within the Sioux Falls Police Department that educates New Americans about the laws and rules in the city
Main Employers for New Americans: Cardinal IG (a glass making plant), hospitals, hotels, restaurants and retail stores, home health caretakers, and daycare centers	Main Employers for New Americans: Smithfield (a meatpacking plant), Starmark, hospitals, restaurants and retail stores, banks (usually in the mail division), call centers (for those who speak English well), hotels, home health caretakers, and daycare centers
Churches (provide mentors and tutors, unity services, and worship space to New American congregations)	Churches (provide mentors and tutors, unity services, and worship space to New American congregations)

fighting was about nationality, class, and race. The poor, mostly rural, white kids claimed that Southern Sudanese believed "they were all that, MTV look-a-likes, the way they dress, et cetera," because they dressed like urban Black teens with big jerseys, baggy jeans worn low, and jewelry, uncommon attire in Sioux Falls among the majority of students. In response to the fighting, Morgan organized a "diversity dinner" with forty students and their parents and sent the message that the school would "not tolerate intolerance."

Fighting discrimination is more than combating extremists and physical acts of violence. Discrimination also works in subtle ways, for example, when a social service worker provides one client a list of further resources to help them stretch their resources to the end of the month but does not provide the same information to the next client, or when a receptionist at a medical clinic allows some clients to check in late but not others, or when teachers use family members as interpreters, which violates Section 601 of Title VI of the Civil Rights Act of 1964 that requires all programs or activities receiving federal funding to provide language interpreters and specifically states that family members should be avoided if at all possible. All these practices have been occurring in Sioux Falls and Fargo, but at the same time, individuals have developed programs to combat discrimination. For example, Laurie Metcalf, the director of the Community Health Center in Sioux Falls, cowrote a grant with the resettlement agency to create a community health outreach team for New Americans. Thanks to the success of their grant, the Health Center began offering team-based primary care, well-child visits, dental exams, immunizations, HIV/AIDS early intervention, healthcare case management, and family planning services to New Americans and other low-income families, and provides qualified interpreters to those who need them. A similar affordable and team-based community healthcare program exists in Fargo through the Family HealthCare clinic. In 2001, in response to the surge in refugees to the city, the clinic began offering medically trained interpreters for patients with language barriers and leads trainings for new medical interpreters.

Preventing discrimination by establishing strong social programs that address health, education, housing, language barriers, and economic inequality in the first few months after refugees arrive is not only humanitarian—it pays off for cities economically. Although often viewed as helpless, vulnerable, dependent on government aid, or reaping scarce resources that those born in the United State are not, refugees have proven time and time again that they are creative, resilient, and entrepreneurial. In July 2017, a report by the Department of Health and Human Services showed that refugees bring in more government revenue than they cost in social services over time (*New York Times* 2017). In the report *From Struggle to Resilience: The Economic Impact of Refugees in America,* researchers argue that debates about resettlement policy are usually framed as a humanitarian issue, but "it is often the economic impact of refugees that leave the most enduring impression" (New American Economy 2017a). In 2015, immigrants were almost twice as likely to start a new business as native-born Americans. These studies show that while refugees receive initial socioeconomic assistance upon arriving in the United States, they see sharp income increases in subsequent years. After twenty-five years in the country, people who came to the US as refugees have an average median household income that is $14,000 higher than the average for all American households and their rates of entrepreneurship outshine those of other immigrants. In other words, the money that cities and the federal government put into refugee resettlement is largely repaid.

To evaluate the economic impact of refugees and facilitate their integration, in 2016 Fargo applied to become one of twenty communities selected for a Gateways for Growth Challenge (gatewaysforgrowth.org/), a bipartisan national program that partners with the organization Welcoming America to integrate New Americans into communities across the country. Welcoming America is a national organization that provides toolkits in social entrepreneurship to make cities across the country more inclusive (welcomingamerica.org). Launched in 2015, Gateways for Growth cities promote citizenship through entrepreneurial enterprises and seek to improve public safety and access to services and to advance education and workforce goals to help regions compete in the global economy. The study that Gateways for Growth conducted in Fargo found that "the 10,663 immigrants and refugees living in Fargo helped create or preserve 490 local manufacturing jobs that would have otherwise vanished or moved elsewhere" (New American Economy 2017a). However, relative to their population—unlike some other American cities—refugees and immigrants own a small number of businesses in Fargo, which suggests that there are barriers to their full participation in the city's economic life. Emerging Prairie, an organization focused on helping startups and building stronger entrepreneurial networks in Fargo found in a 2019 study that less than 3 percent of small businesses in the city were immigrant owned even though foreign-born residents make up 5 percent of the population, and 11.3 percent of immigrants held advanced degrees compared with just 5.8 percent of the US-born population.

In 2015, Sioux Falls earmarked $170,000 to help organizations train New Americans to fill more than two thousand job vacancies in the city, mostly in manufacturing and transportation (Sneve 2015). Pushing New Americans into meatpacking plants and other low-skill positions does not acknowledge the range of skills that they have. The city's investment in such training represents an implicit recognition that countering discrimination, eliminating barriers to full participation in society, and designing programs that facilitate New American–

owned businesses is a social and economic benefit that goes beyond individual workers or companies.

Dialogue and Training

Dialogue and training are key to preventing discrimination, decreasing misinformation, and promoting inclusion. Acknowledging diversity, fighting discrimination, and preparing for new forms of diversity helps cities reap the benefits of receiving New Americans while avoiding debilitating social conflicts. Fargo and Sioux Falls have learned that it takes a coordinated city-wide effort, not just a few individuals or organizations, to facilitate cross-cultural dialogue and incorporate diversity into urban life. Kathy Hogan, former Director of Cass County Services in Fargo, told me that it takes a whole community to resettle refugees because "cultural differences make a lot of people uncomfortable." I asked her in 2008 whose responsibility it was to educate people about refugees and New Americans moving to Fargo and she quickly replied, "Well, it's everyone's. It's everyone's . . . You learn it in your neighborhoods, you learn it in your churches, you learn it in your schools. But it is hard, you know . . . to think that this is gonna be a simple thing is unrealistic."

"People say they are afraid of refugees," Jessica Thomasson, CEO of Lutheran Social Services in North Dakota from 2014 to 2019, told me, "but it has more to do with scarcity . . . People believe that there are limited resources. They see that their community is changing, and they feel like they are losing their identity." "Even people of faith," she explained, "feel like refugees are going to physically harm them . . . It's not an intellectual argument, it is visceral, unnamed, and emotional." As such, when Thomasson leads discussions about refugee resettlement to groups of people, she works to move beyond feelings and establish facts about international migration, refugee resettlement, and the economic and social benefits of incorporating diversity in a community.

In 2005, at the behest of students, the Sioux Falls school district initiated a "Race Concerns Task Force." After further consideration, they changed the name to "Diversity Task Force," connoting a more expansive understanding of human differences that goes beyond race. Viewing race as a primary form of human difference privileges whiteness as the norm, while at the same time diminishes other forms of diversity, such as religion, language, sexuality, political differences, and cultural practices. The task force became a coalition of public and private organizations and students to address increasing cultural and racial diversity to the city. The group created a program to talk about diversity that aired on local radio and television stations. They also designed a billboard campaign with signs that read "Respect Yourself, Respect Me. Diversity: It's What We Have

FIGURE 3.2.   Billboards in Sioux Falls in 2005 that display "Respect Yourself. Respect Me. Diversity. It's what we have in common"

in Common" featuring photographs of students of color (figure 3.2). The goal was to "promote a safe and respectful Sioux Falls for all citizens" (Society for Human Resource Management 2008, 31). Southern Sudanese student Thomas Madut wanted people to think beyond race: "You need to judge them by what they say and what they do," he said.

The billboards meant to educate and call attention to social inequities, violence, and prejudice that result from human differences, but they arguably entrenched racial differences by equating "diversity" with "people of color." Whiteness, too, must be viewed as a race if diversity is understood to be more than skin deep. Some people in Sioux Falls recognized this. When I asked Principal Morgan to speak more about race in Sioux Falls, he stressed the need for a broader, anti-essentialist understanding of diversity that included race but also class, rural/urban differences, (dis)abilities, and sexualities among the student body. However, these other forms of diversity did not raise the same concerns—or garner as much media attention—as refugees and concomitant concerns about race and religion, which was equated with foreignness and hence unworthiness by some.

In July 2005, Beatrice Stanley, an elected city official, wrote a letter to the *Argus Leader* newspaper calling for a moratorium on resettlement because she believed refugees were not receiving enough support. A relatively wealthy and influential Christian white woman in her sixties in 2005, Stanley had been volunteering with refugees for more than twenty years and spent countless hours and capital supporting them. She told me in 2005 that she believed refugees should have a twelve-member team, for at least a year, to help them adjust to life in the United States, "preferably for a lifetime" and felt it was *extremely* irresponsible" to bring refugees to Sioux Falls without this level of support. She aimed her critiques at Lutheran Social Services, arguing they "dumped" more refugees in Sioux Falls than the city could manage. While some refugees do need an extraordinary amount of support, most do not. Stanley's approach overlooks the fact that most refugees become self-sufficient in the United States relatively quickly, within eight months, and many have unique skills and an entrepreneurial spirit.

In August 2015, Damon Ouradnik started a petition on Change.org, which called on the North Dakota Cass County legislature to end refugee resettlement to the Fargo region. Nearly 3,300 people signed it. Of the 1,099 people who reported their location on the petition, 82.5% of them were from North Dakota or Minnesota and about half were from Fargo, West Fargo, or Moorhead. Nativist us/them comments on the petition argued refugees were accessing undeserved services and goods that US-born residents cannot and viewed refugees as "illegals" who "hated America." There was deep concern that tax money was supporting noncitizens and that refugees needed to assimilate faster. A counter petition was created to bring *more* refugees to the region, which was signed by 163 people, mostly locals from Fargo, West Fargo, and Moorhead (Erickson 2020, 136–137).

Both antiresettlement positions, written ten years apart, targeted refugee resettlement as a problem to be solved, not a benefit. Stanley believed that refugees were not getting enough support whereas Ouradnik and his supporters believed refugees were getting too much. Neither position acknowledged the economic and social benefits that New Americans bring to cities. In order to challenge both nativist and paternalistic approaches to refugee resettlement, people in Sioux Falls and Fargo have been creating opportunities between New Americans and members of the dominant population to exchange stories and dispel myths and false information. Narrative 4 is a North Dakota State University–sponsored global story-telling program that facilitates a two-day story exchange between New Americans and US-born residents. On the first day, partners tell each other a story from their own lives. The next day, they tell one another's stories to the larger group as if it were their own. The central idea is that by exchanging stories, people can develop radical empathy that goes beyond political, socioeconomic, and cultural divides. Damon Ouradnik participated in the event after a friend convinced him that it would be beneficial, and he was paired with an immigrant business owner from Ghana (Lussenhop 2017). Ouradnik left before the end of the event, insisting that he was most concerned about the cost of resettlement, not about race, but there is more evidence to suggest that, over time, refugees are more of an economic benefit to cities than a cost.

On July 25, 2017, what started as a parking dispute turned into a verbal alter-
cation between Amber Hensley, a white woman from North Dakota, and three
Somali-American women, sisters Sarah and Leyla Hassan and Rowda Soyan.
They hurled personal insults about one another's appearance until things esca-
lated when Hensley warned, "We're gonna kill all of ya. We're going to kill every
one of you fucking Muslims." Twenty-one-year-old Sarah Hassan recorded the
incident and posted it online. The accounting firm where Hensley worked reported hundreds of complaints about her behavior, which resulted in her termi-
nation. Fargo police chief David Todd called for a reconciliation meeting between
Hensley and the sisters. During that meeting, Hensley learned that the Hassans
endure ongoing prejudice based on their dress (both wear hijabs) and their nationality, while the Hassans learned that Hensley's father was killed in Iraq.
Hensley publicly apologized to the young women and they accepted her apol-
ogy; the women became friends and invited one another to Muslim and Christian holiday celebrations (Erickson 2017). As in the example above, when a
principal in the Sioux Falls school district organized a dinner to bring parents
and students together to talk about diversity, Chief Todd recognized the need
for dialogue to broach intercultural disputes and the results were palpable.

Partnerships with Other Intercultural Cities

Cities don't exist in a vacuum; they are interconnected. People, goods, and ideas
move within and through cities and are connected to others all over the world,
which is why they should rely on and cooperate with one another to succeed.
When Fargo experienced the largest surge of refugees in its modern history (since
wars against Native Americans and European colonization and settlement of the
region) and struggled with the influx, hundreds of refugees moved from Fargo
to Sioux Falls where the structures were marginally better able to support them.
(As a caseworker in Sioux Falls, I worked with refugees who were initially resettled to Fargo.) When Somali refugees were looking for smaller, safer cities in
the northeastern United States, hundreds of them moved to Lewiston, Maine,
and the city struggled with the influx. Like Fargo and Sioux Falls, Lewiston has
learned to work with the new residents but conflict and discrimination were
problems initially (Besteman 2016). Small and midsized cities across the United
States that had been relatively unaccustomed to international migrants, including refugees, until the 1980s and 1990s, experienced parallel forms of diversity
shock when refugees and immigrants began moving into their municipalities
(Massey 2008). Refugee resettlement is strongly reliant on public/private partnerships from the international to the national and local level. The Office of
Refugee Resettlement and voluntary agencies lead national meetings for cities

participating in the resettlement program, but to be more successful, cities must go beyond resettlement networks to engage in intercultural diversity work more broadly. Job availability in both low- and high-skill labor markets and institutions of higher education also bring new forms of diversity to the region. Moreover, there is more to refugees than their refugee status. Among refugees, there are differences in religion, race, ethnicity, sexuality, marriage practices, ability, education, political views, and more. By cooperating with one another, cities can better attract refugees and immigrants while at the same time prepare for the range of differences and similarities that exist within and between populations.

There are numerous programs to assist cities with these partnerships, including national organizations such as Welcoming America and Gateways for Growth, which I mentioned previously. On a regional level, networks of intercultural communities would benefit small and midsized cities by strategizing how to attract and maintain diversity and fight discrimination. Lincoln and Omaha, Nebraska, Des Moines and Cedar Rapids, Iowa, and Worthington, Minnesota have attracted relatively large New American populations relative to their size, drawn to agricultural work and jobs in meatpacking plants and other businesses. According to the mayor of Worthington, "without immigrants . . . [the city] would likely be a community in decline" (Immigrant Law Center of Minnesota 2020).

In addition, municipalities can consider expanding their network beyond the United States. In a globalized world, cities must be cognizant that they are dependent on people, services, and economies beyond municipal and even national boundaries. Cities in the United States can become members of Integrating Cities (http://www.integratingcities.eu/), a partnership between EuroCities and the European Commission that seeks common solutions for shared challenges, especially in regard to immigration. Currently Rochester, Minnesota, is the only city in the United States that has become a member of this network. The Council of Europe's Intercultural cities program "supports cities in reviewing their policies through an intercultural lens and developing comprehensive intercultural strategies to help them manage diversity positively and realise the diversity advantage" (Council of Europe, n.d.). In 2020, there were 139 participating cities, most of which are in Europe, but some are in Turkey, South Korea, Morocco, and Australia.

Small and midsized cities in the United States are recognizing the benefit of New American residents. However, discrimination remains a barrier to full integration into society. Small and midsized cities can benefit by promoting themselves as intercultural, diverse spaces but only if they are willing to recognize diversity and name differences, fight discrimination, and insist on dialogue and training. Doing so will attract capital and residents who desire to live in diverse urban places that are smaller, safer, and more affordable than large metropolitan centers.

Conclusion

Accommodating difference and diversity is never complete; it is an ongoing process. Though actors and institutions change, successful intercultural cities are predicated on a shared political commitment to acceptance of difference and diversity, not on a particular race, religion, ethnicity, or nationality (Wood and Landry 2008, 65). There are many ways to approach diversity management in local government. From an intercultural perspective, the problem that cities face is not so much one of diversity but of difference (White 2018, 22). Because each city has a unique constellation of differences and histories, each city must take into consideration its own particular history and demographics as well as policy at the local, municipal level.

The transformations in policies and practices that I have summarized here as a result of refugee resettlement—and the list is not exhaustive—sowed the seeds for future intercultural policy to take root at the municipal level. In August 2017, Sioux Falls Mayor Mike Huether and Fargo Mayor Tim Mahoney signed a compact by the Anti-Defamation League and The United States Conference of Mayors to fight extremism, bigotry, and white supremacy, and promote justice, equality, diversity, and inclusivity.

In October 2019, President Trump issued an executive order giving unprecedented power to state and local government in deciding whether or not they wanted to accept refugees. In December 2019, the city councils of Sioux Falls and Fargo and county commission offices of Minnehaha and Cass Counties, respectively, voted unanimously to extend the refugee resettlement programs in their cities, but the numbers of refugees coming to the United States is at a historic low. The President ultimately decides how many refugees will be allowed to enter the United States in a given fiscal year. In 2019, Trump set the ceiling for 2020 at a historic low of 18,000 refugees. Comparatively, in 2016, President Obama set the ceiling at 110,000 refugees. For most of its history, refugee resettlement has been a bipartisan program, supported by Democrats and Republicans, faith-based organizations, and secular humanitarian organizations. Until 2019, refugee resettlement had been a federal program that demonstrated the United States' commitment to humanitarianism and immigration. Giving local populations more leeway in whether to accept refugees places a burden on advocates each and every year to defend their programs, taking time away from the work of supporting refugees to integrate into their host cities. It also prevents family reunification cases, challenges a uniform, comprehensive federal approach to resettlement, and allows misinformed, xenophobic residents, such as Ouradnik, more voice and power. As a result of lower refugee admittance ceilings, resettlement agencies across the country are laying off employees and there are fewer refugee workers to fill jobs.

Had Fargo or Sioux Falls been given the choice to opt out of the resettlement program ten or twenty years ago, they may have been tempted to do so, driven by lack of coherent intercultural policies or knowledge about and experiences with refugees and immigrants, and fear. In 2019, Mayor Mahoney reported to AP news that Fargo has "33 businesses that say they will take as many (refugees) as they could" (MacPherson 2019), not to mention countless intercultural friendships and partnerships that have formed as a result of refugee resettlement. Teachers testified at the meetings to the positive impact of refugee resettlement in schools. Mayor Mahoney told me in 2016 that he sees New Americans recruiting others to the region because there are jobs in North Dakota, as well as safety, good schools, and affordable housing. Fargo and Sioux Falls have transformed into destination cities with increasing numbers of New American-owned restaurants, shops, and grocery stores. "People used to have to go to Minneapolis or Winnipeg to see things like that," Mayor Mahoney told me.

Despite the lessons learned in Fargo and Sioux Falls, refugee resettlement remains controversial, both regionally and nationally. Bismarck, the capital of North Dakota with a population of 95,000 that is 95 percent white, has resettled significantly fewer refugees than Fargo—only about 30 annually compared to 400 annually—and had not been facing the same kinds of tensions that Fargo had. That changed in 2019, when the Burleigh County Commission voted only narrowly, three to two, to extend the resettlement program to that city, making national headlines in the process (Kaleem 2020; Farzan 2019). The state of Texas rejected the resettlement of new refugees, despite the support of mayors in Houston, Dallas, and Austin to continue their programs. As of January 2020, nineteen Republican and twenty-three Democratic governors and some one hundred localities had consented to receive refugees; just seven states had not agreed (Jordan 2020).

My research shows that opposition to resettlement creates frictions that make it more difficult for cities to realize the many benefits that New Americans—and diversity more broadly—generate. Adopting an intercultural policy framework that acknowledges diversity, fights discrimination, and promotes dialogue can help cities avoid such difficulties. Such an approach, as well as partnering with other cities that have experienced resettling refugees, can help prevent misinformation, discrimination, and the rejection of refugees, who have proven to help cities be more resilient.

References

Bernat, Frances. 2019. "Immigration and Crime." In *Oxford Research Encyclopedia of Criminology and Criminal Justice*. Oxford University Press. Article published April 2017; last modified August 28, 2019. https://doi.org/10.1093/acrefore/9780190 264079.013.93.

Besteman, Catherine. 2016. *Making Refuge: Somali Bantu Refugees and Lewiston, Maine*. Durham, NC: Duke University Press.

Council of Europe. n.d. "Intercultural Cities Programme." Accessed September 7, 2020. http://www.coe.int/en/web/interculturalcities.

Data USA. 2015. "City profile." https://datausa.io/profile/geo/sioux-falls-sd/.

Data USA. 2016. "Fargo, ND & Sioux Fall, SD." https://datausa.io/profile/geo/fargo-nd /?compare=sioux-falls-sd#demographics.

Erickson, Jennifer. 2012. "Volunteering with Refugees: Neoliberalism, Hegemony, and (Senior) Citizenship." *Human Organization: Journal of the Society for Applied Anthropology* 71, no. 2 (June): 167–175. https://doi.org/10.17730/humo.71.2.152h584 3163031pr.

Erickson, Jennifer. 2017. "Race-ing Fargo." Member Voices, *Fieldsights*, August 5, 2017. https://culanth.org/fieldsights/race-ing-fargo.

Erickson, Jennifer. 2020. *Race-ing Fargo: Refugees, Citizenship, and the Transformation of Small Cities*. Ithaca, NY: Cornell University Press.

Farzan, Antonia Noori. 2019. "A North Dakota County Was Poised To Be First To Bar Refugees under Trump's Executive Order. Residents Said No." *Washington Post*, December 10, 2019. https://www.washingtonpost.com/nation/2019/12/10/north -dakota-county-votes-allowing-refugees-settle-under-trump-executive-order/.

Ferguson, Danielle. 2017. "White Nationalist Posters Spotted in Sioux Falls." *Argus Leader*, September 9, 2017. https://www.argusleader.com/story/news/2017/09/09 /white-nationalist-posters-spotted-sioux-falls/646719001/.

Ferree, Paul, and Peter W. Smith. 2013. "Employment and Wage Changes in Oil-Producing Counties in the Bakken Formation, 2007–2011." *Beyond the Numbers: Employment and Unemployment* 2, no. 11 (April). https://www.bls.gov/opub/btn /volume-2/employment-wages-bakken-shale-region.htm.

Forum of Fargo-Moorhead. 2001. "Valley to the World." December 9–11, 2001.

Guo, Jeff. 2015. "Where Refugees Go in America." *Washington Post*, September 11, 2015. https://www.washingtonpost.com/news/wonk/wp/2015/09/11/where-refugees-go -in-america/?utm_term=.3fae4539933d.

Hagen, C. S. 2017. "White Supremacist Fliers Hit Fargo Streets." *High Plains Reader*, August 25, 2017. http://hpr1.com/index.php/feature/news/white-supremacist-fliers-hit -fargo-streets/.

Hargreaves, Steve. 2013. "North Dakota Grows Five Times Faster than the Nation." *CNN Money*, September 18, 2013. https://money.cnn.com/2013/06/06/news/economy /north-dakota-economy/index.html.

Henry J. Kaiser Family Foundation. 2017. "Poverty Rate by Race/Ethnicity." https:// www.kff.org/other/state-indicator/poverty-rate-by-raceethnicity/?currentTime frame=0&sortModel=%7B%22colId%22:%22Location%22,%22sort%22:%22asc %22%7D.

Immigrant Law Center of Minnesota. 2020. "Immigrants Building Worthington." March 9, 2020. https://www.ilcm.org/latest-news/immigrants-building-worth ington/.

Institute on Taxation and Economic Policy (ITEP). 2015. "South Dakota." January 13, 2015. https://itep.org/whopays/south-dakota/.

Jordan, Miriam. 2020. "Judge Halts Trump Policy that Allows States To Bar Refugees." *New York Times,* January 15, 2020. https://www.nytimes.com/2020/01/15/us/refu gees-states-trump.html.

Kaleem, Jaweed. 2020. "North Dakota Was an Immigrant Haven—Until Trump Was Elected." *Los Angeles Times,* January 9, 2020. https://www.latimes.com/world -nation/story/2020-01-09/refugees-bismarck-north-dakota-trump.

Lussenhop, Jessica. 2017. "Can a Life-Swap Exercise Stop a Community Tearing Itself in Two?" *BBC,* May 4, 2017. http://www.bbc.com/news/world-us-canada-39727185#.

MacPherson, James. 2019. "North Dakota Gov. Burgum Embraces Trump Refugee Order." *Associated Press,* November 19, 2019. https://apnews.com/21450cf7ccc2444 5b790bb7835daca99.

Majumder, Maimuna. 2017. "Higher Rates of Hate Crimes Are Tied to Income Inequality." *FiveThirtyEight,* January 23, 2017. https://fivethirtyeight.com/features /higher-rates-of-hate-crimes-are-tied-to-income-inequality/.

Massey, Douglas, ed. 2008. *New Faces in New Places: The Changing Geography of American Immigration.* New York: Russell Sage Foundation.

Mider, Zachary. 2014. "South Dakota, Little Tax Haven on the Prairie." *Bloomberg Businessweek,* January 9, 2014. https://www.bloomberg.com/news/articles/2014-01 -09/south-dakota-dynasty-trusts-tax-haven-for-rich-families.

New American Economy. 2017a. "From Struggle to Resilience: The Economic Impact of Refugees in America." June 19, 2017. http://www.newamericaneconomy.org/research /from-struggle-to-resilience-the-economic-impact-of-refugees-in-america/.

New American Economy. 2017b. "Is There a Link between Refugees and U.S. Crime Rates?" February 7, 2017. https://research.newamericaneconomy.org/report/is -there-a-link-between-refugees-and-u-s-crime-rates/.

New York Times. 2017. "Rejected Report Shows Revenue Brought in by Refugees." September 19, 2017. https://www.nytimes.com/interactive/2017/09/19/us/politics/docu ment-Refugee-Report.html?smid=tw-share&blm_aid=569361&_r=0.

Office of Refugee Resettlement (ORR). 1983. "Report to the Congress: Refugee Resettlement Program." U.S. Department of Health and Human Services. January 31, 1983. https://www.acf.hhs.gov/orr/resource/archived-office-of-refugee-resettlement -annual-reports-to-congress.

Office of Refugee Resettlement (ORR). 1996. "Report to the Congress: Refugee Resettlement Program." U.S. Department of Health and Human Services. Pages A3–A9. January 31, 1996. https://www.acf.hhs.gov/orr/resource/archived-office-of-refugee -resettlement-annual-reports-to-congress.

Office of Refugee Resettlement (ORR). 1999. "Report to the Congress: Making a Difference." U.S. Department of Health and Human Services. Pages A4–A11. January 31, 1999. https://www.acf.hhs.gov/orr/resource/archived-office-of-refugee -resettlement-annual-reports-to-congress.

Office of Refugee Resettlement (ORR). 2006. "Report to the Congress." Table 4: Arrivals by State of Initial Resettlement 2002–2006. Department of State, Department of Homeland Security, Department of Health and Human Services. January 31, 2006. https://www.wrapsnet.org/resources/.

Office of Refugee Resettlement (ORR). 2009. "Report to the Congress." Table 4: Arrivals by State of Initial Resettlement 2007–2009. Department of State, Department of Homeland Security, Department of Health and Human Services. January 31, 2009. https://www.wrapsnet.org/resources/.

Office of Refugee Resettlement (ORR). 2016. "Preferred Communities." U.S. Department of Health and Human Services. January 8. http://www.acf.hhs.gov/programs/orr /programs/rph.

Office of Refugee Resettlement (ORR). 2018. "Reports to the Congress." Chart II-6: Summary of Refugee Arrivals by State for FY 2010–2018. Department of State, Department of Homeland Security, Department of Health and Human Services. January 31, 2018. https://www.wrapsnet.org/resources/.

Ousey, Graham C., and Charis E. Kubrin. 2009. "Exploring the Connection between Immigration and Violent Crime Rates in U.S. Cities, 1980–2000." *Social Problems* 56, no. 3 (August): 447–73.

Scannell, Kara, and Vanessa Houlder. 2016. "US Tax Haven: The New Switzerland." *Financial Times*, May 8, 2016. https://www.ft.com/content/cc46c644-12dd-11e6 -839f-2922947098f0.

Schmidt, Helmut. 2016. "Of the Languages F-M Students Speak at Home, Somali is Second to English." *Inforum*, May 2, 2016. http://www.inforum.com/news/4022491 -dozens-languages-f-m-students-speak-home-somali-second-english.

Sneve, Joe, 2015. "Immigrants, Refugees Tapped for Workforce Development." *Argus Leader*, April 21, 2015. http://www.argusleader.com/story/news/2015/04/20/immi grants-refugees-tapped-workforce-development/26100435/.

Society for Human Resource Management. 2008. "Enterprising Leadership." https:// community.shrm.org/HigherLogic/System/DownloadDocumentFile.ashx ?DocumentFileKey=4f20338b-cd9d-c0b9-4995-.f13859961571.

Vertovec, Steven. 2007. "Super-diversity and Its Implications." *Ethnic and Racial Studies* 30 (6): 1024–54. https://doi.org/10.1080/01419870701599465.

Walker, Mark. 2014. "Language Line Helps Officers Avoid Getting Lost in Translation." *Argus Leader*, October 8, 2014. https://www.argusleader.com/story/news/crime /2014/10/08/translating-justice-police-need-interpreters/16942619/.

White, Bob W., ed. 2018. *Intercultural Cities: Policy and Practice for a New Era*. London: Palgrave Macmillan. https://doi.org/10.1007/978-3-319-62603-1.

Wood, Phil, and Charles Landry. 2008. *The Intercultural City: Planning for Diversity Advantage*. New York: Taylor & Francis.

SHAKING OFF THE RUST IN THE AMERICAN SOUTH

Deindustrialization, Abandonment, and Revitalization in Bessemer, Alabama

William Grady Holt

Typically, images of the modern American South focus on sunbelt boomtown and edge-city developments such as Atlanta's Perimeter Center, Houston's River Oaks, and the Dallas Galleria area (Garreau 1991).[1] We know much less about small southern industrial cities that have followed development patterns found in northern and Midwestern communities. One such example is Bessemer, Alabama, a small city adjacent to Birmingham that was once a productive industrial center but is now a poor, majority-Black city with 26,472 residents. Tracing its history and examining its recent and current revitalization efforts illustrate the challenges and opportunities facing industrial suburbs and also remind us that the Rust Belt narrative extends beyond the Northeast and Midwest.

This chapter begins by examining the industrial origins and eventual decline of Bessemer, Alabama. First developed in the 1890s as a planned industrial city, Bessemer is located on the western end of an industrial corridor running from Birmingham's west side through other former industrial towns, including U.S. Steel's southern headquarters in Fairfield. Unlike northern and Midwestern small cities, southern industrial cities were legally segregated by race, and back-office staff reporting to out-of-state corporate headquarters ran most plants (Scribner 2002). The combination of an increasingly globalized steel market and the aftermath of the region's civil rights violence in the 1960s and 1970s led to major declines as larger plants as well as smaller local mills started to close (Doss 2018). As plants shuttered, people left, with retail following. By the 1980s Bessemer began to see major population loss just as the city's African American majority gained political power.

Next, the chapter examines the relatively fruitful efforts to revitalize the city's industrial base as well as its downtown area through the late twentieth and early twenty-first centuries. During the 1980s, Bessemer began a downtown redevelopment program focused on streetscaping and retaining small businesses while simultaneously attracting smaller distribution centers to the newly opened I-459 beltway on its southwestern edge. By the early 2000s, the city's government sought to maintain its tax base by building new retail and entertainment centers within city limits. These developments attracted shoppers from outside the city who lived in the growing western exurbs between Birmingham and Tuscaloosa, some drawn by the opening of a Mercedes-Benz assembly plant in Vance, Alabama. The city used these funds to help finance the development of new recreational facilities in the downtown core, directly targeting Bessemer residents by focusing on improving their quality of life (BCOC 2018a).

More recently the city has scored some economic development successes. The most important is the landing of two distribution centers, one for Amazon and one for the online auto retailer Carvana. It has also benefited from regional economic development efforts centered on the western side of the Birmingham Metropolitan Region. Whether these achievements will benefit the deeply impoverished residents of Bessemer remains to be determined.

Finally, the chapter considers the needs and desires of Bessemer's citizens. As part of the US EPA's College/Underserved Community Partner Program (CUPP), Bessemer worked with nearby Birmingham-Southern College (BSC) on redevelopment proposals as well as a community survey. In addition to receiving technical support for some renewal initiatives and for grant writing, the partnership with BSC has enabled local residents to express some of their concerns and priorities. Many of their desires align with past or current redevelopment measures, but some conflicts exist. Ultimately, Bessemer's fortunes may depend on the ability of local, regional, and state leaders to reconfigure the community to fit into a globalizing, service-oriented economy.

By tracing the development, collapse, and redevelopment of Bessemer, this chapter examines postindustrial revitalization strategies in a primarily blue-collar, African American small city located within a small metropolitan region. It highlights the strategies that local and state leaders have employed, including business recruitment, quality-of-life improvements, and regional development initiatives that have begun to turn Bessemer's fortunes around. Whether this revitalization work will generate an inclusive prosperity that successfully addresses the city's deep inequalities remains an open question. Berube (2019) argued that although many small cities face depopulation and loss of industrial jobs, those such as Bessemer that are located within small metros should be places for investment because they are well positioned to benefit from regional initiatives. The discussion that follows shows how one older industrial city within a small metro area has dealt with some of its social and economic challenges. Although not a typical American postindustrial city, Bessemer nevertheless illustrates the broad experiences of once-prosperous, now-struggling manufacturing centers.

The Rise and Fall of Industrial Bessemer

After the 1860s American Civil War, southern civic leaders realized that the American South needed to move beyond its agrarian economic base and into the industrial era. The New South movement's leaders argued that the region should grow by attracting northern businesses, mechanizing agriculture as slavery ended and incorporating former slaves into the labor force (Davis 1990). Northern industrialists, including steel barons from the Pittsburgh area and New York investors, became interested in Jones Valley, a region containing iron, limestone, and coal, the key elements needed for steel production. In 1871, the Elyton Land Company, a British consortium heavily financed by these American industrialists, began development of a new planned city to be known as Birmingham, for its British industrial namesake. The Tennessee Iron and Coal Company (TCI) and the Sloss-Sheffield Steel and Iron Works (Sloss) developed the largest blast furnaces in the region. As the American South's largest industrial corridor emerged along what would become the US 11 highway, the area southwest of Birmingham attracted other outside investors. These included Henry F. DeBardeleben who developed Bessemer, an industrial mill and mine settlement that the Bessemer Land and Improvement Company (BLIC) established (Doss 2010).

Bessemer grew through both private and public initiatives. It began as a private planned industrial town incorporated in 1887. DeBardeleben planned a grand town, complete with relocated 1884 New Orleans' Cotton Exposition buildings and a Carnegie Library (Doss 2018; City of Bessemer 2018.). In 1915, the Jefferson County government decided to build a satellite courthouse for the county's west side in downtown Bessemer. After a fire destroyed the city's fire department, which was located in the City Hall, in the mid-1930s, Bessemer received funding from President Roosevelt's Works Progress Administration (WPA) to construct a new City Hall with a civic auditorium. In the 1890s Bessemer became a boom town that locals referred to as The Marvel City. It competed with nearby rival Birmingham, which had earned the nickname The Magic City because locals thought the iron and steel boom created the place from nothing, as if by magic (Crenshaw 2018c; JCHA 2014, 3–4).

Bessemer proved an attractive site for northern investment. The Pittsburgh Plus pricing system dictated that despite an advantageous location close to the source of abundant raw materials, Southern steel and iron suppliers would charge buyers the same price for producing in Bessemer as in Pittsburgh. This arrangement enabled Pittsburgh- and New York-based investors to avoid competition and retain control over steel production in Bessemer. These financiers and industrialists also took advantage of the American South's Jim Crow peonage system, which conscripted people to work in the mills and mines, and its low union membership rates to reduce production costs. Other industries soon moved to Bessemer. In 1899 the United States Iron Pipe and Foundry Company (U.S. Pipe) acquired the Howard-Harrison Iron Company, a local company started in 1889. In 1929, Pullman Car & Manufacturing Corporation of Alabama incorporated as a wholly owned subsidiary of Pullman, Inc., primarily building railroad cars.

Dependence on outside investment left Bessemer vulnerable to instability and eventually to decline. The city's manufacturing employment base meant that it experienced high levels of unemployment during recessions. In 1907, an economic downturn forced TCI to sell stock to United States Steel (U.S. Steel), which resulted in an eventual takeover. In return for the first stock purchase, U.S. Steel organized a welfare program for sick and injured employees, made infrastructure improvements, and invested in local schools. The 1930s depression impacted Bessemer's industries significantly, resulting in unemployment rising and population temporarily declining. The city recovered during World War II, and its population grew steadily until the 1960s. At that point, the combination of steel's increasingly globalized production with the negative international attention that Birmingham and Alabama received during the Civil Rights era precipitated a major economic decline from which Bessemer is still trying to recover (BCOC 2018a, 2018b; Burnett 2011).

After consistent growth from the late nineteenth century until the 1970s, the city's population began to drop. From a base of 4,544 in 1890 it had reached 33,663 residents by 1970. Notably, Bessemer's decline came about a decade later than comparable population losses in many industrial small cities in the Northeast and Midwest. The difference in timing occurred in part because some companies initially shifted production to facilities in the American South with lower labor costs before moving them to other countries. The city's first postwar population decline occurred between 1970 and 1980, when it lost 1,699 residents. Plant closings fueled this downturn. Pullman produced just over one million freight cars between 1929 and 1980 but began to reduce its output before selling the facility to Trinity Industries in 1984, which closed the plant and thus eliminated 3,500 jobs. This is one illustration of the perils small cities face when they depend on only a few large employers (JCHA 2014, 3–4).

It is worth noting that Bessemer's late-twentieth-century decline was not linear. Bessemer population grew 5.6 percent between 1980 and 1990, from 31,729 to 33,497, as some industrial plants continued operations (World Population Review 2020). The city's 1990 population was just 166 people shy of its population peak in 1970. Also, residents who split family commutes between Birmingham and Tuscaloosa began moving into far western suburbs, including Bessemer. The opening of the Mercedes-Benz assembly facility in Vance, Alabama, drew more people into the metro area's western side. Nevertheless, by the 1980s population instability and job loss took a dire toll on Bessemer. Large industrial employers scaled back or closed, as did many major stores, leaving large gaps in downtown development. Property value decreased in adjacent neighborhoods. After its payroll peaked at 15,000 in the early 1960s, nearby U.S. Steel began layoffs in the early 1980s, resulting in 7,500 lost jobs. Additionally, there were large spikes in local unemployment, which at times exceeded 30 percent (Chavez 1982).

Since 1990 Bessemer has lost population every decade, and its remaining residents have experienced increased social and economic distress. The greatest drop occurred between 1990 and 2000 as the city's population declined 11.4 percent, from 33,497 to 29,672. From 2000 to 2010, Bessemer saw a slightly smaller decrease of 7.5 percent as the population fell to 27,456. As of 2019, the Census Bureau reported that Bessemer's population had declined another 3.6 percent, leaving it with an estimated 26,472, a figure similar to the city's population during the late 1940s. This decline is due not only to departures following the loss of industrial jobs but to an increased death rate among its aging population. Both trends left a growing number of the city's homes vacant (Poe 2018). In 2019 the city's median household income was $31,610, considerably lower than the Birmingham metro average of $56,409 (according to 2018 estimates). The current median property value is $83,500 with a 53.3 percent homeownership rate. Only 13.8 percent of the population had earned a four-year college degree. All these figures place Bessemer well below Birmingham metro averages (ACS, n.d.).

This decay has occurred in the context of significant racial conflict. Bessemer has long been a majority-Black city, but whites held most of the political power until the 1980s. Jim Crow strictures and regional resistance to the Civil Rights Act of 1964 and the Voting Rights Act of 1965 prevented Blacks from exercising power until 1986. At that point in *Tolbert & Petty v. City of Bessemer* (2.84-c.v.00893 UWC (N.D. Ala. 2005)), a federal judge ruled that the city's three-person city commission, elected at large, was illegal. The city then elected its first majority-Black City Council, with each member representing a specific district. Quitman Mitchell, who was part of the new majority, became Bessemer's first Black mayor in 1990. By 2019, African Americans made up an estimated

71.2 percent of the city's population, and whites accounted for just 22.8 percent. This transition to more democratic representation occurred with and may well have fueled Bessemer's economic decline and population loss.

Attempts at Revival

In the decades since Bessemer's decline began, civic and community leaders have tried various strategies for revival and the restoration of the city's tax base. First, the city wanted to retain retail to attract shoppers from newer suburbs. Second, city officials worked with state-level agencies to provide financing and tax abatements for existing and new manufacturing plants as well as brownfield reclamation. Next, city officials aggressively pursued federal funds to redevelop the downtown core's streetscapes while creating new opportunities for mixed-use restoration of historic properties, including residential options targeting blue-collar workers. Finally, to deal with public health issues and attract new people, city officials have focused on the development of recreational facilities as well as healthier food options for residents' quality of life.

Bessemer's downtown evolved in a manner similar to those in other small cities. During the first half of the twentieth century it contained a mix of municipal buildings, local and national retailers ranging from department stores to five-and-dimes, and entertainment, including movie theaters and restaurants. By the early 1960s the relatively high-wage blue-collar jobs began attracting strip malls along US Highway 11 and bringing in national retailers such as K-Mart and Zayre. By the late 1960s the US-11 corridor had attracted three indoor malls: Five Points West, Western Hills, and Westlake. Downtown Bessemer saw its shoppers go to these new developments, which in turn lured the Pizitz store from the city center to the Western Hills mall (Hollis 2010, Birmingham Rewound 2008).

Public policies fueled these changes. As in other American cities, federally funded highway construction—in Bessemer's case the opening of Interstate 20/59 along the edge of town—coupled with federally subsidized home loans encouraged people to buy homes outside downtown. Also, the 1960s Civil Rights Movement ended racially based housing restrictions, giving Blacks more opportunities to purchase homes. Subsequently, whites began leaving Bessemer and moving to adjacent towns such as Hoover. Straddling the Jefferson and Shelby County lines, Hoover incorporated in 1967. The city has remained about 75 percent white since its population was first counted during the 1970 census (ACS, 2018.).

Local redevelopment work has long emphasized retail and entertainment options, a strategy that has had mixed results at best. While the downtown retained some assets such as the Bright Star Restaurant, an upscale eatery founded during the 1910s that originally catered to steel executives, and Simmons Sporting Goods, a local retailer specializing in guns, it continues to struggle economically. Despite efforts to re-landscape the city center, many storefronts have remained vacant. In the 1990s the municipal government organized a downtown revitalization plan with development guidelines for the area. As national retail shifted from indoor regional malls to outdoor power centers, city leaders were able to attract a new Lowe's on the edge of downtown and adjacent to I-20/59. On the far west side of the city limits, city officials used tax abatements and development incentives for Colonial Trust Properties to build Tannehill Promenade, a $75 million, 350,000 square foot retail center with five major anchors and a multiplex, which opened in July 2008. Bessemer annexed the property and provided a guarantee of $13.5 million in site infrastructure work as well as an additional $1 million for the multiplex. The city's strategy helped it capture sales tax revenue from residents living outside the city limits but still shopping in Bessemer. However, the continuing shift to online shopping coupled with the COVID-19 pandemic's impacts has limited the revenue the city can capture from traditional retail. And in supporting this more suburban location, the city has undercut downtown, forcing it to rethink its approach to revitalizing that district in an era of declining brick and mortar shopping.

Attracting new industry and warehouses has also been a staple of Bessemer's pursuit of economic revival. The Bessemer Industrial Development Board (BIDB), originally set up in the 1990s, began extensive investment in businesses located in previously vacant historic structures in the mid-2010s under the leadership of Mayor Kenneth Gulley. Additionally, the BIDB established a business incubation system with two locations, one of them in the downtown area. This incubation facility has successfully graduated many businesses that maintain operations in Bessemer. In May 2007, US Pipe announced that it would invest $45 million in a state-of-the-art ductile iron pipe plant adjacent to its current facility (Graham & Co. 2010). This is the first new ductile iron plant facility constructed in the United States in fifty-five years. The new plant created one hundred jobs and the company promised not to relocate. Opened in the mid-1980s, the I-459 beltway created development opportunities for new industrial parks. These opportunities did not emerge until the early 2000s when city leaders began to pursue them. The city built on its industrial infrastructure by bringing in new distribution facilities for firms such as Milo's Tea and Dollar General that took advantage of its extensive railroad connections and interstate access. The upscale Austrian gun manufacturer Steyr Arms opened their only US facility near I-459. It included a factory and tactical training center for law enforcement, and the company has announced plans for a $29 million expansion. Taking advantage of Bessemer's small commercial airport, Steyr attracts wealthy private gun owners across the country who want to design custom products as well as try out the professional ranges.

In the central city, former industrial sites saw new life with twenty-first-century industries and manufacturers. The old Pullman site became a reclaimed brownfield when BLOX, an architectural firm specializing in the production of prefabricated hospital rooms and facilities, took over part of it. The property's massive structure became an incentive for this new manufacturing operation (Azok 2016). After a delay due to a drop in prices for recyclables, the city opened a downtown recycling center that the Alabama Environmental Council initially managed (Chambers 2019).

More recent efforts have included a new approach to downtown revival centered on the redevelopment of civic buildings. In 2017, the City opened a new $6 million City Hall facility to replace the current, dilapidated structure. Jefferson County invested recently in the construction of a new county courthouse in Bessemer's downtown. The state Department of Human Resources constructed a new office adjacent to the new courthouse. All three projects replaced blighted and abandoned properties, including the last remaining original DeBardeleben buildings relocated from New Orleans. With proper planning vision, these original structures might have provided some uniqueness to the downtown area. However, with that opportunity long gone, the new structures freshened up dilapidated downtown blocks, expanding the city's core while offering opportunities to redevelop other vacant and abandoned properties. Bessemer also implemented traffic signal and sidewalk upgrades and replaced the outdated 1980s streetscaping around the County Courthouse and the old city hall, although there is further work to be done in this area. Although a few local restaurants and antique stores have emerged, and the city has plans for further work, it is too soon to assess the impact of these measures.

Like many small cities, Bessemer has also begun to pursue quality-of-life improvements for local residents as an economic development strategy. Mayor Kenneth Gulley, first elected in 2010 has spearheaded these efforts. Gulley's administration dealt initially with a limited tax base as well as job and population losses. By 2021, it had helped add $800 million in investments and almost 8,000 jobs, spurring interest from private homebuilding companies (Reed 1988; Toraine Norris, interview by author, April 14, 2021). The city set aside $250,000 annually to combat blight through the implementation of a demolition program. This plan is popular with local residents who were tired of overgrown lots creating pest problems as well as abandoned homes providing shelter for criminal activities. The city currently works with Habitat for Humanity to construct new homes within Bessemer and as of 2021 has several projects underway, including

50 new homes in the Hopewell area (Toraine Norris, interview by author, April 14, 2021). Finally, the Red Rock Ridge and Valley Trail System, a US Department of Transportation TIGER (Transportation Investment Generating Economic Recovery)–funded project started in 2012 is underway. This greenway project creates a network connecting communities (including those in Bessemer) throughout Jefferson County. The trail system includes sidewalks and bike lanes to improve bike and pedestrian connectivity. In Bessemer, the three-mile High Ore Line Trail opened in 2019 (Freshwater Land Trust 2019). This trail integrates Bessemer to other areas of Jefferson County while connecting new city facilities such as the recreation center to downtown. Constructed by the city, the new center includes indoor aquatic pools, exercise facilities, and a senior center. The recreation center provides a new city hub for residents to connect with each other. This facility is adjacent to the trail network and in walking distance from local schools (Toraine Norris, interview by author, March 27, 2018).

This focus on recreation assets addresses another key problem that Bessemer faces. Alabama ranks consistently among the most obese states in the nation with an approximate obesity rate of 35.7 percent. In Jefferson County alone, approximately 66 percent of all adults are either overweight or obese. Alabama ranks second in the nation with the highest rate of diabetes at 14.6 percent, and it ranks third in the nation for the rate of those with hypertension at 40.4 percent (Howton 2018; JCHD 2018).

Bessemer's leadership recognized that one of the keys to improving local health, a vital part of successful revitalization, is to combat food insecurity. Until recently there were no viable fresh food options for the downtown area and its adjacent neighborhoods. A small group of people invested in the community attempted a grass roots effort to create a downtown farmer's market in May 2013. However, the market has thus far been unsuccessful due to issues with its remote location on the downtown edge as well as with marketing. A move in 2020 to the Bessemer Recreation Center aimed to boost sales as well as to include more Black farmers. The city and its leaders used the Local Foods, Local Places grant funds to create a plan for the marketing and implementation of the farmer's market to help spur interest and consumer traffic in the downtown area while giving historically underserved residents access to healthy food options. The Bessemer Local Foods Education Network operates a seasonal outdoor farmers market in the downtown area as well as an indoor market at the University of Alabama-Birmingham (UAB) West Medical facility with both accepting SNAP electronic benefits transfer (EBT) payments and Double Bucks, a program matching SNAP-eligible food purchases with an EBT card dollar for dollar up to $20 per day (Bessemer Farmers Market, 2020.).

Because the market's primary customer base downtown has been senior citizens, its leaders would like to attract younger residents. The city plans to establish a year-round market downtown with a storefront component and pavilion. Originally, the city sought to redevelop the former city hall into a community food kitchen where local nonprofits would manage distribution as well as provide a site for local producers to process goods in a commercial-grade facility. This plan was dropped when the property drew interest from developers seeking to create downtown housing. The city wants to use vacant land as community gardens that help beautify its neighborhoods, give residents additional buy-in to their community, and offer access to healthy, fresh foods. Finally, the city would like to develop the former Sunset Homes public housing site property as an urban farm/gardening project. Housing units were demolished in this area after flooding damaged them during Tropical Storm Lee in 2011. The property consists of 25 acres in a federally designated flood plain (Holt, Norris, and Openshaw 2018).

Recent Successes

Bessemer's more recent business attraction efforts have landed two substantial distribution operations. The most notable of these is an Amazon fulfillment center. While numerous large North American cities pursued Amazon's second executive headquarters, Bessemer went after a regional fulfillment center, building on its working-class base as well as capitalizing on the extensive railroad and later expressway networks originally built for twentieth-century industrial and commercial activity. In June 2018 Amazon announced plans to construct a $325 million, 855,000 square foot advanced robotics fulfillment center on 133 acres of U.S. Steel property located off I-20/59, promising 1,500 full-time jobs. Opening in March 2020, the center soon employed almost 6,000 full and part-time employees (Toraine Norris, interview by author, April 14, 2021; ADC, 2018.; Crenshaw 2018a).

Amazon's decision to open their first Alabama fulfillment center in Bessemer, an estimated $325 million investment, depended on major financial incentives from government. The Jefferson County Commission and Alabama Power each offered $3.3 million incentive packages. Jefferson County's incentives went for roadway improvements and reimbursement to Amazon for capital investment. Bessemer's city council approved occupational tax rebates between 50 percent and 65 percent depending on the actual number of Amazon employees. Amazon received a 50 percent occupational tax rebate on their first 1,000 to 2,000 jobs and 60 percent on the next 2,001 to 3,000 jobs, with the rebate percentage increasing up to 65 percent with additional jobs added (Crenshaw 2018b). Bessemer's incentive package included limited building fees to a one-time $2,000 charge as well as a $5,000 business license fee cap for ten years. Also, Bessemer allocated $40,000 for a new municipal bus stop at the center.

In turn, Bessemer expected to receive a substantial boost. The city estimated that the Amazon facility would bring in about $800,000 to $1 million in additional school taxes (Kopolowitz 2018). The company offered full-timers up to $3,000 per year in reimbursements for as many as four years of education or training that results in certificates, commercial driver's licenses, and two- or four-year college degrees. Amazon guaranteed wages to start at $15.00 per hour, not including benefits, for full-time employees (Edgemon 2018; Kopolowitz 2018; Crenshaw 2018c).

Bessemer's leadership built on the successful landing of the Amazon site by luring a Carvana Distribution Center to town. Announced in November 2019, the online car retailer's Bessemer hub will manage fulfillment for Alabama and surrounding states. The company will also house inspection, maintenance, and photography at this facility. Spending $40 million of its own funds for construction and equipment, Carvana expected their new facility to employ 450, with an average salary exceeding $35,000 (Thornton 2019). Bessemer leaders viewed both the Amazon and Carvana facilities as major opportunities for local high school and technical school graduates to find employment nearby.

Bessemer leaders took a realistic approach to capitalizing on the landing of Amazon and Carvana as they sought to attract new residents and rebuild the city's downtown. Instead of trying to build luxury condos for the affluent medical and student markets, such as those in downtown Birmingham, Bessemer's housing plans focus on affordable price points to attract new workers at Amazon and Carvana as well as those working at existing distribution centers such as Milo's Tea and Dollar General, which employ 300 and 700 people respectively. Local leaders saw a market for these workers who are young, many without children, and looking for an urban living experience. Such an approach may also avoid some of the pitfalls of gentrification, by accommodating rather than displacing existing residents. So, although it initially considered the former city hall for a relocated farmer's market and retail center, Bessemer reconceived this property as a residential development. In March 2021, Bessemer approved the sale of the former city hall building to 1800 BCH, a subsidiary of Wisconsin-based Scott Crawford, Inc. and partner Cardinal Capital for $200,000 (Collins 2019; Toraine Norris, interview by author, April 14, 2021). Crawford, Inc. plans a $10 million mixed-use housing development with fifty residential units and 4,000 square feet of retail space, with a late 2022 opening date planned. Parking for new residents will be available in the former city hall spaces in an adjacent municipal lot. Crawford, Inc. partnered with three other subpartners (Hull 2019). The project is an outgrowth of Bessemer's new Amazon facility, as expanded local employment opportunities in turn attracted new residential development (Thornton 2020).

As downtown Bessemer starts to emerge as a site for residential development, a few entrepreneurs have seen an opportunity in providing amenities for the new residents. Abandoned for almost forty years, the Lincoln Theater, designated for African Americans during the Jim Crow era, used to show popular commercial films. Bessemer natives Donald and Mary Sanders Holland along with their son, actor Andre Holland, purchased the facility, which most recently served as a furniture storage warehouse. The Hollands bought the theater in 2017 for about $40,000. Their goal is to save the 4,000 square foot theater and transform it into a cinema, restaurant, and bookstore. The Hollands received a historical façade grant of up to $100,000 from Bessemer, which makes the project eligible for a 20 percent federal match of funding spent to rehabilitate a building in the city's National Historic District (Colurso 2019).

The Amazon fulfillment center is only part of a larger redevelopment pattern along the west side of metro Birmingham. This region is transitioning from steel, mining, and heavy manufacturing to assembly and distribution facilities. The Jefferson County Economic and Industrial Authority began diversifying the region's economy in the late 1990s. The Jefferson Metropolitan Park, located west of Bessemer in McCalla, was their first project. The Metropolitan Park is home to distribution and light manufacturing industries, including Publix, Home Depot, Plastipak (a water bottle manufacturer), and Gestamp, a Spanish-based auto parts manufacturer supplying the Mercedes-Benz plant in nearby Vance. Adjacent to the Metropolitan Park is Norfolk Southern Railway's intermodal facility loading shipping containers between rail and trucks. Later, rival CSX built an intermodal facility on the former Pullman site in Bessemer. So, while many projects are being developed through the City of Bessemer, they are often sought in conjunction with Jefferson County and State of Alabama economic agencies and many seek to revitalize the entire western corridor of Birmingham (Carter 2018). In May 2020, Bessemer received a $300,000 US EPA brownfield site assessment grant providing for reviews of twelve Phase I and nine Phase II locations, with plans to transform them into future development opportunities (Swain 2020).

Understanding Community Needs

The record of redevelopment efforts in Bessemer suggests an uneven appreciation of the needs and desires of local residents. While a focus on downtown revival, increased amenities, and greater quality of life stand to benefit the city's mostly Black, mostly poor and working-class citizens, investments in retail shopping with highway access have been more oriented toward serving shoppers from the wider region and in some respects have undercut retail expansion in the urban core. The recent success in landing the Amazon and Carvana distribution centers may trigger a new cycle of investment, but the relatively low wages offered by these employers may not be sufficient to revive the economic fortunes of a deeply impoverished city such as Bessemer. If it does, it will require more consistent attention to the wishes of community members as well as business interests in the planning and redevelopment process.

Bessemer recently formed a partnership with Birmingham Southern College (BSC) to help it pursue a more inclusive and effective planning process through an EPA initiative. Whereas some cities can rely on research conducted with large, well-funded state universities that have numerous graduate students, many smaller cities may have to look at other options. As part of the US EPA's Environmental Justice Division, the College/Underserved Community Partnership Program (CUPP) provides mechanisms for delivering technical assistance to underserved communities via local colleges and smaller universities. Through student internships and capstone projects, these communities receive technical support at no cost while they provide students applied experiences. In 2016, the US EPA's CUPP Program matched Bessemer with Birmingham-Southern College (BSC), a 1,200-student, undergraduate liberal arts college located nearby on Birmingham's western side. Although EPA Region 4 canceled the CUPP Program in 2019, it laid the groundwork for an ongoing partnership between Bessemer and BSC (US EPA, n.d.).

BSC has provided resources to generate a deeper understanding of Bessemer's needs and the challenges it faces. The college's Urban Environmental Studies (UES) Program provides students a liberal arts approach to addressing environmental issues in urban areas. The UES Program focuses on sustainability in four areas: environmental, economic, sociopolitical and cultural. Also, BSC pairs UES students with those in architectural studies, sociology, public health, and poverty studies to provide technical assistance from urban design plans to surveys for the city through class team projects and senior individual major capstones.

The BSC UES Program collaborated with the city through CUPP on preplanning efforts for the Sunset Farms and former city hall sites. This college/small city partnership grew from the college's initial Western Area Initiative focused on Birmingham neighborhoods directly adjacent to the institution and its work to identify community needs. BSC has worked with the Bessemer Local Food Education Network, a nonprofit community organization that manages the city's farmers markets and coordinates efforts of local producers. BSC has also supported the city's Housing Authority in its attempts to reuse no longer viable properties as well as to promote healthy food options for those in active housing sites. Bessemer's leadership is committed to the implementation of local food options that will promote downtown redevelopment and increase overall community health and access to healthy food options. The city will pursue viable funding options for this implementation as well as work to ensure that there are match-funding options available for implementation. Through the BSC and Bessemer partnership established through the CUPP program, the city has pursued funding options for these projects. While the technical planning for both Sunset Farms and the former city hall building materialized, a joint grant application between the city and college to the USDA to finalize the Sunset Farms master plan and begin construction was not successful. However, by developing the grant proposal, the city has a base from which to pursue other funding options.

To help ensure that redevelopment efforts were responsive to community interests, BSC and Bessemer developed a citywide needs-assessment survey that was administered by BSC in spring 2018. BSC surveyed two hundred city residents. Respondents included seventy-two men and 128 women. There were 144 Blacks, fifty-one whites, two Latinos, two Native Americans, and one biracial subject in the sample. Thirty-one respondents were aged 18–29, seventy-nine were aged 30–49, seventy-two were aged 50–69, and eighteen were aged 70 or over. Of the two hundred respondents, sixty-four had some ties to Bessemer's industrial workforce. Of these, fifty-two had family members who had either worked or were working in local industrial jobs. This included former employees of now-departed companies such as Pullman and Stockham Pipe and Valve as well as those working at currently active firms such as U.S. Pipe and Mercedes-Benz. Twenty-three respondents either worked or had worked in an industrial job.

One important finding from the survey had to do with crime. A problem Bessemer faces in its revitalization efforts is its image as a crime-ridden community. Based on local reporting by television stations, the *Birmingham News*, and the AL.com website (a combination of content from the Birmingham, Huntsville, and Mobile newspapers), Bessemer is a dangerous place. However, a content analysis of coverage by *The Birmingham News* and *The Birmingham Times* (an African American newspaper) showed that *The Birmingham News* attributed many violent crimes to Bessemer that had actually occurred in Birmingham's western neighborhoods or in other west-side towns. The content study showed no positive stories about Bessemer in *The Birmingham Times* whereas the majority of stories in *The Birmingham News* were about new projects and civic activities in Bessemer (Blankenship 2018). The BSC survey followed up on this content analysis by distributing a crime victimization questionnaire, asking if the respondent or immediate family member had been a victim of crime in the past year. It suggested that the city's reputation for violence and lawlessness was overstated. Of respondents, only twenty-three reported being crime victims and 173 did not. The twenty-three reported crimes included two murders, one sexual assault, three robberies, five home burglaries, and one stolen car. The remaining eleven crimes involved minor property theft and car break-ins. As Bessemer moves forward with redevelopment, the reality and perceptions of criminal activities should be addressed. This concern is especially relevant as the city attempts to attract residents to the downtown.

Outdoor recreation, walkable neighborhoods and safer communities are other key areas that residents want to see expanded, although there is some disagreement about priorities. Respondents viewed Bessemer Recreational Center, with its indoor pool, workout facilities, senior and youth programs, as a major asset to the city. Residents noted that not only did they like having the facilities in town but wanted city officials to continue developing projects focusing on their quality of life. Few were aware of the rails-to-trails programs that started in 2017, but that number should grow as more people use it. Also, residents wanted the city to continue to attract stores catering to middle-class shoppers and family restaurants. They were concerned about the recent closure of national retailers at Tannehill Promenade, including JCPenney, and the lack of fresh food restaurants. However, as noted city economic development officials face an uphill battle dealing with national retail trends that have shifted toward online sales. Also, there is a tension between older residents who want national family chains such as Applebee's or Ruby Tuesdays, and younger residents who seek locally sourced food options. This division reflects the difficult choice a reviving small city faces as it strives to balance the interests and desires of established members of the community while it attracts newcomers.

Conclusion

Although small American cities face many of the challenges large cities do, they face particular constraints and distinctive opportunities. (Connolly 2010; Peterson 1981). Berube (2019) argued convincingly that efforts to revitalize smaller, economically underperforming communities need to find a middle ground between the "U-Haul school," an approach that encourages people to relocate to regions with greater economic opportunities, and propping up distressed communities through government spending. Although revitalization measures in cities such as Bessemer have and likely will continue to focus on business development and the creation of amenities to attract new residents, they need to do so with the interests of local residents, many of whom are poor and minorities, in mind. With sufficient resources in hand, their smaller size may permit them to do so more completely and more nimbly than can larger cities.

City leaders have limited power to deal with globalization or industry shifts due to technology (Peterson 1981). However, proactive small-city leaders can make attempts to adapt to these trends faster than larger cities, just as states have served as labs for national policy innovations. Although located in the American South, Bessemer's history follows a pattern seen typically in the US Northeast and Midwest. Until relatively recently, local leadership has followed the standard, business-centered redevelopment playbook, building on existing downtown anchors and maintaining a city tax base by ensuring that suburban-type retailing and industries remain within the city limits. More recently, the city has used some of this tax revenue to construct facilities that directly benefit local residents' quality of life. Through the US EPA's CUPP Program, Bessemer has been seeking to incorporate a more robust sense of community needs into its planning and revival work. However, as shown by the Amazon and Carvana projects, business attraction requires hundreds of millions of public dollars from federal, state, county, and municipal sources—funds that might otherwise address the more immediate needs of local residents. Bessemer received global attention in 2021 when the Retail, Wholesale, and Department Store Union sought unsuccessfully to unionize local Amazon workers. As small cities shift from industrial to wholesale and distribution centers, such conflicts seem likely to arise. How much a community benefits from the arrival of these and other firms over the long term will depend on how well it is able to capture the resources they generate.

It should be noted that Bessemer's fortunes depend not only on municipal action. The city often benefits from being part of the regional economic redevelopment of metro Birmingham's entire western side, which has created connections and access to job opportunities for local residents across municipalities. However, while Bessemer has profited from these linkages, it has also experienced some setbacks. Most notable is the University of Alabama Birmingham's decision to relocate the UAB West Hospital from downtown Bessemer to a new site in McCalla along I-459. For the first time in fifty-five years Bessemer will not have a hospital in the city (Kopolowitz 2018b). As in the case of other regional decisions, the interests of Bessemer's residents did not weigh heavily in this decision. Further, as has often been the case, Bessemer leaders are seeking to turn a loss that came about because of a decision that was out of their hands into an opportunity by transforming the former hospital into a nursing home facility with doctors' offices. If this Southern, majority–African American, deindustrialized small city is to revive within a globalized, service-oriented economy, it will need to make these and other improvements with the concrete needs of its citizens in mind.

Notes

1. This chapter was presented at the 2018 Small Cities Conference, Ball State University, Muncie, Indiana. This research is part of the US EPA's College/Underserved Communities Partnership between the City of Bessemer, Alabama, and Birmingham-Southern College.

References

Alabama Department of Commerce (ADC). 2018. "How Amazon Picked the Prime Site For Its First Alabama Fulfillment Center." Accessed July 28, 2020. https://www.madeinalabama.com/why-alabama/success-stories/how-amazon-picked-the-prime-site-for-its-first-alabama-fulfillment-center/.

American Community Survey (ACS). 2018. US Census Bureau. Accessed October 22, 2020. https://www.census.gov/programs-surveys/acs/data.html.

Azok, Dawn. 2016. "Building BLOX: Alabama Architecture Firm Makes Mark on Healthcare with Innovated Process." *Made in Alabama*, August 25, 2016. http://www.madeinalabama.com/2016/08/blox.

Berube, Alan. 2019. *Why Midsize Metro Areas Deserve Our Attention*. Washington, DC: Brookings Institution. https://www.brookings.edu/research/why-midsized-metro-areas-deserve-our-attention/.

Bessemer Area Chamber of Commerce (BCOC). 2018a. *Bessemer*. Vol. XIII.

Bessemer Area Chamber of Commerce (BCOC). 2018b. "Historic Downtown Bessemer." Accessed March 27, 2018. http://downtownbessemer.blogspot.com.

Bessemer Farmers Market. 2020. Accessed July 27, 2020. https://www.bessemerfarmersmarket.com/.

Birmingham Rewound. 2008. "Pizitz at Five Points West: Birmingham's Original 'Dead Mall.'" April 22, 2008. http://birminghamrewound.com/old_5pw_pizitz.htm.

Blankenship, Jesslyn. 2018. "Changing the Public's Perception on Crime: Impact of News Media, Urban and Social Planning on Crime Prevention in Bessemer." Senior Project, Urban Environmental Studies Program, Birmingham-Southern College.

Burnett, Jason. 2011. *Early Bessemer*. Charleston, SC: Arcadia.

Carter, Robert. 2018. "Amazon's a Big Deal, but West Jefferson's Economic Rebirth is Bigger and Broader." *BirminghamWatch*, July 19, 2018. https://birminghamwatch.org/amazons-big-deal-west-jeffersons-economic-rebirth-bigger-broader/.

Chambers, Jesse. 2019. "Alabama Environmental Council Seeks To Put New Recycling Center in Downtown Bessemer." *AL.com*, March 6, 2019. https://www.al.com/spotnews/2013/10/alabama_environmental_center_s.html.

Chavez, Lydia. 1982. "U.S. Steel to Close Big Alabama Mill." *The New York Times*, May 22, 1982. http://www.nytimes.com/1982/05/22/business/us-steel-to-close-big-alabama-mill.html.

City of Bessemer. 2018. "History of Bessemer." Accessed March 27, 2018. https://www.bessemeral.org/about-bessemer/.

Collins, Alan. 2019. "Old Bessemer City Hall Sold to Developer." *WBRC.com*, May 9, 2019. https://www.wbrc.com/2019/05/09/old-bessemer-city-hall-sold-developer/.

Connolly, James J., ed. 2010. *After the Factory: Reinventing America's Industrial Small Cities*. Lanham, MD: Lexington.

Colurso, Mary. 2019. "There's New Life at Bessemer's Historic Lincoln Theatre, Thanks to Actor Andre Holland and Family." *AL.com,* September 12, 2019. https://www.al.com/life/2019/09/theres-new-life-at-bessemers-historic-lincoln-theatre-thanks-to-actor-andre-holland-and-family.html.

Crenshaw, Solomon. 2018a. "Touchdown! Bessemer Celebrates Scoring Deal to Secure Amazon Center." *BirminghamWatch*, June 22, 2018. https://birminghamwatch.org/touchdown-bessemer-celebrates-scoring-deal-secure-amazon-center/.

Crenshaw, Solomon. 2018b. "Bessemer OKs Tax Rebate, Fee Reductions and Transit Service to Bring in Amazon Center." *BirminghamWatch*, June 12, 2018. https://birminghamwatch.org/bessemer-oks-tax-rebate-fee-reductions-transit-services-bring-amazon-center/.

Crenshaw, Solomon. 2018c. "The Way Things Used to Be: Officials Recall Bessemer's Heyday while Approving Incentives to Lure in Amazon." *BirminghamWatch*, June 7, 2018. https://birminghamwatch.org/way-things-used-officials-recall-bessemers-heyday-approving-incentives-lure-amazon/.

Davis, Harold. 1990. *Henry Grady's New South: Atlanta, A Brave and Beautiful City*. Tuscaloosa: University of Alabama Press.

Doss, Faye L. "Bessemer." *Encyclopedia of Alabama*. Article published December 9, 2010; last modified August 17, 2020. http://www.encyclopediaofalabama.org/article/h-2996.

Edgemon, Erin. 2018. "Jefferson County, Bessemer to Consider Incentives to Lure Amazon." *AL.com*, May 31, 2018. https://www.al.com/news/birmingham/2018/05/jefferson_county_bessemer_to_c.html.

Freshwater Land Trust. 2019. "Now Open: High Ore Line Trail to Red Mountain Park." August 2, 2019. http://freshwaterlandtrust.org/high-ore-open/.

Garreau, Joel. 1991. *Edge Cities: Life on the New Frontier*. New York: Anchor.

Graham & Co. 2010. "80-Job Pipe Coating Plant Coming to Bessemer." *Birmingham News*, January 12, 2010. http://www.grahamcompany.com/news/80-job-pipe-coating-plant-coming-to-bessemer/.

Hollis, Tim. 2010. *Pizitz: Your Store*. Charleston, SC: History Press.

Holt, William, Toraine Norris, and Joe Openshaw. 2018. "Development of Urban Food Production, Processing and Distribution in Bessemer." Grant Application. US Department of Agriculture's Farmers Market and Local Food Promotion Program. Unpublished manuscript.

Hull, Christine. 2019. "New Apartments, Retail Space Coming to Historic Former Bessemer City Hall." *Bham Now*, April 23, 2019. https://bhamnow.com/2019/04/23/new-apartments-retail-space-coming-to-historic-former-bessemer-city-hall/.

Jefferson County Historical Association (JCHA). 2014. "Bessemer Plant Made Pullman Standard's One Millionth Rail Car." *Jefferson County Historical Association Newsletter*, July 2014.

Kopolowitz, Howard. 2018a. "Bessemer City Council Gives Mayor Go-Ahead to Make Deal with Amazon on Facility." *AL.com*, June 12, 2018. https://www.al.com/news/2018/06/bessemer_city_council_gives_ma.html.

Kopolowitz, Howard. 2018b. "UAB Medical West to Move from Bessemer to McCalla." *Al.com*, October 26, 2018. https://www.al.com/news/birmingham/2018/10/uab-medical-west-to-move-from-bessemer-to-mccalla.html.

Peterson, Paul. 1981. *City Limits*. Chicago: University of Chicago Press.

Poe, Kelly. 2016. "U.S. Steel Lays Off 200 More Workers in Fairfield." *AL.com*, March 18, 2016. https://www.al.com/business/2016/03/us_steel_lays_off_200_more_wor.html.

Reed, Adolph. 1988. "The Black Urban Regime: Structural Origins and Constraints." In *Power, Community, and the City*, edited by M. P. Smith, 138–189. Comparative Urban and Community Research, Vol. 1. New Brunswick, NJ: Transaction.

Scriber, Christopher MacGregor. 2002. *Renewing Birmingham: Federal Funding and the Promise of Change, 1929–1979*. Athens: University of Georgia Press.

Swain, Sharron Mendel. 2020. "Bessemer Got a $300K Brownfield Grant—Why This is Good News." *Bham Now*, May 19, 2020. https://bhamnow.com//2020/05/19/bessemer-brownfield-grant-good-news.

Thornton, William. 2019. "Carvana to Build $40 Million Bessemer Distribution Center, to Hire 450." *Al.com*, November 5, 2019. https://www.al.com/business/2019/11/carvana-to-build-40-million-bessemer-distribution-center-to-hire-450.html.

Thornton, William. 2020. "$10 Million Bessemer Project Would Use Former City Hall." *AL.com*, April 22, 2020. https://www.al.com/business/2019/04/10-million-bessemer-project-would-use-former-city-hall.html.

United States Environmental Protection Agency (US EPA). 2019. College/Underserved Community Partnership Program. Accessed January 2, 2019. https://www.epa.gov/environmentaljustice/collegeunderserved-community-partnership-program.

World Population Review. 2020. "Bessemer, Alabama Population 2020 (Demographics, Maps, Graphs)." Accessed October 22, 2020. https://worldpopulationreview.com/us-cities/bessemer-al-population.

Part II

PATTERNS AND STRATEGIES

5

THE ECONOMIC FORTUNES OF SMALL INDUSTRIAL CITIES AND TOWNS

Manufacturing, Place Luck, and the Urban Transfer Payment Economy

Alan Mallach

As the industrial revolution spread across the United States during the nineteenth and early twentieth centuries, it spawned a few outsized manufacturing centers such as Detroit and Pittsburgh that became global icons of American industrial might. At the same time, it created hundreds of smaller cities and towns that were dependent on manufacturing not only for their prosperity but for their very existence. These cities and towns range from still-important regional centers like Allentown, Pennsylvania, or Dayton, Ohio, to far smaller places such as the factory towns strung like beads along the Monongahela and Ohio Rivers.

As larger cities like Pittsburgh and Baltimore have revived over the last roughly two decades, commentators have noted the extent to which smaller industrial cities have lagged their larger counterparts in terms of revival and regrowth (Longworth 2008; Tumber 2012; O'Hara 2010). Although the reasons for larger cities' revival are complex and multifaceted, three central themes appear consistently significant: the role of global educational and medical institutions (Harkavy and Zuckerman 1999; Gurwitt 2008), the emergence of the twenty-first-century city as a center of consumption (Clark 2011), and the in-migration of university-educated millennials (Moos, Pfeiffer, and Vinodrai 2017).

Since the 1950s, the share of the US economy devoted to health care and to higher education has grown rapidly. In 1950, the United States spent $12 billion on health care ($117 billion in 2014 dollars). In 2014, with a national population slightly more than double that of 1950, we spent just over $3 *trillion* as a nation for health care—more than twenty-five times what we spent in 1950. Of that total, nearly $1 trillion went for hospital care. Over the same period, spending on medical research, although a small part of the total, went from under $1 billion (in 2014 dollars) in 1950 to $46 billion in 2014—almost fifty times what it was in 1950. The growth in higher education spending, although not as precipitous, has outpaced population growth by a factor of more than four.

Although economic changes have put large industrial cities at a competitive disadvantage with respect to manufacturing, decisions made long ago to found the institutions that have become today's global centers of health care and higher education placed the same cities in a strong position to capitalize on the transformation of higher education and health care (often known as "eds and meds"). Growth in institutions such as Johns Hopkins in Baltimore, the University of Pittsburgh (Pitt) and University of Pittsburgh Medical Center (UPMC), and the Cleveland Clinic has fueled the revival of those cities. These institutions are not just larger than but qualitatively different from the colleges and community hospitals of smaller cities.

Eds and meds in a city like Pittsburgh are a global industry and the city's dominant economic engine. Tens of thousands of students from all over the world gravitate to its universities, and UPMC is the largest nongovernmental employer in the state of Pennsylvania with a $13 billion operating budget. These are export industries in the truest sense, attracting billions of dollars from the outside to fuel the local economy and spinning off cutting-edge biotech and IT businesses and drawing others, while their students and employees fuel commercial spending, entertainment, and residential revitalization.

Canton, Ohio, a representative small industrial city of 71,000, also has an eds and meds sector, with two community hospitals and Malone University, a Quaker-oriented institution with around 1,600 students. The hospitals meet the health care needs of the city and nearby communities, whereas most of Malone University's students come from the surrounding region, and only half live on campus. These and their counterparts in similar small cities are important community assets and provide some jobs but otherwise add little to the city's economy. From an economic perspective, if Pitt is Central Park, Malone is a community playground.

The University of Pittsburgh has over eleven thousand full-time employees compared with Malone's 250, and an annual operating budget of $2.1 billion compared with $32 million. Not only do research universities have larger student bodies, faculty, and administrative staff, but their faculty and staff make far more; the average full professor at Yale makes nearly $200,000 for her nine months' work, compared with $65,000 for her counterpart at Malone University. Johns Hopkins University spent $2.3 billion on R&D in 2015, whereas Pitt and Carnegie Mellon spent $1.1 billion. By comparison, even large commuter universities generate little research activity; Youngstown State University's student body is more than half the size of Johns Hopkins', but YSU spent only $3.3 million on R&D in 2015, or slightly more than *one-thousandth* as much.

As urban economies have been molded by eds and meds, erstwhile industrial cities have been reinvented as centers of consumption, characterized as "entertainment machines" (Clark 2011) or Michael Sorkin's more pejorative "theme parks" (1992). Cities are increasingly places where wealth is spent rather than created, and perhaps should be seen more as "consumption machines" than as "entertainment machines," growing by providing the services and amenities sought by a consumption-oriented society. As bluntly put by Glaeser, Kolko, and Saiz (2001), "attractive cities will thrive; unpleasant cities will decay."

Amenities, which can be a scenic waterfront or a cluster of theaters and restaurants like Cleveland's Playhouse Square, are not merely the product of consumption demand but are themselves generators and multipliers of demand, by drawing people with money to spend and potential wealth-creating skills to cities. A critical part of this is what Clark calls the "scene." When enough amenities cluster in one area to form a critical mass, they create scenes. *Scenes* draw people together to share activities, to behave in different but specific ways, to participate in a distinctive shared atmosphere, and to define their identities by sharing the scene with other like-minded people. Scenes also offer young unattached people the greatest opportunity to make friends and identify potential romantic partners.

Many factors contribute to drawing the millennial generation to these cities, but the presence of a "scene" is a critical element. The millennials who set the pace for urban revival cluster in areas that offer the amenities that most resonate with their interests and life style. These areas not only have restaurants, cafes, and music venues but also have high densities and lively mixtures of different activities on the same block or even in the same building. It is not without reason that the reinvention of historically nonresidential downtowns as heavily residential mixed-use areas is a prominent feature of the urban revival (Birch 2009).

All this depends on the existence of a critical mass at various levels; or, put differently, the emergence of an agglomeration economy; or, as defined by Glaeser (2010), "the benefits that come when firms and people locate near one another together in cities and industrial clusters." Ultimately, all the complex synergies of economic transformation, consumption, scenes, and selective inmigration are dependent on the benefits of agglomeration, creating a critical mass of amenities as well as the knowledge spillovers and thick labor market needed to create and sustain a postindustrial economy (Moretti 2012).

To the extent that critical mass is a function of population size, small cities are at an inherent disadvantage attempting to compete with larger cities on the basis of the same assumptions about revival grounded in the linked dynamics of an export-oriented eds and meds sector, a strong consumption economy largely driven by millennial in-migration (Mallach 2018). Although there are exceptions, as I discuss in the next section of this chapter, they are rare.

Small cities' disadvantage is not attributable, as O'Hara (2010, 26) suggests, to their being "specifically designed to not have the kind of diversity and vibrancy that Jane Jacobs points to as essential to urban growth." That is certainly true of the mill towns of the Monongahela Valley and elsewhere but not of cities like Dayton, Ohio, or Trenton, New Jersey, which in their heyday contained vibrant downtowns and neighborhoods, robust cultural and educational institutions, and substantial social and economic, as well as racial and ethnic, diversity. Their disadvantage lies in their inability to aggregate the necessary activities—institutional, economic, cultural, or otherwise—capable of creating sustainable critical mass. What that means, in turn, is that revival strategies mirroring what might be called the "creative class" strategies of larger cities are likely to yield far more limited results in most smaller cities.

Two Contrasting Models of Small-City Economic Vitality

If small cities cannot find a path to success by emulating the large city revival model that I have summarized above, what paths to success are available to them? Whereas I conclude this chapter by looking directly at that question, it serves as a useful frame for examining two types of small city that appear to show, at least for the moment, considerable economic vitality. I refer to these two city types as production cities and, for reasons that are apparent, well-positioned cities.

Production Cities

Despite alarmist reports, manufacturing in the United States is far from dead. Although a smaller part of the US economy than in its heyday, in 2018 manufacturing employed nearly 13 million people, equal to 8.5 percent of the US workforce, and generated $2.3 trillion in GDP, equal to 11.4 percent of the total GDP (National Association of Manufacturers 2019). Much of this activity has historically taken place in small towns and cities, and it continues to do so, arguably more than in larger cities, whose early-twentieth-century steel mills and auto plants became the dinosaurs of the changing economy.

The importance of manufacturing to a local economy can be easily discerned by looking closely at Ohio. In 2015, the manufacturing sector employed 25 percent or more of the county's workforce in twenty-five of Ohio's eighty-eight counties, indicating that those counties' economies are heavily dependent on manufacturing. Although by themselves those numbers prove nothing about the economic vitality or well-being of these counties or their residents, a closer look at these counties offers some insights into those considerations.

All twenty-five are small-city, small-town, or rural counties, although four lie within the penumbra of a larger city's metropolitan area. The largest central place in any of the twenty-five counties, Findlay, has a population of slightly more than forty thousand; in ten counties, the largest central place has a population under ten thousand. Most of these central places are actually towns rather than cities.

Table 5.1 shows salient features of the fifteen counties containing a central place with a population over ten thousand. The table suggests that on the whole these counties and their small cities are doing well. The 2016 unemployment rate was below the statewide average in twelve of the fifteen counties, and median household income was above the statewide average in ten of the fifteen and significantly (more than 10 percent) below in only one county. Even more notably, the family poverty rate was lower than either the state or national rate in fourteen of the fifteen counties. Although the number of manufacturing jobs declined by 23 percent nationally between 2002 and 2015, those jobs declined by only 10 percent in these fifteen counties; in four counties, their number actually grew.

The industrial mix in many of these counties is highly diversified, as shown in table 5.2 for Greenville and for Darke County, located in western Ohio along the Indiana border. The county's principal manufacturers, of which all but two are located in Greenville, are a mix of direct consumer products (small appliances, awards, and dry ice) and supply chain products (automotive parts and coatings, electric motors, and oil filters). In a vote of confidence for the area, the Midmark Corporation announced that it would build its new technology center in 2018 in Versailles, adding another ninety-seven jobs to the area (Chalmers 2017). This is a very different model from the traditional single-industry company town.

Cities like Greenville and Celina in Mercer County are not wealthy, but they suggest solid economic well-being, with few vacant storefronts in their neat, often carefully restored downtowns and well-maintained older houses on tree-lined streets. While both cities boast at least one coffee place where one can buy a latte, reflecting how much espresso drinks have become a mainstream taste, most downtown stores cater to a population that is working class but not poor. Moreover, challenging the assumption that prosperity is dependent on a college degree, the share of the population with a bachelor's or higher degree in fourteen of fifteen counties (the exception is Union County, which is becoming an exurban adjunct of Columbus) is significantly below either statewide or national levels.

TABLE 5.1. Production counties in Ohio

COUNTY	PRINCIPAL CITY/TOWN	PRINCIPAL CITY/TOWN POPULATION	MANUFACTURING JOBS OUT OF TOTAL JOBS (%)	RESIDENTS WITH BA OR HIGHER DEGREE (%)	MEDIAN HOUSEHOLD INCOME ($)	UNEMPLOYMENT RATE (%)	MANUFACTURING JOBS 2002	MANUFACTURING JOBS 2015	CHANGE 2002–2015 (%)
Darke	Greenville	13,227	25.1	13.1	47,043	4.1	4,101	4,486	9.4
Logan	Bellefontaine	13,370	25.9	21.1	51,136	4.2	7,444	5,048	−32.2
Defiance	Defiance	16,494	26.1	15.8	50,822	4.8	6,037	3,993	−33.9
Union	Marysville	22,094	26.3	29.1	71,282	3.8	11,734	8,450	−28.0
Marion	Marion	36,837	26.5	12.3	43,557	5.0	8,125	6,320	−22.2
Miami	Troy	25,058	27.2	21.1	53,432	4.3	12,503	11,356	−9.2
Hancock	Findlay	41,202	27.9	25.8	51,604	3.6	11,262	12,296	9.2
Madison	London	10,058	28.1	16.4	58,326	3.8	3,617	4,125	14.0
Van Wert	Van Wert	10,846	28.5	17.2	50,547	4.0	2,678	2,958	10.5
Huron	Norwalk	17,012	28.6	13.5	48,838	6.5	9,394	5,795	−38.3
Wayne	Wooster	26,119	29.9	21.5	51,363	3.9	13,815	13,669	−1.1
Sandusky	Fremont	16,309	36.1	14.8	49,032	5.5	10,497	9,741	−7.2
Champaign	Urbana	11,793	36.4	16.5	53,673	4.5	4,074	3,987	−2.1
Shelby	Sidney	21,229	44.4	17.1	56,169	4.1	14,242	12,024	−15.6
Mercer	Celina	10,400	46.0	16.8	55,220	3.2	3,653	6,297	72.4
Total							123,176	110,545	−10.3
Ohio			13.1	26.7	50,674	4.9	884,923	676,315	−23.6
US			8.7	30.3	55,322	7.4			−22.7

Sources: Data from US Census Bureau's On-The-Map; 2012–2016 5-year American Community Survey; Bureau of Labor Statistics

TABLE 5.2. Principal manufacturers in Darke County, Ohio

COMPANY NAME	PRODUCT	LOCATION	EMPLOYEES
Whirlpool Corp.	Household appliances	Greenville	1,200
Greenville Technology	Plastic automotive parts	Greenville	865
Midmark Corp.	Medical, dental, and veterinary equipment	Versailles	820
FRAM group	Oil filters	Greenville	450
PolyOne Designed Structures & Solutions	Specialized polymer materials	Greenville	170
Norcold, Inc.	Recreational refrigeration (small refrigerators for recreational vehicles)	Gettysburg	166
BASF Corp.	Automotive coatings	Greenville	154
Neff Motivation	Awards	Greenville	116
Continental Carbonic	Dry ice	Greenville	116
Ramco	Electric motors, stators, and rotors	Greenville	114

Source: Data from Darke County Economic Development.

This brief description strongly suggests that for these small cities and counties, manufacturing not only remains viable as a business model for the local economy but sustains a healthy level of prosperity for the people of the community. This model is radically different from the far more widely publicized urban revival model of larger cities. Notable, however, is that all the cities (or towns) that share this business model are quite small, raising the question of whether it offers any meaningful lessons for planners in cities of even fifty thousand, let alone 150 thousand, population. Although whether and to what extent this model could be replicated elsewhere and if so, under what conditions, are questions beyond the scope of this chapter, they are well worth exploring both as research questions and as important concerns of public policy.

Well-Positioned Cities

Well-positioned cities represent another version of smaller industrial cities. While the economic vitality of production cities is based on indigenous export-oriented manufacturing production, the economic vitality of well-positioned cities is based on either their good fortune to be situated in a strong region or close enough to a major outside source of economic activity to build a viable local economy around their regional location—a variation on what Reese and Ye (2011) have referred to as "place luck"; or, more rarely, on having inherited from previous generations an institution or facility of such magnitude or recent growth that by itself it provides the city with a strong economic base. Although these cities are fortunate in some ways, they remain challenged in other respects.

While many erstwhile industrial cities have eds and meds institutions that contribute to their economic vitality, in only one does an institution all but single-handedly provide the economic base—New Haven, Connecticut. New Haven was historically an industrial city, in which Yale University played only a modest economic role; well into the 1960s, "beyond frequent scrapes between the students and the townspeople, Yale had little to do with the city around it" (Powledge 1970, 25). Today, as a global institution, Yale dominates New Haven's economy. The university and its affiliated hospital employ nearly 25,000 people or roughly one out of every three people who work in New Haven, whereas the university's 12,000-strong student body accounts for one of every eleven city residents. When one adds the effects of the university's spending, the dollars spent by its workers and student body, and the thousands of jobs and hundreds of businesses that the spending supports, it is probably not an overstatement that Yale accounts for three-quarters of the city's economy.

No other small industrial city houses such an outsize institution capable of single-handedly driving the local economy to such an extent, although many, including Muncie, Bethlehem, and Albany, have major educational institutions that support much of the local economy. Indeed, the small industrial cities that appear to be most successful economically are those that combine proximity to a strong regional economy with strong local institutions.

Hollingsworth and Goebel (2017) ranked a sample of small and medium-sized industrial cities on a number of indicators. The five cities that scored highest were Grand Rapids, Michigan; Worcester and Lowell, Massachusetts; Bethlehem, Pennsylvania; and Albany, New York. All five can readily be characterized as well-positioned cities. Grand Rapids, which at a population of nearly 200 thousand may or may not be considered a small city, not only has a strong manufacturing base but anchors an economically strong region; GDP growth in the Grand Rapids-Wyoming Metropolitan Area from 2011 to 2016 was nearly 36 percent, compared with the national level of 21 percent (Bureau of Economic Analysis 2017).

Both Worcester and Lowell are within the Boston metropolitan area, which of 382 metropolitan areas had the ninth highest rate of GDP growth from 2011 to 2016. Both cities have commuter rail links to Boston and house major higher educational institutions, particularly Worcester, with a strong array of institutions led by nationally known Clark University and the University of Massachusetts Medical School. Bethlehem, in a moderately strong metropolitan area, benefits from its proximity to the New York City area—which provides the principal market for its casino—as well as the presence of Lehigh University. Finally, Albany is not only arguably close enough to New York to benefit from its economic strength but as the capital of New York State, hosts a large state government workforce while it also contains one of the largest public universities in any small industrial city, the University at Albany, with an enrollment of nearly 18,000 students.

This brief recitation is not meant to suggest that success was inevitable for these cities. In each case, to varying degrees, they have pursued economic development strategies that have enabled them to capitalize on their locational and other assets, notably Lowell's successful reuse of historic industrial buildings and Bethlehem's highly productive repurposing of the closed Bethlehem Steel plant, once the mainstay of the city's economy. In contrast to the production cities discussed earlier, however, the elements of revival for the well-positioned cities are those for the large industrial cities albeit writ smaller: eds and meds as a major economic base; attraction of a well-educated younger population, including in Lowell's case, significant numbers of Boston commuters; and growth of the consumption economy, featuring arts, culture, and entertainment as well as residential redevelopment of downtowns. However, it is these cities' positions within their regional settings that enable them to pursue that strategy, whereas other cities cannot.

Despite their relative success, these cities continue to face the challenges of America's older industrial cities, including entrenched poverty and inequality, substandard housing, and distressed neighborhoods. That said, their growth at least gives them the potential to address those issues, a potential that may be largely absent elsewhere. It is notable that despite the loss of its long-standing steelmaking economy, Bethlehem today has a poverty rate only modestly higher—and an unemployment rate lower—than the national average.

Finally, while the replicability of the production model is uncertain, the positioning model, which is more a matter of fate than of design, appears to offer even less replicability potential. That raises the central question of this chapter: what happens to those cities that have lost their historic industrial role but cannot follow either of these paths to economic revival?

Small Cities and the Urban Transfer Payment Economy

A few miles south of the Italian city of Ravenna, a magnificent Byzantine basilica stands among fields and pastures (figure 5.1). It was dedicated in 549 CE in the heart of the long-vanished city of Classe, a major naval base under the Roman emperors that became an important commercial port in the Mediterranean basin from the fifth to the seventh centuries (Augenti and Boschi 2013). Although Classe suffered the usual depredations during the years following the end of the Roman Empire, it was ultimately destroyed by Mother Nature. Located at the southern

FIGURE 5.1.   The Basilica of Sant'Apollinaris in Classe

Source: © 2020 Google US Dept. of State Geographer. © 2020 GeoBasis-DE/BKG.

edge of the Po River delta and the recipient of vast deposits of silt brought down from the mountains by the river, "between the 7th and 9th centuries the port was gradually buried, as a result of the combined action of the sea and the hinterland's rivers [. . .] The ancient Classe disappeared from the surface, becoming part of the countryside around Ravenna" (Augenti and Boschi 2013, 3). The effects of the river have gradually extended the coastline outward, and the church, the only surviving remnant of the city, is now four miles from the seacoast.

In ancient times, cities like Classe that lost their economic purpose as ports, trading centers, or mining towns simply disappeared. Today, in the United States as in other developed nations, cities do not disappear; instead, their historic economic base is replaced by a system of financial transfers that sustains a local population without regard to its level of economic activity in the conventional sense; I call this system the urban transfer payment economy. I explore its features and effects in four small cities that could be considered exemplars of this economy to provide a sense of its ramifications without trying to present a detailed economic model of its workings.

Dissecting the Urban Transfer Payment Economy

Transfer payments, almost all from the public sector, are redistributional payments derived from sources outside a local jurisdiction to provide social and economic support within that jurisdiction, either through direct income supports

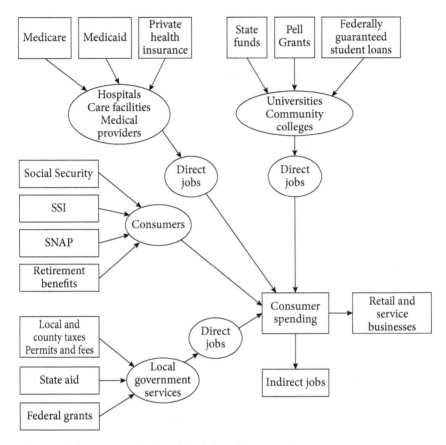

FIGURE 5.2. A simplified model of the urban transfer payment economy

to residents such as Social Security, housing vouchers, or Supplemental Nutrition Assistance Program (SNAP) (food stamps); through payment for services that those residents need but cannot afford to buy with their own resources, such as Medicare; or by subsidizing institutions that bring outside funds into the jurisdiction, such as public universities or military bases. In this broad definition, I also include funds coming from outside the jurisdiction to support local government services, including county tax revenues collected from outside the city and spent in the city, as well as state and federal aid to local governments. A simplified model of the urban transfer payment economy is shown in Figure 5.2.

Direct payments to individuals provide them with purchasing power that they use to consume goods and services, whereas payments that flow to hospitals, universities, and local government bodies translate into jobs for doctors, teachers, and public officials as well as large numbers of support personnel and vendors. These payments then drive consumer spending and indirect employment, although

because high-level employees as well as the proprietors of urban businesses generally live in suburban areas, much of this leaks out of the urban jurisdiction that
received the initial flow of resources. Table 5.3 shows the principal components of
the urban transfer payment economy and how they affect the local economy.

Of these sectors, income supports are most widely characterized as transfer
payments. The level of income supports in the four small cities is shown in
table 5.4, along with national data for purposes of comparison. A far larger percentage of households in these four cities rely on income supports, which make
up a far larger share of aggregate household income than they do nationally. Most
dramatic, perhaps, is the extent to which specific-purpose supports such as SNAP
benefits and housing subsidies pervade these cities' economies; roughly two of
five households receive SNAP benefits, and roughly half of all renter households
receive housing subsidy, either through a housing choice (Section 8) voucher or
by occupying a housing unit built under a public sector subsidy program such
as public housing or the low-income housing tax credit. Even more significantly,
nearly two out of three households with children in these cities receive SNAP
benefits. This highlights the extent to which poverty, low wages, and unemployment, as I subsequently discuss, are a hallmark of the urban transfer payment
economy.

It is relatively easy to map income supports, because detailed small area data,
albeit with a hefty margin of error, is provided by the American Community
Survey. No similar source provides equivalent small area data across jurisdictions and institutions for other types of transfer payment, so that one must rely
on illustrative examples for much salient information.

Fortunately, a variety of those examples are available. As table 5.5 shows, the
three transfer-payment driven sectors—health care, education, and government—
make up a disproportionate share of the jobs compared with statewide levels in
each city. Local government is a somewhat special case, because other than intergovernmental transfers and grants-in-aid, local government revenues derive
from the productivity of the local economy; in other words, income taxes are
collected when people have income, property taxes are collected when property
has value, and so forth. Thus, local government both supports the transfer payment economy by drawing federal and state funds and is a beneficiary of it by
virtue of the taxes it collects from those supported directly by that economy.

The scale of intergovernmental transfers is largely a function of state policy
with regard to local government. New Jersey is particularly generous in that respect; nonlocal public funds, almost entirely from state government, amount to
$117.2 million, which is 53 percent, of the municipal budget of Camden, the state's
most distressed city, and $388 million, which is 97 percent of the budget of the
local school district. Put differently, in what is admittedly an apples-and-oranges

TABLE 5.3. Principal components of the urban transfer payment economy

CATEGORY	ELEMENT	DIRECT IMPACTS	INDIRECT IMPACTS
Income support	Social security	Consumer spending	Earnings of local businesses
	Other retirement benefits	Consumer spending	Salaries and wages of workers in retail and services
	SSI, TANF, and other public assistance benefits	Consumer spending	
	Housing choice vouchers	Rental spending	Earnings of local landlords
			Investment in local real estate
			Landlord payments to contractors and vendors
	SNAP	Food spending	Earnings of local businesses
			Salaries and wages of workers in retail and services
Support for government and social service sector	Countywide taxes, fees and other revenues	Salaries and benefits for government employees	Consumer spending
		Payment for delivery of public services and capital investment	Payment to contractors and vendors
	State and federal grants	Salaries and benefits for government and nonprofit sector employees and contract service providers	Consumer spending
		Payment for delivery of public services and capital investment	Payment to contractors and vendors

(continued)

TABLE 5.3. (continued)

CATEGORY	ELEMENT	DIRECT IMPACTS	INDIRECT IMPACTS
Support for health care sector	Medicare	Salaries and benefits for employees and contract service providers in health care	Consumer spending
	Medicaid and CHIP	Capital investment in and maintenance of health care infrastructure	Payment to contractors and vendors
	Blue Cross/Blue Shield and other private insurance		
Support for higher education sector	Pell grants	Salaries and benefits for higher education employees and contract service providers	Consumer spending
	Federal student loans	Capital investment in and maintenance of higher education infrastructure	Payment to contractors and vendors
	State operating and capital support	Student spending	
	Federal grants		

TABLE 5.4. Income supports in United States and four small cities

	UNITED STATES	SAGINAW, MI	YOUNGSTOWN, OH	CHESTER, PA	JOHNSTOWN, PA
Households with social security income (%)	30.2	36.1	38.8	34.8	42.5
Households with SSI (%)	5.4	15.8	13.9	13.6	17.1
Households with other retirement income (%)	18.3	20.9	20.7	18.2	21.3
Households receiving SNAP benefits (%)	13.0	42.6	38.9	40.5	38.8
Households with children <18 receiving SNAP benefits (%)	21.6	60.2	67.9	61.4	62.2
Number of households with housing choice vouchers	2,265,478	1,075	1,433	1,224	468
Number of households in subsidized housing	5,220,819	3,737	4,504	2,278	1,829
Percentage of all households receiving rental subsidy[a] (%)	6.4	24.8	22.0	30.2	24.0
Percentage of all renter households receiving rental subsidy[a] (%)	17.5	63.0	50.6	48.1	47.3
SHARE OF AGGREGATE HOUSEHOLD INCOME DERIVED FROM EACH SOURCE (%)					
Social Security	7.1	15.3	15.3	12.6	18.8
SSI	0.7	4.2	3.4	3.4	4.3
Public assistance	0.1	0.4	0.8	0.6	0.6
Other retirement income	5.8	10.3	10.9	7.1	9.0
Total of all sources	13.7	30.2	30.4	23.7	32.7

Sources: Income and SNAP data from 2012–2016 5-year ACS; housing choice vouchers from US Department of Housing & Urban Development (through PolicyMap); subsidized housing from National Housing Preservation Database

[a] Many residents of subsidized housing projects also hold vouchers, resulting in a large but indeterminate duplication of the total number of units in the two categories. As many as 1/3 to 1/2 of all vouchers may be duplicated. As a result, the percentages shown in the table inflate the share of subsidized housing in the population and in the rental housing stock, probably by 5 to 10 percent.

TABLE 5.5. Share of primary jobs by sector in 2015 (%)

CATEGORY	SAGINAW, MI	YOUNGSTOWN, OH	CHESTER, PA	JOHNSTOWN, PA
Health care and social assistance	37.8	26.1	20.5	26.1
Educational services	3.1	11.7	20.0	3.6
Public administration	4.8	7.8	6.5	3.8
Total	45.7	45.6	47.0	43.5
Michigan	27.5			
Ohio		26.6		
Pennsylvania			29.5	29.5

Source: Data from US Census Bureau LEHD Origin-Destination Employment Statistics (On-The-Map).

comparison, the more than $500 million that the state and federal government spend to support local government services and public schools in Camden is equivalent to more than 50 percent of Camden residents' aggregate household income. Chester, Pennsylvania, gets far less direct state aid, but $12 million (27 percent) of its general fund revenues come from its share of state gambling taxes levied on Harrah's Philadelphia Casino and Racetrack, which despite its name is in Chester and not Philadelphia.

Public nonresearch colleges and universities in smaller industrial cities, which are the majority of higher education institutions in such cities, depend heavily on state and federal resources. With nearly 13,000 students and a 145 acre campus close to Youngstown's downtown, Youngstown State University (YSU) is the largest single contributor to the city's economy. YSU is a product of the transfer payment economy. While state appropriations cover a significant part of its expenses, its largest single source of operating revenue is the federal government, largely through the federal direct student loan program, which covers the majority of its students' tuition costs (table 5.6). Without this support, YSU could not exist.

This is not a criticism of either the university or the federal programs that sustain it. Indeed, they are both critically important; without the availability of federal loans and grants, millions of young people would be unable to obtain a higher education today. In 2019 to 2020, the federal government made nearly 5 million Pell grants and guaranteed over 11 million student loans. The point is that that aid is not only a benefit to students but also covers half of YSU's operating budget, most of which is wages and salaries of YSU employees, and is a critical mainstay of Youngstown's economy.

The same situation holds for medical care. Although it is not possible to obtain comprehensive local data that shows the distribution of funds by source going through the entire local health care system, a few data sources shed some

TABLE 5.6. Youngstown State University revenue breakdown for 2015–2016 fiscal year

SOURCE	CATEGORY	AMOUNT ($ THOUSAND)	PERCENTAGE OF TOTAL REVENUES (%)
State of Ohio	Operating support	41,814	24.0
	Capital support[a]	8,539	4.9
Federal government	Direct Student Loan Program	63,048	36.2
	Pell Grants	20,159	11.6
	Other student aid	3,566	2.0
	Research & Development	1,083	0.6
	Other	2,052	1.2
Total federal and state		140,261	80.5
All other		34,051	19.5
Total[b]		174,312	100.0

Source: Data from Youngstown State University Single Audit Report, June 30, 2016.

[a] State funds characterized as capital support are actually used for major maintenance and upgrading of existing facilities, and are shown as annual revenues, as distinct from bond proceeds used for new buildings and expansion of existing buildings, which are not included.

[b] This figure excludes $23.9 million shown in the audit as auxiliary revenues, which include such areas as housing room and board and bookstore, and which are in large part derivative of revenues shown in the table.

TABLE 5.7. National health care expenditures by source 2015

SOURCE	AMOUNT ($ BILLION)	PERCENTAGE OF TOTAL (%)
Medicare	646.2	20.2
Medicaid	545.1	17.0
Other federal programs	121.1	3.8
Total federal	1,312.4	40.9
Other[a]	482.8	15.1
Private health insurance	1,072.1	33.4
Out of pocket	338.1	10.5
Total	3,205.6	100

Source: Data from Center for Medicaid and Medicare Services.

[a] Other category includes other third-party payers, public health services, and investment. The majority of these funds come from the public sector, including federal, state, local government, and school district resources.

light on the extent to which outside resources, primarily federal, drive health care spending. Table 5.7 shows the national distribution of health care costs by source of funds.

It is well known, of course, that the great majority of health care costs in the United States are covered by insurance rather than direct payment by consumers, although some readers may not be aware that federal insurance spending now substantially exceeds private insurance. In an affluent community, however, health care costs are offset by the insurance and tax payments of individuals and employers, generated largely from private sector economic activity. In cities that are part of the urban transfer payment economy, these costs are almost entirely covered by outside, largely public-sector transfers. To the extent that some health costs are covered by private insurance, that is largely paid by public-sector, education, or health care employers in the form of either employee or retiree health benefits.

It is worth exploring briefly whether the framework of the urban transfer payment economy can or should be extended to other types of communities in the United States. There are a number of communities, such as military bases and state capitals, that arguably are as economically dependent on outside transfers of cash—whether directly through tax collections or indirectly through federal appropriations—and that generate little revenue to offset those transfers. I would argue that there is a fundamental difference between such communities and those that I characterize as part of the urban transfer payment economy. In essence, from an economic standpoint, the purpose of the cash transfers is to purchase services that government has determined to be essential—in the case of state capitals, the various services that the state provides its residents, and in the case of a military base, the defense of the United States. It would be hard to argue that Youngstown or Saginaw provide an essential service to the state or nation.

Residents of cities in the urban transfer payment economy disproportionately receive health care benefits through the public sector, as shown in table 5.8. While the extent of Medicare coverage is essentially a function of the age distribution of the community—Medicare coverage is nearly universal for people over 65 years, with almost no regard to income—the extent of Medicaid and other means-tested coverage, particularly for children, is a function of the poverty of these cities and their residents. Without the benefits made available through Medicaid, the Children's Health Insurance Program (CHIP), and SNAP (shown in table 5.4), the overwhelming majority of children living in these cities would have little or no means of sustenance or health coverage.

Health care spending represents a massive infusion of transfer payments into cities dependent on the transfer payment economy. Although many such cities lack universities, most above a modest minimum size have hospitals and ambulatory care providers. In 2012, total revenues of health care providers in Youngstown totaled $845 million, of which $500 million was generated by the city's two hospitals. Although most of these revenues do not remain in the city, they nonetheless represent the largest single element in the city's economy.

TABLE 5.8. Reliance on public sector health insurance by insurance type and age category

CATEGORY	UNITED STATES	SAGINAW, MI	YOUNGSTOWN, OH	CHESTER, PA	JOHNSTOWN, PA
Public health insurance by type for total noninstitutionalized population:					
Medicaid or other means-tested insurance alone (%)	14.2	39.1	36.0	29.3	32.8
Medicare alone or with supplements (%)	16.3	17.8	21.0	16.3	25.0
Other[a] (%)	2.5	3.4	3.7	4.8	2.8
Total public insurance (%)	33.0	60.3	60.7	50.4	60.6
Percentage with public sector health insurance by age category					
Under 6 (%)	44.2	84.0	86.7	71.9	72.5
6 to 17 (%)	36.3	72.5	76.3	65.9	80.4

Source: Data from 2012–2016 5-year American Community Survey.
[a] Category includes Medicaid in combination with other insurance

This discussion leads to a clear conclusion: while all parts of the United States benefit from the system of transfer payments that has emerged over the past many decades, the cities described here depend on it. To summarize the dynamics of the urban transfer payment economy,

- A large percentage of the population, particularly children and the elderly, are directly dependent on income supports, whether direct in the form of Social Security or indirect in the form of SNAP or housing choice vouchers;
- A second large percentage hold jobs that are in turn dependent on transfer payments to health care, social service, and education providers;
- A third large percentage, including retailers, consumer service providers and their employees and vendors, are dependent on the consumer spending of the first two categories; and
- Finally, local government and its employees and vendors are dependent on the tax and other revenues generated as a result of the first three categories.

Although each of these cities has some residual manufacturing activity as well as other export industries, such as Chester's casino, they are modest by comparison; an educated guess would be that collectively they are unlikely to represent more than a quarter of the economic activity in each city. The urban transfer payment economy enables these cities to survive, rather than to disappear as Classe did over a thousand years ago. Survival, however, is a low bar. In the next section, I explore what it means to a city and its residents to be dependent on the urban transfer payment economy.

Life in the Urban Transfer Payment Economy

The urban transfer payment economy, as it operates in cities like Saginaw or Johnstown, in the context of a modern postindustrial society is a subsistence economy. As these cities have shifted from manufacturing to their current economy, they have undergone dramatic declines in their standard of living and quality of life. Table 5.9 shows current conditions and trends for the four cities and for the United States.

This is hardly surprising. Income supports are not designed to foster a high standard of living but to provide minimum subsistence. Although many of the beneficiaries of the transfer payment economy, in particular professional and managerial personnel in local government, health care, and higher education, earn good salaries, few live in the cities where they work; 88 percent of all jobs paying $40,000 or more in 2015 in Youngstown were held by commuters, and the same was true for 94 percent of all such jobs in Chester. Hence most of the indirect economic effects of those jobs, except for the occasional latte, are felt in the city's suburbs, where most of each region's commercial activity takes place, or even farther afield. People who live in the city are less likely to be in the workforce and, if they are in the workforce, far more likely to be unemployed. Even those who work full-time and year-round typically earn only about two-thirds of national average earnings.

The pervasive poverty of these cities is compounded by their continued long-term population loss. All four cities have lost substantial parts of their peak population, in some cases in a trend that has persisted since 1930, nearly ninety years. The combination of poverty and population loss has created extremely weak housing market conditions, shown in the extraordinarily high levels of housing vacancy, the extremely low prices for which houses sell if they sell at all, and other factors shown in table 5.10. Vacant properties make up more than 1 out of 10 of all units in these four cities, although the most powerful impression an observer gets in Johnstown is less the number of vacant houses than the pervasive dilapidation of so many of the occupied ones.

The weakness of the housing market in these cities is further exemplified by the low volume of sales, suggesting that many properties, when their current owner moves, are not sold at all and end up being added to the ranks of abandoned properties, and by the low ratio of mortgages to sales, indicating not only

TABLE 5.9. Social and economic characteristics for United States and four small cities

	UNITED STATES	SAGINAW MI	YOUNGSTOWN OH	CHESTER PA	JOHNSTOWN PA
Peak population		98,265	170,002	66,039	66,993
Peak year		1960	1930	1950	1930
Estimated population (2016)		48,948	64,312	33,988	19,712
Change (%)		−50.1	−63.2	−48.5	−70.6
Poverty rate, 2000 (%)	12.4	28.5	24.8	27.2	24.6
Poverty rate, 2016 (%)	15.1	34.7	38.0	36.9	37.0
Poverty rate in population under 18, 2000 (%)	16.1	40.2	37.3	36.9	37.5
Poverty rate in population under 18, 2016 (%)	21.2	46.0	60.3	51.2	60.4
Median family income in 1969 ($2016)	63,183	65,846	59,828	56,078	52,927
Median family income in 2016 ($)	67,871	34,356	32,507	32,971	32,946
Change 1969–2016 (%)	+7.4	−47.8	−47.3	−41.8	−47.8
Adults with BA or higher degree, 1970 (%)	10.7	6.3	5.4	3.1	3.4
Adults with BA or higher degree, 2016 (%)	30.3	11.4	12.0	10.3	11.7
Unemployment rate, 2000 (%)	3.7	7.7	5.8	9.9	5.8
Unemployment rate, 2016 (%)	7.4	17.7	16.8	19.0	15.7
Homeownership rate, 1970 (%)	62.9	67.7	67.6	51.2	46.0
Homeownership rate, 2016 (%)	63.6	60.7	56.7	37.3	49.4

Sources: Data from US Census 1970 and 2000; 2012–2016 5-year ACS; sales price data for US from National Association of Realtors, and for cities from Boxwood Means and PolicyMap.

TABLE 5.10. Housing market conditions in United States and four small cities

	UNITED STATES	SAGINAW, MI	YOUNGSTOWN, OH	CHESTER, PA	JOHNSTOWN, PA
Other vacant housing[a] in 2000 (%)	2.0	4.3	2.8	8.2	4.2
Other vacant housing in 2016 (%)	4.1	12.1	11.6	15.4	14.6
Median sales price in 2006 ($)	221,900	43,000[b]	24,000	25,000	25,000
Median sales price in 2015 ($)	222,400	21,652	22,925	17,950	19,990[c]
1–4 family properties	92,614,000	20,428	28,304	11,373	8,880
Number of sales in 2015	5,745,000	739	781	478	212[d]
Sales as percentage of inventory (%)	6.2	3.6	2.8	4.2	2.4
Mortgages originated[e] in 2015	3,650,000	133	147	32	57
Mortgages as percentage of sales (%)	63.5	18.0	18.8	6.7	26.9

Source: Inventory data from 2000 Census and 2012–2016 5 year ACS. National median sales price for existing houses from National Association of Realtors, city sales price and volume data from Boxwood Means and PolicyMap. Purchase mortgages from Home Mortgage Disclosure Act (HMDA) reports.

[a] The residual category used by the Census Bureau to identify vacant properties that are not on the market either for sales or rental, nor are being held for seasonal or occasional use; in other words, a rough surrogate for properties that have been abandoned by their owners.

[b] 2007

[c] 2014

[d] 2014

[e] For home purchases

that the great majority of transactions are cash transactions but that in all likelihood the great majority of purchasers are investors rather than homebuyers. Given the low sales prices and the high ratio of rental income to house price, particularly for tenants with housing choice vouchers, it is likely that the majority of these investor buyers are the investors that I have characterized elsewhere as *milkers*—people who plan to put little money into the properties, make their profit through cash flow in a few years, and then walk away (Mallach 2014).

By any measure, cities that are dependent on the urban transfer payment economy show severe deficits in terms of living conditions, quality of life, housing markets, and opportunities compared to the rest of the United States. Not only are cities like Johnstown and Saginaw desperately poor communities, but they offer only one way by which most of their residents can escape poverty, that is, to leave and go elsewhere. They will never disappear like Classe, as long as the transfer payment economy continues to exist, but the question remains—is there an alternative to sustained, long-term extreme deprivation and lack of opportunity for these cities? Although I do not presume to suggest I have the answer, after a discussion of the role of economic development strategies and leadership in the fate of cities in the urban transfer payment economy, I close with a few observations on that question.

Fighting the Tide: The Role of Leadership and Economic Development Strategies

In contrast to production cities, which have maintained or regrown a manufacturing base, and well-positioned cities, which have with some success replaced their manufacturing base with a postindustrial economic base integrated into a larger metropolitan area, transfer payment dependent cities have done neither. This is not for lack of trying. All four cities have made major efforts, often with substantial state or federal support, to recruit new sources of economic activity.[1]

Thanks in part to the Keystone Opportunity Zone, a Pennsylvania program that provides firms with generous relief from both state and local taxes along with a major investment by the state's Department of Transportation, Chester's Delaware River waterfront has seen the construction of not only the casino and racetrack mentioned previously but also a 400,000 square foot Class A office building and an 18,500-seat stadium hosting a professional soccer team.

Johnstown's story is striking. From his election in 1974 until his death in 2010, Johnstown's Congressman John Murtha devoted himself to funneling over $2 billion in federal money into his hometown (Zengerle 2009), earning him a reputation as Washington's "king of pork" (CBS 2008). Murtha's largesse gave Johnstown a cluster of federally subsidized facilities, including the Murtha Airport, characterized by one writer as "the airport for nobody" (Karl 2009), the John P. Murtha Regional Cancer Center, the Joyce Murtha Breast Cancer Center, the Murtha Center for Public Service and National Competitiveness at the University of Pittsburgh-Johnstown (a major beneficiary of Murtha's earmarks), and the National Drug Intelligence Center, described at the time of its opening as a "wasteful display of political patronage that primarily benefits the constituents of one Democratic Congressman" (Hinds 1993). The Center was closed and its functions reassigned to facilities elsewhere in 2012.

Youngstown, which maintains a professional economic development staff in City Hall, has had some success luring firms to industrial parks it has created by acquiring, cleaning up, and subdividing two former steel mill sites for use by small and medium-sized manufacturing and distribution facilities. These industrial parks provide some benefits in terms of employment and constitute a significant part of the city's property tax base.

The extent to which Murtha's largesse sustained a viable economy for Johnstown during his lifetime is questionable, although the evidence is not compelling; since then, however, although perhaps providing some marginal quality-of-life benefits, his projects have clearly made little or no contribution to building a sustainable local economy. Similarly, Youngstown's industrial parks have not changed the basic trajectory of the local economy; as a city staffer ruefully acknowledged to me, nearly all the workers in those firms live in the city's suburbs.

One cannot fault Youngstown's planners, who are doing the best they can with the tools and assets at their disposal and at least are pursuing a coherent strategy. The number of manufacturing jobs has remained largely the same over the last fifteen years in that city, albeit only 10 percent of the city's jobs, but might well have dropped significantly without their efforts. Youngstown remains, however, a desperately poor city. Although we address the question of whether there is anything that Youngstown or another similar city could do that would significantly shift its economic trajectory in the closing section of this chapter, it seems clear that these cities' determined economic development efforts have not had such an effect. This is not surprising, as the supporting evidence of the efficacy of the sorts of economic development strategies that characterize these cities' efforts is weak; as Richard Schragger (2016, 13–14) pointed out in his brilliant book *City Power*, "any claim that cities have transformed themselves through improved policies of capital attraction and retention is seriously overstated." Reese and Ye (2011) similarly found no association between economic development policies and economic health.

Closely related is the role of local political, civic, or institutional leadership. The importance of leadership in setting a city's course is a familiar trope in the literature on urban politics and public sector management (Hennessey 1998; Osborne and Gaebler 1992; Van Wart 2005, among many others), with Judd and Parkinson (1990, 295) asserting that "leadership is a crucial variable in determining how cities respond to economic change." A number of recent publications have pointed to the role of leadership in addressing the particular challenges faced by small cities (Kodyryzcki and Munoz 2009; Hollingsworth and Goebel 2017). In the context of the transfer payment–dependent cities discussed previously, that raises the question: is strong, effective leadership capable of making a significant difference?

Despite their conscientious efforts, neither of the last two publications cited makes a compelling case for the potentially transformative effect of leadership independent of locational or other economic advantage. Both adopt an ex post facto approach to the question; after identifying the more successful cities, they ask knowledgeable local informants or economic development professionals to identify the reasons for these cities' resurgence. Under these circumstances, it is only to be expected that the informants would attribute their cities' success to design rather than to the workings of a benevolent providence.

Along with Reese and Ye (2011), Erickcek and McKinney (2004) are among the few who have made a systematic attempt "to identify particular public policies which have the potential to increase the economic viability of smaller metropolitan areas and cities" (1), in their case by comparing the features and economic performance of 212 small metropolitan areas. Of the eight distinct clusters the authors found, only one, those with "growing university/government/business complexes" showed significant positive deviation from the trend line. Although the authors—arguably grasping at straws—conclude by speculating that policy may have played a role, they reluctantly admit the possibility that what their evidence actually supports is that those areas "were lucky to have universities, state capitals, or large firms to fall back on as the economy changed" (25).

To be sure, one can find examples where leadership clearly mattered. The reopening of the Providence River in Providence, Rhode Island, and the related investments championed by then-mayor Vincent Cianci unquestionably had a strong effect on that city's fortunes; at the same time, however, Providence had strong locational and other assets that enabled strong local leadership to leverage those assets with their investment. Similar examples can be found elsewhere. In the absence of those assets, however, the sort of leadership that focuses on visible economic development activities is not likely to lead to significant change in these cities' underlying condition. This conclusion is reinforced by the painful reality that these cities have severely limited resources to hire and retain competent professional staff—for economic development or anything else—as well as a severely limited talent pool from which to draw political and civic leadership.

Conclusion: The Prospects for Transfer Payment-Dependent Cities

If the benefits of economic development strategies appear illusory, the question remains: is there anything that Youngstown, Chester, or any other similarly situated city can do to significantly shift its economic trajectory? In some respects, the answer may well be no. Cities—especially small ones that cannot benefit from agglomeration—cannot invent economies but must operate within the range of options provided by the larger regional, national, and global economies. As suggested previously, from a macroeconomic perspective the revival of industrial cities like Baltimore and Pittsburgh can be seen as little more than a chain reaction flowing from the expanding role of the higher education and health care sectors in the United States economy and the fortuitous location of critical components of both sectors in those cities, coupled with intergenerational changes in consumer preferences reflected in the millennial migration. Those cities, to be sure, did not sit idly by, but their actions responded to those changes rather than initiate them.

Over the past decades, those forces have worked against many small cities such as the four described here. That does not mean that other opportunities may not arise. Some accounts suggest that Youngstown may have the ability to benefit significantly from the growth in the fracking industry, as well as the parallel decline in natural gas prices (Schwartz 2014; Mundahl 2017), to rebuild a strong manufacturing sector. Similarly, Chester's location only 12.5 miles from the heart of Center City Philadelphia, with frequent commuter rail service to both Philadelphia and Wilmington, suggests that *some* economic opportunities should exist for that city over and above a casino and soccer stadium. What those opportunities might be, however—particularly because Philadelphia, although reviving, is far from an economic powerhouse fueling regional growth like Boston or New York—remains unclear.

Although cities should take advantage of whatever idiosyncratic opportunities that may arise, history suggests that there are few intentional strategies in terms of what is conventionally termed economic development that these cities can pursue that are likely to lead to meaningful change. That, in turn, suggests that one should look at the future of these places through other than a conventional economic development lens and explore other pathways of increasing their prosperity and that of their residents.

One such pathway may be through immigrant or refugee attraction. Bosnian refugees have thrived in the upstate New York city of Utica (Hartman 2014), and the Ahiska or Meskhetian Turks have done well in Dayton, Ohio, where they are credited with stabilizing the distressed Old North Dayton neighborhood (Navera 2014; Preston 2013). Dayton, indeed, has pursued a high-profile immigrant-welcoming strategy, which appears to have attracted other, albeit smaller, immigrant communities, as well (Preston 2013). There is little to be lost and much potentially to be gained through efforts to attract immigrants and refugees, although the settlement patterns of refugees often have more to do with the fortuitous location of resettlement agencies or sponsors than with any overt city strategy, and the potential for conflict between immigrants and long-time residents should not be ignored.

I would argue that an even more important strategy is to focus on building human capital, particularly with respect to local education systems, in the hope that raising the level of human capital will increase a city's competitive position (Glaeser 1994; Glaeser, Scheinkman, and Shleifer 1995). That is not an unrealistic prospect; there is a strong body of global research supporting human capital development as an economic growth strategy; Reese and Ye (2011) point out that public school graduation rates are positively correlated with economic health. Even if such a strategy does not change the city's economic trajectory, it will increase the degree to which the city's young people can find attractive opportunities elsewhere. That, of course, would be significantly to their benefit if not to the benefit of the city as a place.

Another approach, more specific to place, would be to try to increase the localized impact of the transfer payment system by reducing the leakages that currently mean that most of the resources the system provides leave the city, and in many cases, the immediate region. That could involve measures to increase the number of jobs for city residents—particularly those currently unemployed or without stable employment—in local hospitals and universities; measures to increase local procurement of goods and services by those institutions; and measures to encourage more of the middle- and upper-income workers in those institutions to live inside the city. Any such approach would require that service providers address simultaneously education and workforce development on the one hand, and the attractiveness and quality of life of the city on the other, to encourage people who benefit from greater job opportunities to remain in these cities rather than leave them for their suburbs, which are typically affordable to almost anyone with even a modest but stable income.

Any such efforts would be enhanced by more robust regional governance, which is all but nonexistent in the metropolitan areas surrounding transfer payment–dependent cities. This is likely, however, to be at best a remote prospect in the foreseeable future; moreover, the lack of significant regional economic growth and the limited fiscal capacity of nearly all jurisdictions within the larger regions in which most of these cities are located not only increases the potential opposition to such measures but means that their effect would be less than in more prosperous regions.

Moving their cities to embrace building human capital and improving quality of life as systematic strategies for change represents the real challenge for local leadership in these cities, far more than fostering transactional activities such as luring casinos and building industrial parks.

In the final analysis, however, strategies both to increase skills and job opportunities and to rebuild the physical and social quality of life of a city like Chester or Saginaw would require a major infusion of public resources, well beyond what would be possible from local sources. In today's political climate, one must concede that such a commitment appears unlikely. That could perhaps change in the future. These cities and their regions are an important part of what has been called the forgotten America, the left-behind working-class communities of flyover country that are being paid increased, although to this point largely rhetorical, attention. That attention may ultimately lead to action. The only plausible alternative is an indefinite perpetuation of the status quo and the continuing immiseration of large numbers of American towns and cities.

Notes

1. The discussion covers three of the four cities. Although Saginaw has pursued a variety of economic development strategies, none raise the distinctive issues that arise from the activities of the other three cities. It is worth noting, however, that in 2011, in recognition of the city's significant population loss and vacant land, Saginaw designated a largely vacant 350 acre (roughly 5.5 square miles) area as a "green zone," with the intention of allowing it to revert to nature. Judging from a recent Google search, the project appears to have been abandoned in 2015.

References

Augenti, Andrea, and Federica Boschi. 2013. "Classe (Ravenna): An Abandoned Town in an Urbanized Landscape." In *New Research for Archaeological Heritage Protection and Territorial Planning: Proceedings of the 17th International Conference on Cultural Heritage and New Technologies 2012, Vienna*. Vienna, Austria: Museen der Stadt Wien—Stadtarchäologie. https://www.chnt.at/wp-content/uploads/eBook_CHNT17_Augenti_Boschi.pdf.

Birch, Eugénie L. 2009. "Downtown in the 'New American City'." *The Annals of the American Academy of Political and Social Science* 626, no. 1 (November): 134–53. https://doi.org/10.1177/0002716209344169.

Bureau of Economic Analysis. 2017. *Gross Domestic Product by Metropolitan Area, 2016*. https://www.bea.gov/newsreleases/regional/gdp_metro/gdp_metro_newsrelease.htm.

CBS News. 2008. "Meet Congress' 'King of Pork'." April 4, 2008. https://www.cbsnews.com/news/meet-congress-king-of-pork/.

Chalmers, Christina. 2017. "Midmark Moves Headquarters to Austin Landing: Versailles Campus Will Remain." *Daily Advocate*, Nov. 14, 2017. http://www.Dailyadvocate.Com/News/43730/Midmark-Moves-Headquarters-To-Austin-Landing.

Clark, Terry Nichols. 2011. *The City as an Entertainment Machine*. Lanham, MD: Lexington Books.

Erickcek, George A., and Hannah McKinney. 2004. *"Small Cities Blues": Looking for Growth Factors in Small and Medium-Sized Cities*. Upjohn Institute Working Paper, No. 04-100. Kalamazoo, MI: W.E. Upjohn Institute for Employment Research. https://research.upjohn.org/cgi/viewcontent.cgi?article=1117&context=up_workingpapers.

Glaeser, Edward L. 1994. "Cities, Information and Economic Growth." *Cityscape* 1, no. 1 (August): 9–48. https://www.huduser.gov/Periodicals/CITYSCPE/VOL1NUM1/ch2.pdf.

Glaeser, Edward L., ed. 2010. *Agglomeration Economics*. Chicago: University of Chicago Press.

Glaeser, Edward L., Jed Kolko, and Albert Saiz. 2001. "Consumer City." *Journal of Economic Geography* 1, no. 1 (January): 27–50. https://doi.org/10.1093/jeg/1.1.27.

Glaeser, Edward L., José A. Scheinkman, and Andrei Shleifer. 1995. "Economic Growth in a Cross-Section of Cities." *Journal of Monetary Economics* 36, no. 1 (August): 117–43. https://doi.org/10.1016/0304-3932(95)01206-2.

Gurwitt, Rob. 2008. "Eds, Meds and Urban Revival." *Governing*, April, 44–50.

Harkavy, Ira Richard, and Harmon Zuckerman. 1999. *Eds and Meds: Cities' Hidden Assets*. Washington, DC: Brookings Institution, Center on Urban and Metropolitan Policy.

Hartman, Susan. 2014. "A New Life for Refugees, and the City They Adopted." *New York Times*, August 10, 2014.

Hennessey, J. Thomas. 1998. "'Reinventing' Government: Does Leadership Make the Difference?" *Public Administration Review* 58, no. 6 (November-December): 522–32. https://doi.org/10.2307/977579.

Hinds, Michael DeCourcy. 1993. "Center for Drug Intelligence Opens, But Some Ask if It Is Really Needed." *New York Times*, November 17, 1993.

Hollingsworth, Torey, and Alison Goebel. 2017. *Revitalizing America's Smaller Legacy Cities*. Cambridge, MA: Lincoln Institute of Land Policy. https://www.lincolninst.edu/publications/policy-focus-reports/revitalizing-americas-smaller-legacy-cities.

Judd, Dennis, and Michael Parkinson. 1990. "Patterns of Leadership." In *Leadership and Urban Regeneration,* edited by Dennis Judd and Michael Parkinson, 295–307. Newbury Park, CA: Sage.

Karl, Jonathan. 2009. "Welcome to the Airport for Nobody." *ABC News*, April 23, 2009. http://abcnews.go.com/Business/Politics/story?id=7412160.

Kodyryzcki, Yolanda, and Patricia Munoz. 2009. *Lessons from Resurgent Cities*. Boston: Federal Reserve Bank of Boston. https://www.bostonfed.org/publications/annual-reports/2009/lessons-from-resurgent-cities.pdf.

Longworth, Richard C. 2008. *Caught in the Middle: America's Heartland in the Age of Globalism*. New York: Bloomsbury.

Mallach, Alan. 2014. "Lessons from Las Vegas: Housing Markets, Neighborhoods, and Distressed Single-Family Property Investors." *Housing Policy Debate* 24 (4): 769–801. https://doi.org/10.1080/10511482.2013.872160.

Mallach, Alan. 2018. *The Divided City: Poverty and Prosperity in Urban America*. Washington, DC: Island Press.

Moos, Markus, Deirdre Pfeiffer, and Tara Vinodrai, eds. 2017. *The Millennial City: Trends, Implications, and Prospects for Urban Planning and Policy*. London: Routledge.

Moretti, Enrico. 2012. *The New Geography of Jobs*. Boston: Houghton Mifflin Harcourt.

Mundahl, Erin. 2017. "Rust Belt No More: Chemical Plants Bringing Manufacturing Jobs Back to Youngstown." *Inside Sources*, June 25, 2017. http://www.insidesources.com/chemical-plants-manufacturing-jobs-youngstown/.

National Association of Manufacturers. 2019. "2019 United States Manufacturing Facts." Washington, DC: National Association of Manufacturers. https://www.nam.org/state-manufacturing-data/2019-united-states-manufacturing-facts/.

Navera, Tristan. 2014. "The Rise of Dayton's Ahiska Turkish Community" *Dayton Business Journal,* April 25, 2014.

O'Hara, Paul. 2010. "Model Cities, Mill Towns and Industrial Peripheries: Small Industrial Cities in Twentieth-Century America." In *After the Factory: Reinventing America's Industrial Small Cities*, edited by James J. Connolly, 19–48. Lanham, MD: Lexington Books.

Osborne, David, and Ted Gaebler. 1992. *Reinventing Government: How the Entrepreneurial Spirit Is Transforming Government.* Reading, MA: Addison-Wesley.

Powledge, Fred. 1970. *Model City: A Test of American Liberalism: One Town's Efforts to Rebuild Itself.* New York: Simon and Schuster.

Preston, Julia. 2013. "Ailing Midwestern Cities Extend a Welcoming Hand to Immigrants." *New York Times,* October 6, 2013.

Reese, Laura A., and Minting Ye. 2011. "Policy versus Place Luck: Achieving Local Economic Prosperity." *Economic Development Quarterly* 25, no. 3 (August): 221–36. https://doi.org/10.1177%2F0891242411408292.

Schragger, Richard. 2016. *City Power: Urban Governance in a Global Age.* New York: Oxford University Press.

Schwartz, Nelson. 2014. "Boom in Energy Spurs Industry in the Rust Belt." *New York Times,* September 8, 2014. https://www.nytimes.com/2014/09/09/business/an-energy-boom-lifts-the-heartland.html.

Sorkin, Michael, ed. 1992. *Variations on a Theme Park: The New American City and the End of Public Space.* New York: Hill & Wang.

Tumber, Catherine. 2012. *Small Gritty and Green: The Promise of America's Smaller Industrial Cities in a Low-Carbon World.* Cambridge, MA: MIT Press.

US Census Bureau. n.d. LEHD Origin-Destination Employment Statistics (2002–2017). Washington, DC: US Census Bureau, Longitudinal-Employer Household Dynamics Program, accessed on February 15, 2018 at https://onthemap.ces.census.gov.

Van Wart, Montgomery. 2005. *Dynamics of Leadership in Public Service: Theory and Practice.* Armonk, NY: M.E. Sharpe.

Zengerle, Jason. 2009. "Murthaville: The City that Pork Built." *New Republic,* Sept. 1, 2009. https://newrepublic.com/article/68877/murthaville.

6

WHERE DO SMALL CITIES BELONG?

The Case of the Micropolitan Area

J. Matthew Fannin and Vikash Dangal

This chapter examines some of the problems that arise as official Micropolitan Statistical Area definitions change over time. In particular, it addresses the policy challenges facing struggling small cities and other regions with intermediate population densities that result from the volatility of this classification. Changes in these criteria can have a substantial impact on the people- and placed-based development efforts that aim to revitalize such places.

We take several steps to demonstrate the variability of these census-based regional classifications and explain its significance. First, we identify the context for placed-based policy and provide examples of how federal agencies' funding formulas create challenges for small cities seeking more control over their own futures. We then provide evidence that existing federal definitions of statistical areas, which are used in federal policymaking, have the potential to reduce the autonomy of these communities. The chapter concludes by offering some potential strategies that can be considered by federal statistical organizations, federal agencies implementing either place-based or people-based programs, and small-city regions attempting to navigate vulnerabilities stemming from the volatility in policy-leveraged regional definitions.

The Policy Context

Place-based policies are spread across all federal government agencies. In many cases, the nature of the policy objectives results in programs that define different categories of place. For example, the USDA's National Agricultural Library has a litany of place-based definitions to address many rural development–based programs both within and outside the USDA (Rural Information Center 2016). Further, agencies such as the Department of Health and Human Services have targeted many programs to deal with the challenges of rural health access, and programs like the Critical Access Hospital program have incorporated place-based dimensions directed by policy (Fannin and Nedelea 2013).

Urban areas are also defined through federal programs. Medicare, for example, is highly dependent on the Metropolitan Statistical Area (MSA) definitions of the Office of Management and Budget (OMB). Healthcare spending represented 17.9 percent of the US Gross Domestic Product in 2016 and Medicare spending represented 20 percent of that total. Medicare differentiates reimbursement rates to hospitals for similar health services based on geographic reimbursement differentials such as the hospital wage index. This index differentiates more expensive health care labor markets from less expensive labor markets by using MSA definitions (Institute of Medicine 2012, 62). As a result, hospitals in counties that move in and out of metropolitan status face sizeable changes in hospital revenue depending on the hospital's Medicare patient mix. For example, the projected 2019 hospital wage index used by Medicare for hospital reimbursement averaged 1.026 for hospitals in counties with metropolitan status but only 0.868 for hospitals in nonmetropolitan counties, meaning that nonmetropolitan hospitals received only 84 percent of what metropolitan hospitals received. A 16 percent reduction in wage reimbursement would have major implications on hospital bottom lines because the average not-for-profit hospital operating margins in 2017 were only 1.9 percent (Kacik 2018). The implications of these lower reimbursement rates have resulted in the federal government's adjusting these base indices to reduce reimbursement disparities. They have also implemented cost-based reimbursement through the Critical Access Hospital program to increase reimbursement of rural hospitals that lack the economies of scale of larger, more urban hospitals.

One very high-profile, place-based development program is the Department of Housing and Urban Development's Community Development Block Grant (CDBG) program. The CDBG program has historically focused on two major programmatic categories. The first category, currently defined as the entitlement program, focuses strategic investments in development projects for geographic areas within MSAs. This program leaves decision-making authority over spending to regional decision makers (US Department of Housing and Urban Development 2020a). The second category of the CDBG program, currently called both the nonentitlement program and the State Community Development Block Grant Program, is structured to give discretion for strategic investment decisions to decision makers at the state level (US Department of Housing and Urban Development

2020b), essentially giving control of development of these nonentitlement regions to the states. Nonentitlement regions include all counties, parishes, and boroughs of the United States that are not classified within an entitlement region, or those outside of MSAs. To the extent that state decision makers' priorities align with the those of nonentitlement region decision makers, these investments can potentially maintain their value in addressing local and regional substate priorities. However, when these nonentitlement program funds are used by state decision makers in ways that deny local leaders a final say on investment, a misalignment may result between state decisions and local priorities, which sometimes produces suboptimal investment from the perspective of local stakeholders.

History of Core Based Statistical Areas (CBSAs)

To better understand the challenges faced by public officials in the nonentitlement regions in the CDBG program and nonmetropolitan hospitals funded by Medicare, one must first look at the history of the place-based MSA definition, which can be traced back to the 1950s (US Census Bureau 2018). The concept of MSAs replaced Metropolitan Districts, which were created in 1910. Following World War II, increasing suburbanization created larger interconnected regions that were supported by a densely populated urban core. These regions comprised *central counties*, designated on the basis of having a central city with a minimum population threshold, and *outlying counties,* which had strong social and economic connection to the central county, measured by commuting patterns and other character elements consistent with metropolitan areas. The combination of the central county or counties and the outlying county or counties made up the entire Metropolitan Statistical Area.

Historically, an MSA was defined by the political jurisdiction of its principal city.[1] However, because political jurisdictions can be changed by local government authorities through such procedures as annexation, over time several constituencies called for the metropolitan definition to be made more objective. The Metropolitan Standards Area Review Project was ultimately formed in the early 1990s to evaluate alternatives to the MSA definition. Their final report (Office of Management and Budget 2000, 8228) led to a new set of rules for data generated from the 2000 US Decennial Census; these rules were roughly kept the same for data generated from the 2010 US Census.

Beginning with the 2000 classification of Metropolitan Statistical Areas, a new category was created, Micropolitan Statistical Areas.[2] Micropolitan Statistical Areas are constructed similarly to MSAs, the primary difference being the population thresholds within the urban clusters. On the basis of Part D in the Federal Register (Office of Management and Budget 2010, 37249–37252), a county with an urbanized area with a population of 50,000 or more would be designated a central county of a Metropolitan Statistical Area, whereas the urban cluster in a Micropolitan Statistical Area contained a population between 10,000 and 49,999. Additional outlying counties would be included if at least 25 percent of the workers living in the county worked in the central county or counties of the Metropolitan or Micropolitan Statistical Area. Consequently, the OMB calls both the Metropolitan Statistical Areas and Micropolitan Statistical Areas a more general category called Core Based Statistical Areas (CBSAs). It has become commonplace to identify those counties that are not a part of either a metropolitan or micropolitan CBSA *noncore* counties.

One of the challenges faced by federal agencies that have chosen to leverage the CBSA definitions for purposes of policy implementation through specific federal programs is that the Metropolitan and Micropolitan Statistical Area standards were not created for applying policy. In fact, the Federal Register states the following:

> The purpose of the Metropolitan and Micropolitan Statistical Area Standards is to provide nationally consistent delineations for collecting, tabulating, and publishing federal statistics for a set of geographic areas. The Office of Management and Budget establishes and maintains these areas solely for statistical purposes.
>
> Metropolitan and Micropolitan Statistical Areas are not designed as a general-purpose geographic framework for nonstatistical activities or for use in program funding formulas. The CBSA classification is not an urban-rural classification; Metropolitan and Micropolitan Statistical Areas in many counties outside CBSAs contain both urban and rural populations. (Office of Management and Budget 2010, 37249)

Despite OMB's officially discouraging the practice, federal agencies continue to leverage CBSA definitions for distribution of federal dollars such as Medicare and CDBG. For small cities, this can be particularly challenging to manage as the definitions create instability over time.

Challenges to Using CBSAs for Federal Program Delivery

Although the desire to create objective definitions is understandable, federal definitions around functional regions with strong social and economic ties are not necessarily stable, which can create unintended consequences for regions over time. Further, when these definitions are used to administer program funding formulas for CDBG, Medicare, and other expenditures, they can create problems for optimal, long-run decision making. The three primary reasons that regional definitions become unstable over time are

1. the volatility of MSAs;
2. the variability in point estimates created by sampling procedures for commuting; and
3. competing hierarchies of regional identification.

Volatility in Metropolitan Statistical Areas

Since the creation of MSAs in the 1950s, the number of counties classified as metropolitan has grown nationally. Primarily, new MSAs are created when new central counties reach the population threshold (currently a 50,000-population threshold for an urbanized area). MSAs can also be created when contiguous counties increase their social and economic integration via increased commuting ties to the central counties. Whereas the population of urbanized areas has some volatility, there is likely to be even greater change in commuting patterns over time.

Two characteristics likely generate much of this volatility. The first is reduced transportation costs for travel between where people work and where they live. As a result, people may cross county boundaries in their normal commutes because they live geographically further from where they work. Second, the strength of local economies outside central counties may erode, resulting in workers in these outlying counties commuting to central counties to obtain employment. Although the commuting patterns of urbanized area residents and residents of contiguous suburban and rural regions move in both directions, academics, policy analysts, and the general public often focus more on the population growth of the urbanized area. This emphasis reinforces the conventional wisdom that commuting patterns primarily flow in one direction—into these central counties and not outward from the center to the periphery.

The reality is that these patterns, while consistent overall, do not hold in every geographic region. Many urbanized areas in the Midwest that were hubs of post–World War II manufacturing have stagnated or declined in population. Further, certain regional retail hubs in the more sparsely populated Great Plains have lost population as the economic base of many of these areas (agriculture and mining) have become more capital- and less labor-intensive. In addition, there are many residents across the United States who live in counties on the knife's edge of commuting thresholds that determine whether they reside inside or outside of a given CBSA. As a result, federal funding formulas that use these definitions result in their eligibility changing from decennial census to decennial census as smaller central cities move inside or outside of the threshold.

EXAMPLE: LOUISIANA

An example of this knife-edge pattern at work in the definition of statistical areas can be observed in the state of Louisiana. The changing Metropolitan Statistical Areas of the state of Louisiana from 1950 through 2010 are highlighted in figures 6.1 through figure 6.7. In 1950, there were only three MSAs in the state of Louisiana: Shreveport, Baton Rouge, and New Orleans. As one follows the changing geography of these areas over the decades, one can observe parishes moving both into and out of various MSAs.

Take the Shreveport MSA as an example. In 1950 (figure 6.1, northwest corner), only Caddo Parish was included in the definition. In 1960 (figure 6.2), Bossier Parish (on the eastern border of Caddo) was added to the Shreveport MSA definition. By 1970 (figure 6.3), a third parish, Webster Parish (on the eastern border of Bossier Parish), was added as the interstate highway system expanded, connecting Caddo Parish workers residing in Webster Parish. Over the next three decades, however, Webster Parish flip-flopped between being in and out of the Shreveport MSA. By the time the MSA definitions based on the 1980 census were released, Webster was no longer an outlying parish of the Shreveport MSA (figure 6.4). In 1990, Webster Parish was again included (figure 6.5) but was later removed from the 2000 definition (figure 6.6), only to come back on the basis of the most recent commuting data used by OMB to calculate 2010 Metropolitan Statistical Areas (2006–10 American Community Survey county commuting statistics) (figure 6.7).

Instability due to Sampling Procedures

The elimination of the long form after the 2000 US Census resulted in the OMB's move from a census approach to a survey approach, and it transitioned to the 2006–10 American Community Survey (ACS) for its county-to-county commuting statistics. As a result, the first challenge of true commuting changes impacting regional definitions was compounded with sampling error.

Each county-to-county commuting estimate comes with a margin of error (MOE). The MOE represents the value (in commuters) that would be added to or subtracted from the commuting estimate to calculate a 90 percent confidence interval. That is, given the sampling procedure, the Census Bureau is 90 percent

FIGURE 6.1. Louisiana Metropolitan Statistical Areas—1950. Data drawn from historical delineation file of the US Census

confident that the true number of commuters between any pair of counties falls within the range of the commuting estimate plus or minus this MOE. Given that OMB uses the point estimate of commuting to determine which counties do or do not belong to a given metropolitan or micropolitan area, true estimates of commuting that fall at the lower bound or upper bound of the confidence interval may result in measurably different CBSAs from what is generated from the official estimates.

Lost Regional Identities due to OMB Definitions

Finally, the OMB delineation of CBSAs recognizes that some delineations are not mutually exclusive; that is, a county may contain an urban cluster of 10,000 or more and thus potentially serve as a central county of a Micropolitan Statistical Area while at the same time it meets the 25 percent threshold of commuting to be considered part of a Metropolitan Statistical Area. OMB delineations

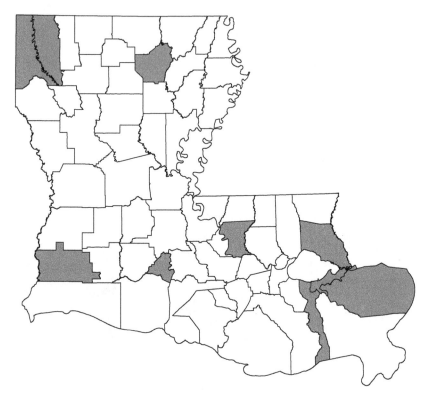

FIGURE 6.2. Louisiana Metropolitan Statistical Areas—1960. Data drawn from historical delineation file of the US Census

state that if a county meets both criteria, the county is treated as an outlying county to the central metropolitan county to which its residents commute for work. This means that a county in which a plurality or majority of its workforce are employed within the county but at least 25 percent commute to a nearby central county of another CBSA will be included in the definition of the larger CBSA. Because the OMB definition defaults to the creation of a smaller number of large multicounty regions at the expense of a larger number of small and medium-sized regions, the regional identity of these smaller, potentially central counties are subsumed in the definition of a larger nearby metropolitan CBSA.

Small cities are at the epicenter of these two challenges to CBSA definitions. Small cities that serve as the centers of small urbanized areas or urban clusters may potentially underrepresent the regional connectedness due to large sampling error in commuting estimates of small neighboring counties. Further, small cities with a long-term regional identity and strong bonding social networks may be drawn in as outlying counties to larger urban hierarchies without measuring

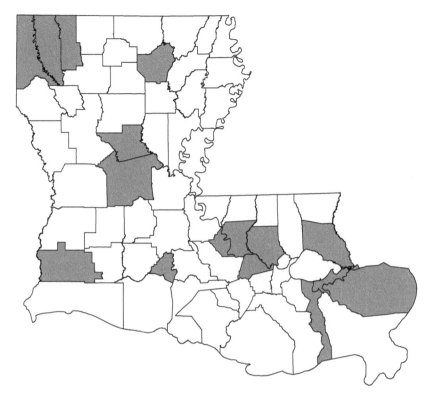

FIGURE 6.3. Louisiana Metropolitan Statistical Areas—1970. Data drawn from historical delineation file of the US Census

the relative strengths of the connections between the smaller and larger regional identities. We attempt to address the magnitude of these issues in the next section.

Understanding the Impact of Changing CBSA Classifications

To address the first and third reasons stated previously that regional definitions become unstable over time, we evaluate the changing classification of counties between CBSAs. In particular, changes in CBSA classification are evaluated between data sourced from the 2000 US Census and 2010 US Census. We expanded the basic three-way classification of CBSAs (metropolitan, micropolitan, and non-core) into a five-way classification that incorporates central and outlying county subsets for metropolitan and micropolitan areas. This approach permits a better

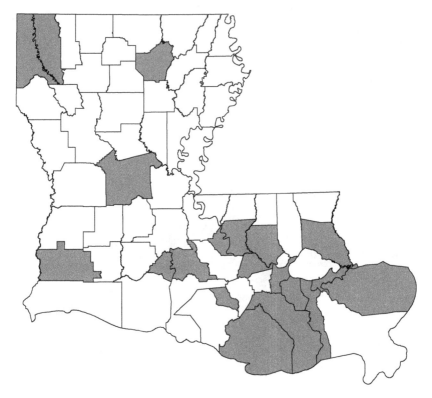

FIGURE 6.4. Louisiana Metropolitan Statistical Areas—1980. Data drawn from historical delineation file of the US Census

understanding of how growth and decline in population, population density, and shifts in commuting patterns move counties between these classifications.

The results of changing CBSA classifications are highlighted in table 6.1, where columns correspond to CBSA classifications (primary and subcategory) using data from the 2010 Census, and rows correspond to the classification of all US counties using data from the 2000 Census. Each row is uniquely identified by two dimensions of CBSA status: the CBSA primary classification (metro, micro, or noncore) and the subcategory of CBSA status (central or outlying). The number shown in a cell at the intersection of a row and column represents the number of counties that were originally in the row CBSA classification in 2000 that became classified in the column CBSA in 2010. For example, the value 42 in the microcentral row/metrocentral column cell represents the 42 counties that were classified as central micropolitan counties in 2000 and then reclassified as central metropolitan counties in 2010.

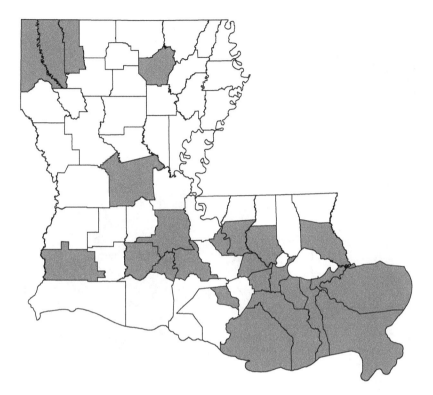

FIGURE 6.5. Louisiana Metropolitan Statistical Areas—1990. Data drawn from historical delineation file of the US Census

Analyzing this table from different directions (row or column) reveals important changes in CBSA classification. For example, the number of counties in cells along the diagonal represents counties that did not change their classification between 2000 and 2010. Of the 3,132 counties analyzed, 2,844 (the sum of all the counties represented in the cells along the diagonal, approximately 91 percent) counties did not change their classification over the 10 year period. The remaining 288 counties (9 percent) underwent changes in their classification during the same 10 year window.[3]

Looking at the counties that did move between classifications, one observes that the initial classification that generated the greatest movement or volatility was micropolitan. Of the 673 counties classified as micropolitan in 2000, 101, which is just over 15 percent, switched to either metropolitan or noncore status in 2010.[4] The volatility of 2000 micropolitan counties was approximately twice as high as either 2000 metropolitan counties (7.84 percent) or 2000 non-core counties (7.35 percent).

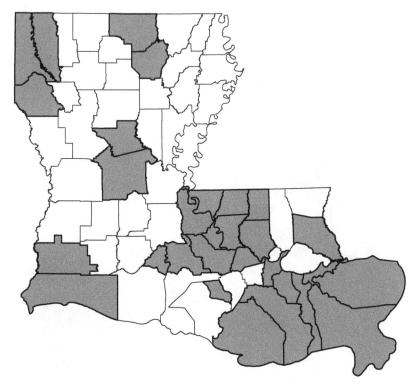

FIGURE 6.6. Louisiana Metropolitan Statistical Areas—2000. Data drawn from historical delineation file of the US Census

From the perspective of 2010 (columns), there appears to be even more volatility for micropolitan areas. Between 2000 and 2010, 65 counties gained micropolitan status.[5] Given that 101 counties lost micropolitan status, there was a net loss of 36 micropolitan counties between 2000 and 2010.

The gains in micropolitan status came primarily from 2000 noncore counties; fifty-four noncore counties became micropolitan in 2010.[6] Reductions in micropolitan status between 2000 and 2010 were split between counties changing to metropolitan and noncore status. There were seventy-one micropolitan counties in 2000 that were reclassified as metropolitan in 2010 and thirty micropolitan counties that were reclassified as noncore over the same period.[7]

The designation of either central or outlying county is important to the consideration of regional identity (point three). Nineteen counties that were classified as central micropolitan in 2000 were reclassified as outlying metropolitan in 2010. While some of these counties may have had their urban clusters decline to below 10,000, many of them were likely counties for which commuting into a neighboring central metropolitan county rose above the 25 percent threshold over the ten-

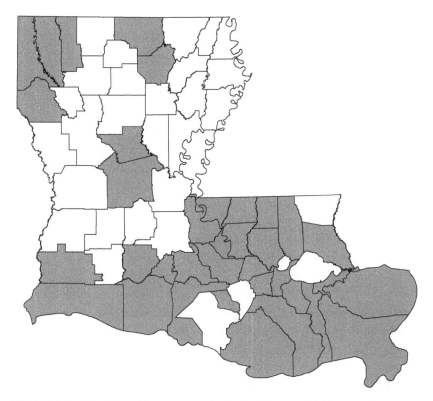

FIGURE 6.7. Louisiana Metropolitan Statistical Areas—2010. Data drawn from historical delineation file of the US Census

TABLE 6.1. Changing classifications of CBSAs between 2000 and 2010

2000 (rows)	2010 (columns)	Metro		Micro		
		Central	Outlying	Central	Outlying	Noncore
Metro	Central	648	12	4	0	0
	Outlying	37	351	7	0	25
Micro	Central	42	19	497	0	15
	Outlying	0	10	1	74	15
Noncore		1	46	36	18	1,274

year period. Consequently, the "tie goes to the metro" rule would be in effect so that these counties would be reclassified as outlying metropolitan even though they contained an urban cluster with a population between 10,000 and 49,999. These counties represent approximately 6.7 percent of *all* county CBSA changes and 18.6 percent of micropolitan county changes between 2000 and 2010.

Policy Implications and Alternatives

As mentioned earlier, CBSAs are used by major federal government agencies in the distribution of funding. A change in a county's metropolitan status has implications for both local autonomy in the use of dollars from programs like Community Development Block Grants and the rate of reimbursement for Medicare. Because metropolitan status generates more funds or at least more control over expenditure of funds, this volatility can result in local governments at the margin attempting to focus on development practices that create sufficient density to define new urbanized areas or maintain such density to keep existing urbanized areas. Unfortunately, such practices may produce suboptimal development patterns, given the mix of placed-based and people-based wealth assets in a county. Small cities are in the crosshairs of these federal programs because in many cases they anchor those regions (smaller metropolitan areas and micropolitan areas) that are most prone to change in status.

Given the volatility faced by micropolitan areas, the three constituencies that have the most influence over how this unstable categorization system impacts these regions should consider strategies that reduce future volatility. First, OMB (and the federal statistical agencies that participate on the OMB committee that recommends CBSA delineations) should consider expanding the delineation range for micropolitan areas. In 2000, the concern that smaller towns with a few characteristics of urban areas should be differentiated from smaller villages and low-density rural populations resulted in the creation of micropolitan areas. Almost twenty years later there is likely more heterogeneity in metropolitan regions than in micropolitan and noncore areas. For example, a subset of the largest US metropolitan regions, sometimes referred to as *global cities*, are less connected economically to the geography surrounding them than to other sister global cities half-way around the world (Badger 2017). Evidence is growing (e.g., see Weber et al. (2017, 113–9)) that the factors that drive some functional quality-of-life characteristics are similar between micropolitan and metropolitan areas. Because the total populations of the largest micropolitan areas and the smallest metropolitan areas are often similar, increasing the minimum population necessary for densely populated census tracts and blocks to be classified as urbanized areas would likely identify a greater number of regions with similar social and economic characteristics. Such a reconfiguration would also distinguish such places from larger global cities.

Federal agencies that use CBSA definitions for formula funding might consider small adjustments to the applications of these definitions. One example might include allowing an outlying county that has metropolitan or micropolitan status to maintain that status if changes in commuting between decennial census periods falls within the margin of error of the initial period. For example, in the 2010 CBSA primary classification there were sixty-seven outlying metropolitan counties that would have been reclassified as nonmetropolitan (either micropolitan or noncore) if their percent commuting had been estimated at the lower end of the 90 percent confidence interval. Another seventy-nine nonmetropolitan counties would have gained metropolitan status at the higher end of the 90 percent confidence interval, potentially jeopardizing future eligibility of rural-centric federal funding formulas. Another possible adjustment to consider is changing rules such as "tie goes to the metro" so that a micropolitan area with strong local labor markets that supply a plurality or majority of their employed residents' jobs can maintain its micropolitan identity as opposed to becoming an outlying county in a larger MSA. Such approaches by federal agencies would reduce the amount of volatility in program formula funding and at the same time allow more optimal long-term development to occur across multiple counties in these CBSA regions.

Finally, small cities that are at the core of these micropolitan and small metropolitan regions should consider a broad regional approach to development. Counties that move into and out of metropolitan or micropolitan status from decade to decade should not be excluded from long-term regional planning, such as regional development districts. They should be included in development discussions consistently to ensure that their small cities can serve as viable and potentially sustainable regional anchors instead of minor, often neglected satellites of larger urban centers and global cities.

Notes

1. The original Metropolitan Districts used a principal city population of 100,000 in 1910. When the 1930 Metropolitan Districts were defined, the threshold for principal city population was reduced to 50,000. This became the basis for the current threshold used from the 1950s (when Metropolitan Districts were called Standard Metropolitan Areas) to the present.

2. This chapter uses 2000 and 2010 to refer to the classification of Metropolitan and Micropolitan Statistical Areas because they correspond to the years in which the data were sourced for the calculation of urbanized areas and commuting levels. The actual formal designation by OMB typically does not occur until the third year after the decennial census (2003 for 2000 and 2013 for 2010).

3. Many individual counties may not recognize that their CBSA classification changed if the change was a subcategory move from inside a primary CBSA.

4. The 101 counties classified as micropolitan in 2000 that switched to either metropolitan or noncore status in 2010 were calculated as $101 = 42 + 19 + 15 + 10 + 15$ or the sum of Micro Central and Micro Outlying rows.

5. The calculation is $65 = 4 + 7 + 36 + 18$.

6. The calculation is $54 = 36 + 18$.

7. The calculations are $71 = 42 + 19 + 10$ and $30 + 15 + 15$.

References

Badger, Emily. 2017. "What Happens When the Richest US Cities Turn to the World?" *New York Times,* December 22, 2017. https://www.nytimes.com/2017/12/22/upshot/the-great-disconnect-megacities-go-global-but-lose-local-links.html.

Fannin, J. Matthew, and I. Cristian Nedelea. 2013. "Performance of the Critical Access Hospital Program: Lessons Learned for Future Rural Hospital Effectiveness in a Changing Health Policy Landscape." *Choices Magazine.* 2(1). http://dx.doi.org/10.22004/ag.econ.148547.

Institute of Medicine. 2012. *Geographic Adjustment in Medicare Payment: Phase I: Improving Accuracy.* Washington, DC: National Academies Press. https://doi.org/10.17226/13138.

Kacik, Alex. 2018. "Not-for-Profit Hospital Operating Margins Continue to Contract." *Modern Healthcare,* September 20, 2018. https://www.modernhealthcare.com/article/20180920/NEWS/180929982.

Office of Management and Budget. 2000. "Final Report and Recommendations from the Metropolitan Area Standards Review Committee to the Office of Management and Budget Concerning Changes to the Standards for Defining Metropolitan Areas; Notice." *Federal Register* 67 (63): 51060–77. https://www.gpo.gov/fdsys/pkg/FR-2000-08-22/pdf/00-20951.pdf.

Office of Management and Budget. 2010. "2010 Standards for Delineating Metropolitan and Micropolitan Statistical Areas; Notice *Federal Register* 75 (123): 37246–52. https://www.federalregister.gov/documents/2010/06/28/2010-15605/2010-standards-for-delineating-metropolitan-and-micropolitan-statistical-areas.

Rural Information Center. 2019. *What Is Rural?* Beltsville, MD: USDA, National Agricultural Library. https://www.nal.usda.gov/ric/what-is-rural.

US Census Bureau. 2018. *History: Metropolitan Areas.* https://www.census.gov/history/www/programs/geography/metropolitan_areas.html.

US Department of Housing and Urban Development. 2020a. *Community Development Block Grant Entitlement Program.* https://www.hudexchange.info/programs/cdbg-entitlement/.

US Department of Housing and Urban Development. 2020b. *State Community Development Block Grant Program.* https://www.hudexchange.info/programs/cdbg-state/.

Weber, Bruce, J., Matthew Fannin, Sam Cordes, and Thomas G. Johnson. 2017. "Upward Mobility of Low-income Youth in Metropolitan, Micropolitan and Rural America." *The Annals of the American Academy of Political and Social Science* 672, no. 1 (July):103–22. https://doi.org/10.1177%2F0002716217713477.

7

CONCEPTUALIZING SHRINKING INNER-RING SUBURBS AS SMALL CITIES

Governance in Communities in Transition

Hannah Lebovits

As the United States rolls into the 2020 election period, suburban communities are gaining significant attention. With the decades-long suburbanization of the Democratic party, the spaces between large urban communities and smaller or more rural ones are a political battleground in most major metropolitan regions (Hopkins 2019). Along with this trend, demographic, housing, and economic data show that these geographies have changed in complex ways: poverty has suburbanized (Kneebone and Berube 2013; Allard 2017), the growth in suburban housing has encouraged more minority suburbanization (Timberlake, Howell, and Staight 2011; Massey and Tannen 2018), the 2008–2009 financial crisis devastated many suburban areas (Lucy 2017), and although jobs continue to sprawl across the region throughout the suburban areas, poor and minority residents are less likely to benefit (Raphael and Stoll 2010).

However, despite our knowledge of the current suburban realities, we lack a clear understanding of how these communities, currently facing complex issues that were once urban in nature, perceive and govern themselves. Particularly in inner-ring, industrial-area communities, where these shifts present significant constraints, a broad understanding of the long-term management and governance response to this transition is missing. Existing research focuses on individual city efforts, particularly one-off projects and economic development plans (Lee and Leigh 2005; Vicino 2006; Hanlon 2008), while the metropolitan-level literature oversimplifies suburban communities, viewing them simply as additional rational-acting units within the region (see Matkin and Frederickson 2009; Hawkins 2010; Jimenez and Hendrick 2010). As a result, little is clear regarding the unique nature of suburban governance as a process and not simply as a series of outputs (practices) in response to inputs (people, property, and businesses). How do older, inner-ring suburban cities see themselves, their goals, their assets, and their weaknesses? How do they make decisions, and what do they prioritize? These are the city-centric questions we have yet to consider in the suburban setting.

In this chapter, I fill this gap by introducing a new framing for inner-ring suburban governance, focused on the complex nature of size, space, and significances: a small-cities approach. At first glance this might seem like an odd choice. Conceptualizations of small cities often focus on those that are geographically central to the region that they are in (core cities), and studies of suburbs often do not focus on suburban communities alone. Instead they view suburbia from an urban-periphery perspective and a metropolitan lens. Indeed, small-cities literature centers the nature of the city as its own comprehensive unit, entirely focused on key aspects of the city such as the commercial district, the cultural aspects of the community, and the experiences of those who live there. Small cities might have their own suburbs but are often perceived as islands, of sorts. Common trends in suburban research, on the other hand, focus on the practices that lead to and manage the process of suburbanization (Ekers, Hamel, and Keil 2012; Hamel and Keil 2015; Addie 2016; Hamel and Keil 2016), the spatial structures of population, economics and housing/land-use characteristics as they relate to the central city and the metropolitan region (Short, Hanlon, and Vicino 2007; Vicino 2008), or broader metropolitan efforts that view suburban and central cities as units engaged in competition or collaboration (Parks and Oakerson 2000; Post and Stein 2000).

Nevertheless, I suggest that viewing shrinking, transitioning, inner-ring suburban communities as small cities enables us to understand the tensions that these cities face between enhancing the value of their smallness and growing diversity and internalizing failure because of their size and the constraints of rapid demographic shifts. In analyzing the master plans of inner-ring suburban communities across a single metropolitan region, I find important small-city tendencies that shape the aspirational documents of these communities. The plans highlight a tendency toward pulling away from a reliance on the central city with particular focuses on generating suburb-specific amenities, identities, and opportunities. The inner-ring suburban cities in this study, although physically connected to the urban core as well as other cities, seek to meaningfully frame themselves as separate from others and uniquely valuable.

As a view into the ways these cities see themselves, these findings have important implications for our understanding of both suburban communities and small cities. Though master plans are ambitious documents and not implementation tools per se, they are coproduced through community-engaged and institution-led efforts, making them an ideal source through which to understand a city's vision, goals, and interests. In recognizing the growing small city tendencies of this particular type of suburb, we can better explore not only the unique needs of these communities but the distinct advantages they possess.

The State of "Shrinking" Inner-Ring Suburban Cities

In the last thirty years, older suburban cities have faced issues that were once urban in nature, especially those in midwestern and northeastern shrinking regions (Tighe and Ryberg-Webster 2019). As minority groups have moved out of the central city into the nearest suburbs, more economically and racially homogeneous whites have sprawled further out into the exurbs (Brueckner 2000). Few states have limited the continued development of suburban layers in any meaningful way, resulting in new pattern of poverty and decline in older, suburban communities. As a collective whole, poverty is rising more rapidly in the suburbs than in the central cities (Kneebone and Berube 2013; Allard 2017). The inner-ring suburbs have been the first to face this increase in poverty as people left the central city in an effort to move people to areas of opportunity, despite the fact that these cities lacked the resources and design to be wholly supportive of racial and economic diversity in any meaningful way (Kneebone and Nadeau 2015). And while poverty rates have risen in all inner-ring suburbs, this change is particularly apparent in the Northeast and Midwest (Orfield 2002; Madden 2003; Mikelbank 2004; Short, Hanlon, and Vicino, 2007; Hanlon 2008).

As a result of historical and current policy making and economic development efforts, those in poverty who can find good-quality, affordable housing in the suburbs will often find these communities to be a "poverty trap" rather than a place of opportunity. Social services are few and far between in these settings and public dollars are mostly allocated to services, including public works, safety and EMS services, and school districts (Murphy and Wallace 2010). Additionally, as many residents of these cities purchased their homes with subprime mortgages, vacancy rates in the inner-ring suburbs have risen dramatically since the housing market crash of 2007–08 (Adhya 2013; Anacker 2015; Lucy 2017), creating additional pockets outside of the central city where homeownership and property-based equity are out of reach for those living in poverty (Kneebone and Nadeau 2015). Indeed, almost 75 percent of homes that secured a mortgage between 2004 and 2008 and subsequently faced foreclosure were in suburban neighborhoods (Schildt et al. 2013).

Shifts in population, demographics, economic vitality, and housing stability have prompted scholars to study suburban spaces through a growth-loss lens (Lee and Leigh 2005; Puentes and Warren 2006; Anacker, Niedt, and Kwon 2017; Airgood-Obrycki 2019; Sarzynski and Vicino 2019). Suburban areas that have undergone any significant transformation in the last 40–50 years have been considered shrinking or in decline, whereas those that have retained wealth, population statistics, white residents, and high-priced housing are considered stable, growing, and successful (Short, Hanlon, and Vicino 2007). As a result, scholars and practitioners have attempted to promote revitalization efforts in suburban communities that include nonwhite, low-income, immigrant, and housing-insecure residents via economic development strategies and attempts to lure new residents to the community (Kneebone and Berube 2013). In some regions, including Ohio (Coleman and Carroll 2018) and Maryland (Vicino 2008), these practices have gained support as valuable methods of recovery and have been shared widely among local governance scholars without significant critical analysis or review. Indeed, the recently published Routledge Handbook of American Suburbs (Hanlon and Vicino 2018) includes pieces that characterize and define suburbs, and yet these pieces do not discuss the governance, that is, the specific processes by which a city runs itself, of these places individually, including the institutional policies and the actions of powerful actors.

The trajectory and current state of older suburban communities indicate a significant need to examine governance in these places. Particularly in Rust Belt regions, where the city and surrounding suburbs are managing economic decline, older, dilapidated housing stock and the movement of residents toward the outer suburbs, it is essential that we understand the priorities and trade-offs of these communities and the environment in which these choices occur. There is a need to add to the current literature on suburbs and small cities by analyzing these vulnerable, small municipalities to recognize the ways in which they govern themselves. As older, inner-ring suburbs face these constraints, we should approach these cities as places of their own.

Considering Suburban Governance Through A Small Cities Approach

As these inner-ring communities are at a particularly heightened state of complexity in which they face multiple challenges at once, a more nuanced approach to understanding their governance is necessary. In focusing so narrowly on the development of land (land use, housing, and infrastructure) or the provision of municipal services, a view of governance as a dynamic, aspirational, and interactive process is lacking. Whereas contemporary research on American suburbs highlights a measure of variability and complexity in the demographic and spatial nature of these places, scholars do not invest significantly in understanding the complexity within them. Instead, I suggest a small-cities framing can illuminate that governance element and enable us to understand the nature of these places.

Broadly, one can argue that every action that a city takes—or does not take—can fall under the heading of *governance*. From accessibility to zoning, whether through institutions of government, networks of people and organizations, or highly personal relationships and social capital, the small and aggregate practices of a community determine the path of the city, shaped by goals of local stakeholders, institutions, and macro-level trends (Dahl [1961] 2005; Lynn, Heinrich, and Hill 2000; Peters and Pierre 2001; Stone 2005). Yet although many local actors associate success with increases to regional population, economic activity, and spatial reach (Molotch 1976), the United States has a long history of romanticizing smaller communities, reveling in the level of engagement, direct democratic process, and local impact that they allow (Tocqueville [1835] 2003; Dahl and Tufte 1973; Newton 1982). Small cities therefore provide a unique and interesting lens through which to study local efforts as they can face a tug-of-war between capitalizing on their smallness as an asset and perceiving their size as a sign of failure (Bell and Jayne 2006).

Although long ignored in favor of a focus on large urban centers, over the last two decades small-city scholarship has picked up significantly. Bell and Jayne led the way in this research in their edited book, *Small Cities: Urban Experience beyond the Metropolis* (2006), in which they highlighted case studies from around the world and described the ways in which important actors and institutions make trade-offs and create a sense of place. Published at around the same time, Ofori-Amoah's (2006) *Beyond the Metropolis: Urban Geography as if Small Cities Mattered* looks at small cities through a geographer's lens with a focus on the form of cities, which is briefly mentioned also in Bell and Jayne's work. Both Bell and Jayne and Ofori-Amoah framed their books with an understanding of small cities as places with fewer than 100,000 people and focused their attention on cities that lie outside our understanding of the metropolitan center. Conversely, in his book *Small Cities USA* (2013), Jon Norman wrote about the economic and demographic trends in core cities with between 100 thousand and 200 thousand people. Norman identified eighty such cities in the United States and tracked them over time, with special attention to four cities in various regions. Norman highlighted the trends of economic activity and racial and economic inequality and showed how similar yet different they are in comparison with larger urban areas.

Unlike the books of Norman and Ofori-Amoah, Bell and Jayne's book was primarily an attempt to highlight governance practices in small cities, as opposed to an urban geography or an economic/social function of medium-sized cities. *Small Cities* (2006) asks the reader to consider how small cities operate differently from larger ones, suggesting that cities that are spatially small and have fewer residents do indeed govern in unique ways. Bell and Jayne framed their book with two perspectives in mind. The first is that size is not merely an adjective that describes the number of people in the city but that it is rather an idea at the heart of our understanding of what it means to be a city. "The discourses of cities—the way they are talked about and thought about by different people," the authors wrote, "have tended to follow the logic that cities should be big things, either amazing or terrifying in their bigness but big, nonetheless. . . . [S]hrinkage is a sign of failure" (5). Indeed, they do not define size as simply a measure of population numbers and argue against the idea that small cities are just small versions of big urban places. They emphasize the small-mindedness of small cities and the "me-too-ism" (1) that small cities display when they attempt to duplicate the actions of larger cities.

Bell and Jayne pointed out several concerns with the me-too approach, including the likelihood that the efforts would not translate into meaningful action at the small-city level. Small cities, they argued, are not below large cities on an urban hierarchy. Instead, they are on a parallel path with large cities, attempting to evolve and shape their future while balancing the tension between the benefits and threats of smallness, specifically in their political and cultural economies, their ability to craft an urbanized experience, and their sense of identity and place making. The second framing perspective that the authors point to is the difficulty small cities face in highlighting their value when so many cities are judged according to their ability to be globalized, economic powers. Indeed, this conflict between associating with the larger global urban experience and recognizing the uniqueness of individual small cities is the central tension in much of the literature on small cities.

The themes highlighted by Bell and Jayne echo those that appear in much of the remaining literature on governance in small cities as well as in classic urban governance texts. Thrift (2000) similarly argued that there is no one-size-fits-all approach to understanding cities or conceptualizing bigness/smallness. Haque (2001) added to the central conflict depicted by Bell and Jayne (2006) and suggested that it can translate into a visioning problem for small cities, in which they may not even be aware of their own value and their ability to engage in a variety of decision-making processes because they associate size with strength/advantage (Haque 2001). While the notion of a hierarchy of cities (Friedmann 1986; Markusen, Lee, and DiGiovanna 1999; Hall 2001) supports the idea that small cities are a tier below large cities and at a disadvantage because of their smallness, small-cities researchers have stressed the potential benefits of being small and far from larger urban centers (Partridge et al. 2008).

Furthermore, small cities are not only important joints in the massive network of regional economic activity (Hardoy and Satterthwhaite 1986) and ripe with social capital to increase economic development (Ring, Peredo, and Crisman 2010), but they have an urban geography and economic governance of their own (Robertson 2001; Smith 2007). In the United States, the ideal of Small Town USA and the Main Street model of economic activity continue to be romanticized as quintessential city forms and functions (Robertson 2001; Norman 2013). Studies of the land-use and economic activity in American small towns often show rates of congestion/crime, more niche and independent retail, mixed-use districts, historical buildings and areas, closely linked residential area, and the lack of a large corporate presence (Robertson 2001, 9). Economic revitalization efforts in small cities tend to focus on the human scale and the idea of re-creating a quaint view of small-town life (Paradis 2000; Burayidi 2001; Robertson 2001; Smith 2007).

In addition to the spatial identity and networks of small cities, small cities have a unique functional identity that influences their role as a platform for social and cultural activity (Garrett-Petts 2005; Bradley and Hall 2006; Waitt 2006). Some small cities in the United States, such as Roswell, New Mexico, are known to be cultural meccas and tourist destinations that have branded themselves with unique identities (Paradis 2002), and many small cities maintain ownership over specific cultural events and festivals to increase their urban edge (Bradley and Hall 2006; Miles 2006). Although these places can struggle to cultivate community and identity despite strong social ties (Leitner 2012), social capital and civic engagement can also be stronger in small cities (Putnam 2000; Oliver 2001; Ring, Peredo, and Chrisman 2010). Indeed, the push toward New Urbanism sought to capitalize on the social element of small-city networks and create small-city spaces even within larger metropolitan regions (Scott 2014).

In considering the nature of older, inner-ring suburban communities, I suggest that governance practices of small cities will be evident in these places. As population growth is a signifier of success in the capitalist North American territories, in a declining context even cities that have always maintained a small size will feel the constraints and opportunities of smallness. As a feedback mechanism, we can expect that the recognition of their smallness acts as a catalyst that triggers and further produces small city governance practices. Additionally, as these communities are physically connected to the central city and share boundaries with each other, we can expect that they will emphasize the need to stand out, not only in municipal service delivery and competition for residents and resources (Tiebout 1956; Savas 1977) but because the efforts of neighboring communities will likely diffuse across the region (Crain 1966; Gray 1973; Walker 1969).

In what specific practices can we expect these suburbs to invest? On the basis of the small-city literature, I suggest three overarching themes of small-city governance, adapted mostly from Bell and Jayne (2006) because their work encompasses the central themes discussed in this section. These include (1) political economic activity designed to improve a city's fortunes, especially in the planning and revitalization of the downtown or Main Street area; (2) the battle to gain an edge in an urban hierarchy in order to attract capital, culture, and people; and (3) the development of a sense of identity, lifestyle, and forms of sociability upon which small cities can more easily capitalize (Bell and Jayne 2006, 15; Paradis 2000; Robertson 2001; Ofori-Amoah 2007; Smith 2007). These three interconnected agendas exemplify the tension between uniqueness and metooism: they are simultaneously similar to large-city focuses and yet especially prevalent in small cities. Although the literature empirically indicates that these themes are generally observed in small core cities because size is a critical factor that generates these governance efforts, we can expect to see them evident to various degrees within small, suburban cities as well.

Methodology

This project focuses on the older suburban municipalities outside the city of Cleveland, several of which began to develop as cities in the late nineteenth century. Located in the northeast section of Ohio, Cleveland is a Rust Belt city that was once a booming industrial center. The area began to suburbanize in the late nineteenth century with the creation of predominantly residential cities outside the city core. These cities were home to the wealthy, and several initially barred Jews, Catholics, and African Americans from residing in their borders. The long history of redlining, blockbusting, and racial housing discrimination in the northeast Ohio area lingers within the private market and continues to impact the region's vitality (Galster 1990; Brennan 2015).

The Cleveland area is highly fragmented, with several layers of suburbs outside the city that make up the thirty-eight cities and several more county subdivisions of Cuyahoga County. As the area deindustrialized, the region faced severe population and industry decline. Today the city of Cleveland and many of the inner-ring suburbs—like many other Rust Belt and midwestern cities and inner-ring communities—continue to lose population and economic opportunities both to outer-ring suburban areas and to other counties and states. For the pur-

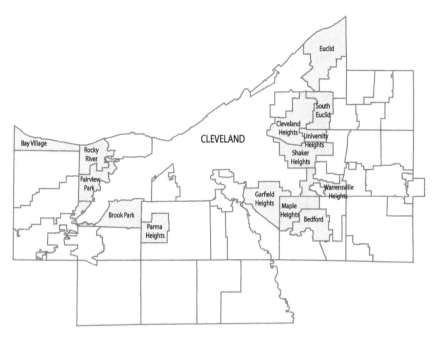

FIGURE 7.1. Map of Cuyahoga County

Note: The shading indicates the cities that are the focus of this chapter. Nineteen cities were identified and the fourteen shaded cities were coded by the author. Map by Cade Deckard.

pose of this case study, suburbs were considered older, inner-ring municipalities when at least 75 percent of their housing stock was built before 1970 and in most cases these cities shared a physical boundary with the city of Cleveland. These two measures, housing stock age and proximity to the central city, are utilized frequently in determining which suburbs are in the inner and outer rings of the MSA (Forsyth 2012). These measurements narrowed the original group of thirty-eight suburban municipalities in the county to a group of nineteen older suburbs. Of these nineteen, data were available from fourteen cities. The cities profiled in this piece are highlighted in figure 7.1.

In order to determine the city's goals and self-perception, each city's most recent master plan was coded in accordance with the governance themes identified in the small-cities literature. Master plans are an interesting and valuable data source because the process of creating and approving a master plan involves the combined efforts of residents, local legislators and administrators as well as other stakeholders such as business owners and landlords. In Cuyahoga County, cities can choose to perform an in-house planning process, or they can partner with the county's planning department to ensure that the process is inclusive and exhaustive. The benefits of a comprehensive plan are well established: the process allows areas to plan for the present as well as the future, assess opportunities for development, find innovative ways to remove obstacles inconsistent with the present/future needs and create incentives to resolve issues and better prepare for future demand (Mandelker, Cunningham, and Payne 2001). However, in the state of Ohio, municipalities are not required to act in accordance with a master plan. Therefore, while the document outlines the priorities of the city, as determined by residents, governmental bodies, and private interests, one cannot say for certain that the plan is a definitive statement of the city's policy actions. Still, the fact that the state does not require a planning procedure prior to building and development and yet cities choose to undergo the expensive and time-consuming process, indicates the value of the document regardless of whether future policymaking follows the exact recommendations of the master plan.

For this study, planning documents were retrieved for each of the cities from a variety of sources including the Cuyahoga County Planning Commission's project webpage, individual city websites and via information requests from the author. Nineteen cities were identified as inner-ring cities according to the housing age measure; however, only fourteen master plans were analyzed for this case study. Five cities could not provide documents in an appropriate format and were thus not included in the study. Because the five cities are not clustered in a single area and do not have specifically unique demographic or social characteristics, the fourteen remaining plans are sufficient for this study.

TABLE 7.1. Information on master plans

CITY	YEAR PLAN WAS ADOPTED/DRAFTED
Bay Village	2016
Bedford	2007
Brook Park	2012
Cleveland Heights	2017
Euclid	2018
Fairview Park	2013
Garfield Heights	1999
Maple Heights	2018
Parma Heights	2017
Rocky River	2018
Shaker Heights	2000
South Euclid	2015
University Heights	2016
Warrensville Heights	2012

As the master plan documents of fourteen of these cities are the main data set, this chapter employs an interpretive paradigm to perform the document analysis and code the documents according to themes outlined in the literature on small-city governance. The process and methodology of coding texts for interpretive research is well stablished (Lincoln 1995; Klein and Myers 1999; Rowlands 2005) and uniquely suited to the goals of this project. The documents were comprehensive and included sections outlining the engagement process for the plan itself, the current state of the city, the community vision, and the policies and practices that the city should execute in order to reach the vision. In accordance with Bell and Jayne's work (2006) and the specific case studies they describe, I identified eleven individual codes that represent aspects of the three major governance themes identified here: political economic agendas, an urban experience that offers a competitive advantage within an urban hierarchy, and the cultivation of a sense of identity lifestyle and forms of sociability. These themes, adapted from Bell and Jayne (2006), and their component parts are shown divided into subthemes in table 7.2.

The purpose of this analysis is to highlight trends and patterns within and between documents that show the aggregated focus of these suburbs as well as the variability between suburban municipalities. As such, the coding and subsequent analysis gives great weight to the individual wording of the texts because the words themselves describe the ways in which those engaging in the planning process see their city and the value they institutionalize within the priorities outlined in the master plan. The codes are distinctive yet related within the social fabric and spatial nature of cities, so that multiple codes could be used to describe the same passage.

The documents were coded by a single coder and received additional review from colleagues. This is not seen as a threat to the legitimacy of the coding because the code definitions are not difficult to understand, and the interpretive research paradigm encourages the researcher to interpret language and make sense of the ontology and epistemology in a manner that highlights the subjective experience of the coder and the text (Rowlands 2005). All documents were coded using the QDA Miner coding software. This software allows a researcher to strip documents of pictures and other nontext items and code individual segments of text. QDA Miner can create charts and graphs to display the frequency of codes and thus allow the researcher to quantify the qualitative measurements.

The text of every document in this analysis followed a similar outline. An executive summary was followed by a description of the city's current state, next a summary of several key goals, and then an in-depth description of each goal and the ways in which the goals can be achieved. Therefore, most of the text of each document was not coded. However, the coding of the vision statements,

TABLE 7.2. Coding descriptions and themes

GOVERNANCE THEME	MEASUREMENT NAME	OVERVIEW
Political economic governance	Intersecting economic activity	Attempt to connect structural economic activity (actual building/shaping of economic spaces and firms) with attempt to create greater global focus and identity.
Political economic governance	Singular product focus	Units and competition with other cities; city economic activity is driven by identity as supplier of single economic item (furniture), and governing authorities create strategies to maintain that singular economic activity
Political economic governance	Cooperation	Combined economic efforts with other political entities close by, balanced with each area's own political/identity/economic concerns.
Political economic governance	Outsizing and tourism	Measured by ability to attract growth that outsizes the size of the city. Large, interesting projects that can become major economic drivers.
The urban hierarchy and competitive advantage	Festivals	Development strategies that market the city through festival and art/cultural experiences. Also used for recreational and sometimes historical/cultural activities.
The urban hierarchy and competitive advantage	Grassroots governance	Building on local qualities through urban grassroots attempts—small entrepreneurs and residents; entrepreneurial governance.
The urban hierarchy and competitive advantage	Cluster and space	Designating space for cultural activity and focusing on attracting a single economic cluster (knowledge-based economy).
The urban hierarchy and competitive advantage	Mythology	An almost tacit, immeasurable nature of the city that creates a brand that might not really reflect any reality or even a desired reality by the residents.

Identity, lifestyle, and forms of sociability	Place making	Architectural innovation, *Widening the Tourist Net*, *SWAGing the Space* (selling brand products), production of new social formations and practices—basically, cities allow for/create a singular space with their own uniqueness that becomes a branded public space/melting pot—cultivating new social practices and norms within a space that provides niche, branded products.
Identity, lifestyle, and forms of sociability	Identity	"Heightened sense for and of place" (Bell and Jayne 2006, 230) and compounds tensions for young people because they see themselves as being in the margins; maintaining and creating mew spaces and boundaries to deal with declining city issues and youth's concerns or ideals for their future.
Identity, lifestyle, and forms of sociability	Capitalizing on big ideas	Can be a shift that stems from a single event or cultural experience/ development. Identity can be inauthentic and built up in the city's mind, especially small cities because they need to be visible to get picked up.

Source: Coding descriptions and themes adapted from Bell and Jayne 2006.

stated priorities, description of the current state of the city and potential strengths and weaknesses, and citizen-led survey does tell an important story of each city's values and governance goals; giving legitimacy to the plan's final recommendations. The percentage of the text of the master plans that were coded varied from 1.8 percent (Garfield Heights) to 28.5 percent (Warrensville Heights) with a mean of 11 percent.

Findings and Analysis

The coded findings indicate that the suburbs in this case study see themselves as their own complex, self-governing cities, with varying degrees of importance given to the governance themes. These findings and the subsequent analysis add nuance to our understanding of suburbs as complex local spaces and set the stage for future research on suburbs as small cities. The coded findings highlight many similarities between inner-ring suburbs and the governance of small cities. In the aggregate, the coding revealed that the governance priorities of suburban municipalities reflect small city themes—particularly in the political economic and social components of small city governance (figure 7.2). The three most frequent individual codes were for *Place making* (29.8 percent), *Intersecting economic*

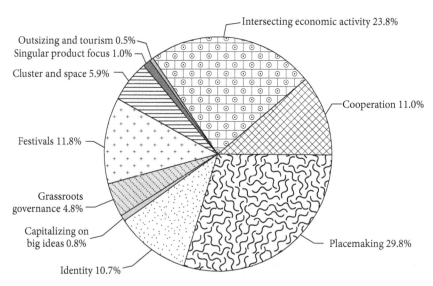

FIGURE 7.2.   Cumulative distribution of codes for all municipalities and their frequency

Note: The *Mythology* code was not used because none of the cities' stated goals related to this theme.

activity (23.8 percent) and *Festivals* (11.8 percent); and the larger governance themes (table 7.2) were fairly evenly distributed with *Identity, lifestyle, and forms of sociability* at 41.3 percent, *Political economic governance* at 36.3 percent, and *The urban hierarchy and competitive advantage* at 22.5 percent.

Nevertheless, the degree to which individual plans prioritized small city governance themes varies in several important ways, as shown in figure 7.2. First, these differences did not seem to tie into city size. Indeed, the cities with the largest and smallest population sizes (Euclid and Bedford, respectively), both displayed complex governance strategies with a variety of codes within their texts. Furthermore, several cities varied from the group, both in individual codes and broader themes. There were also a few cities that prioritized significantly different codes from the others. Some of these coding priorities appear to be similar in cities with similar demographic, economic, and housing trends, but any causal trends are beyond the scope of this particular discussion.

Largest Percentage of Code Distribution (Single Code)

As reflected in the cumulative distribution of codes for the documents (table 7.3), the largest distribution of codes for eleven of fourteen cities was in the *Place making* category, a subtheme of the *Identity, lifestyle, and forms of sociability* category. *Place making* codes were most often focused on city branding and attracting new residents by creating an identity that was unique to the place. The literature on city branding indicates a growing trend among municipalities to brand themselves through slogans, products, and changes to the city form as well as social expressions (Oguztimur and Akturan 2016; Zavattaro 2010). The governance goals of these suburban cities seems in line with this growing trend. However, whereas eleven of the cities prioritized place making over other governance activities, this trend was not evident in Cleveland Heights, Parma Heights, and Warrensville Heights. In Cleveland Heights, the largest percentage of codes were in the Festival category. In Parma Heights, *Intersecting economic activity* had the largest frequency, and the largest percentage of distribution of codes in Warrensville Heights was *Identity*.

Largest Percentage of Code Distribution

In ten of the fourteen master plans (table 7.3) the various subthemes within *Identity, lifestyle, and forms of sociability* were most frequently coded. In Parma Heights, South Euclid, and University Heights the largest percentage of codes were in the *Political economic governance* section, whereas in Cleveland Heights *The urban hierarchy and competitive advantage* code section was the most prevalent.

TABLE 7.3. Coding of individual master plans and comparison to total distribution of codes

	POLITICAL ECONOMIC GOVERNANCE				
	INTERSECTING ECONOMIC ACTIVITY	SINGULAR PRODUCT FOCUS	COOPERATION	OUTSIZING AND TOURISM	TOTAL
Total distribution of codes	23.8	1.0	11.0	0.5	36.3
Bay Village	15.6		10.1		25.7
Bedford	18.1	12.9	1.0	1.8	33.8
Brook Park	26.9	7.9	9.4		44.2
Cleveland Heights	12.6		8.5	0.3	21.4
Euclid	12.4		5.3	0.7	18.4
Fairview Park	22.7				22.7
Garfield Heights	27.6				27.6
Maple Heights	12.0		4.4		16.4
Parma Heights	47.4		8.4		55.8
Rocky River	4.3		30.8		35.1
Shaker Heights	40.2		2.0		42.2
South Euclid	23.1		14.4		37.5
University Heights	13.6		29.8		43.4
Warrensville	28.0		0.8		28.8

(continued)

Indeed, Cleveland Heights's focus on its grassroots, culturally infused nature and the idea that it gives the city a unique advantage put that code section ahead of the other cities in frequency by over 25 percentage points. The suburb is located on the east side of the city of Cleveland and is directly connected to Cleveland's University Circle, a neighborhood in uptown Cleveland that is home to Case Western Reserve University as well as its healthcare facility, University Hospitals, and a number of other cultural and educational facilities. The Cleveland Heights master plan highlights the city's proximity to University Circle and its function as a residential center for those who work in University Circle. It is possible that the strong focus on an urban experience grew out of the spatial and social proximity to the local cultural and educational mecca.

Smallest and Largest Cities, Smallest and Greatest Number of Codes

The cities of Bedford and Euclid (table 7.3) have the smallest and largest populations, respectively, and yet both plans indicated a variety of governance priori-

URBAN HIERARCHY AND COMPETITIVE ADVANTAGE				IDENTITY, LIFESTYLE, AND FORMS OF SOCIABILITY			
FESTIVALS	GRASSROOTS GOVERNANCE	CLUSTER AND SPACE	TOTAL	PLACE MAKING	IDENTITY	CAPITALIZING ON BIG IDEAS	TOTAL
11.8	4.8	5.9	22.5	29.8	10.7	0.8	41.3
20.8	1.8		22.6	51.8			51.8
4.7	1.3	5.4	11.4	34.9	7.3	12.6	54.8
5.8		3.9	9.7	29.3	6.6	10.3	46.2
22.8	18.3	17.7	58.8	14.1	5.7		19.8
2.2	11.2	20.2	33.6	36.0	11.9		47.9
9.0			9.0	68.3			68.3
			0	72.4			72.4
		7.0	7.0	43.2	33.4		76.6
		1.2	1.2	34.1	8.8		42.9
	2.7		2.7	52.8	9.4		62.2
	2.6	6.7	9.3	48.5			48.5
16.7		9.3	26.0	28.0	8.4		36.4
17.0	1.0		18.0	34.6	4.0		38.6
1.8	3.0		5.0	29.7	36.5		66.2

Note: The *Mythology* code was not included in the table because none of the cities' stated goals related to this theme.

ties and complex governance goals. In fact, Bedford's plan included ten of the eleven codes whereas Euclid's focused on only eight. While both plans prioritized cultivating an economic edge in the city, Euclid's was more focused on cultivating a knowledge hub whereas Bedford's plan revealed a strong focus on its role as a location for auto dealerships. Additionally, while Bedford's plan included the greatest number of codes, the Fairview Park and Garfield Heights documents had the fewest small city–themed codes, even though the percentage of coded text varied significantly (14.5 percent and 1.8 percent, respectively). Garfield Heights's plan was particularly sparse despite the city's size, central location in the county, and local population count. The most recent plan was also developed almost twenty years ago and was predominantly focused on housing and environmental concerns such as local draining practices.

Other important findings reveal a strong focus on local economic activity that has little to do with the central city's economic vitality or the role of the suburb as a residential community for people who work in the core. Similar to findings in the literature on revitalizing downtowns in small cities, many of the suburbs in this case study focused on creating vibrant economic spaces and highlighting individual enterprises. For example, Bedford and Brook Park were the cities with the highest frequency of the *Singular product focus* coding, and they are also cities with distinct economic niches. Broadway Avenue in Bedford is the primary regional location for car dealerships, and Brook Park is the home of a large regional Ford plant. Both cities' plans stated that they hope to capitalize on these existing ventures in the future. Likewise, Parma Heights's strong focus on *Intersecting economic activity* included several references to the nearby Shoppes at Parma (previously Parmatown), a large retail center in the neighboring city of Parma that is currently undergoing a large renovation and its own planning efforts.

Euclid is currently a center for jobs in manufacturing and, to a lesser degree, healthcare. Local actors noted the potential to gain an urban advantage through more knowledge-based clusters to create a trifecta of economic activity. Even Cleveland Heights, which clearly prioritized the vitality of Cleveland's University Circle, is interested in creating a space for niche markets to grow within Cleveland Heights's borders. Cleveland Heights and Euclid both discussed the desire to attract residents who will bring an entrepreneurial nature to the community and grow local *Grassroots governance* efforts. Furthermore, Bay Village, Rocky River, and University Heights, the most outlying older suburbs, all stressed the need to cooperate with surrounding cities and the regional government for services and new economic opportunities.

There are also interesting trends regarding the communities' social concerns. Maple Heights and Warrensville Heights have the highest rates of poverty and of African American residents of the suburbs in this case study. These are also the only cities with predominantly African American representation in their local elected offices. The documents of these cities are the only ones that give significant attention to the importance of cultivating a sense of place and identity for young people and the need to create a pathway toward opportunity for young people within the city.

Conclusion

Across the United States—particularly in the northeastern and midwestern regions—suburban communities right outside the central city are struggling. Population loss, industry shifts, housing market fluctuations, and economic upheavals have left many of these primarily residential communities with fewer residents and fewer dollars. Yet, while research in this area tends to focus on measuring these shifts and promoting revitalization tactics, we lack a clear understanding of how these communities in transition are attempting to orient themselves for future success. This chapter adds new insight by suggesting that in the face of additional complexities, inner-ring suburban communities adopt a small-cities approach to governance, maximizing their focus on political-economic activities, a distinctively urban experience, and a sense of place and identity. They do not see themselves as satellites of the urban core or even interrelated units of a metro region but as self-contained cities and self-governed small communities. I test this hypothesis by analyzing master plans of inner-ring suburban communities across a single metropolitan region, in accordance with Bell and Jayne's (2006) small cities framework. The findings suggest that like small independent cities, these communities shape their governance strategies with a focus on urban experiences that do not match the geographic scale of the community, economic plans, and a specific sense of place and identity. These results can compel us to reconsider how we understand suburban governance in such communities, providing valuable insight on the state of these spaces as well as providing targeting recommendations for those seeking to invest in better practices.

Older suburbs outside of Cleveland, Ohio, not only value and prioritize economic and social activity but they mostly approach local governance with little reference to the central city. These cities do not attempt to create slogans or branded locations that borrow from the themes in the urban core. In fact, the opposite seems to be true. Aside from one city, which is spatially close to the urban core's key culture and education district, the documents of other cities do not indicate any comparison to or even competition with the central city for resources or residents. Instead, the documents read as manifestos of fully independent cities looking to become economically successful, attractive places that are culturally appealing and identity specific. In other words, these suburbs see themselves as complex, dynamic small cities of their own. Still, as this research effort focused on the suburbs of a declining region, it is unclear whether this effort to procedurally distance themselves from the core would be evident in growing regions. Future research analyzing suburban communities in the southern and western regions can add to our understanding of this phenomenon.

As we see continued attention to the changing nature of suburban America, the findings in this chapter present a new way to conceptualize and consider the agendas that these cities adopt, providing additional insight to explain political, social, and economic outcomes. Governance practices in these places, whether conscious or not, reflect the inner conflict of small cities. They seek to behave in ways both similar to yet distinct from larger cities. This struggle defines and shapes their aspirational governance documents. Yet, unlike big cities, the unique nature of the small-city outlook might allow suburbs to be more flexible. Small cities can be laboratories of new ideas, social experiences, and economic opportunity. As inner-ring suburban communities invest in governing like small cities, they may supersede the large central city in their ability to cultivate opportunity, identity, and a rich urban experience.

References

Addie, Jean-Paul D. 2016. "Theorising Suburban Infrastructure: A Framework for Critical and Comparative Analysis." *Transactions of the Institute of British Geographers* 41, no. 3 (July): 273–85. https://doi.org/10.1111/tran.12121.

Adhya, Anirban. 2013. "From Crisis to Projects; A Regional Agenda for Addressing Fore-closures in Shrinking First Suburbs: Lessons from Warren, Michigan." *Urban Design International* 18, no. 1 (January): 43–60. https://doi.org/10.1057/udi.2012.31.

Airgood-Obrycki, Whitney. 2019. "Suburban Status and Neighbourhood Change." *Urban Studies* 56, no. 14 (November): 2935–52. https://doi.org/10.1177/0042098018811724.

Allard, Scott W. 2017. *Places in Need: The Changing Geography of Poverty.* New York: Russell Sage Foundation.

Anacker, Katrin B. 2015. "Analyzing Census Tract Foreclosure Risk Rates in Mature and Developing Suburbs in the United States." *Urban Geography* 36, no. 8 (November): 1221–40. https://doi.org/10.1080/02723638.2015.1055931.

Anacker, Katrin, Christopher Niedt, and Chang Kwon. 2017. "Analyzing Segregation in Mature and Developing Suburbs in the United States." *Journal of Urban Affairs* 39, no. 6 (August): 819–32. https://doi.org/10.1080/07352166.2017.1305730.

Bell, David, and Mark Jayne. 2006. *Small Cities: Urban Experience Beyond the Metropolis.* London: Routledge.

Bradley, Andrew, and Tim Hall. 2006. "The Festival Phenomenon: Festivals, Events and the Promotion of Small Urban Areas." In *Small Cities: Urban Experience Beyond the Metropolis,* edited by David Bell and Mark Jayne, 91–104. London: Routledge.

Brennan, John F. 2015. "The Impact of Depression-Era Homeowners' Loan Corporation Lending in Greater Cleveland, Ohio." *Urban Geography* 36, no. 1 (January): 1–28. https://doi.org/10.1080/02723638.2014.956418.

Brueckner, Jan K. 2000. "Urban Sprawl: Diagnosis and Remedies." *International Regional Science Review* 23, no. 2 (April): 160–171. https://doi.org/10.1177/016001700760101 2710.

Burayidi, Michael A. 2001. *Downtowns: Revitalizing the Centers of Small Urban Communities.* New York: Routledge.

Coleman, Chloe, and Tom Carroll. 2018. "A First Suburb Revitalized." *PM Magazine,* November 30, 2018. https://icma.org/articles/pm-magazine/first-suburb-revitalized.

Crain, Robert L. 1966. "Fluoridation: The Diffusion of an Innovation Among Cities." *Social Forces* 44, no. 4 (June): 467–476. https://doi.org/10.2307/2575080.

Dahl, Robert A. (1961) 2005. *Who Governs?: Democracy and Power in an American City.* New Haven: Yale University Press.

Dahl, Robert Alan, and Edward R. Tufte. 1973. *Size and Democracy.* Vol. 2. Stanford, CA: Stanford University Press.

Ekers, Michael, Pierre Hamel, and Roger Keil. 2012. "Governing Suburbia: Modalities and Mechanisms of Suburban Governance." *Regional Studies* 46, no. 3 (April): 405–22. https://doi.org/10.1080/00343404.2012.658036.

Forsyth, Ann. 2012. "Defining Suburbs." *Journal of Planning Literature* 27, no. 3 (June): 270–81. https://doi.org/10.1177/0885412212448101.

Friedmann, John. 1986. "The World City Hypothesis." *Development and Change* 17, no. 1 (January): 69–83. https://doi.org/10.1111/j.1467-7660.1986.tb00231.x.

Galster, George C. 1990. "White Flight From Racially Integrated Neighbourhoods in the 1970s: the Cleveland Experience." *Urban Studies* 27, no. 3 (June): 385–99. https://doi.org/10.1080/00420989020080341.

Garrett-Petts, William Francis, ed. 2005. *The Small Cities Book: On the Cultural Future of Small Cities.* Vancouver, BC: New Star Books.

Gray, Virginia. 1973. "Innovation in the States: A Diffusion Study." *American Political Science Review* 67, no. 4 (December): 1174–85. https://doi.org/10.2307/1956539.

Hall, Peter G. 2001: "Global City-Regions in the Twenty-First Century." In *Global City-Regions: Trends, Theory, Policy,* edited by Allen J. Scott, 59–77, New York: Oxford University Press.

Hamel, Pierre, and Roger Keil, eds. 2015. *Suburban Governance: A Global View.* Toronto: University of Toronto Press.

Hamel, Pierre, and Roger Keil. 2016. "Governance in an Emerging Suburban World." *Cadernos Metrópole* 18, no. 37 (December): 647–70. https://doi.org/10.1590/2236-9996.2016-3702.

Hanlon, Bernadette. 2008. "Fixing Inner-Ring Suburbs in the US: A Policy Retrospective." *International Journal of Neighbourhood Renewal* 1 (3): 1–30.

Hanlon, Bernadette, and Thomas J. Vicino, eds. 2018. *The Routledge Companion to the Suburbs.* New York: Routledge.

Haque, Akhlaque. 2001. "Does Size Matter? Successful Economic Development Strategies of Small Cities." In *Downtowns: Revitalizing the Centers of Small Urban Communities,* edited by Michael A. Burayidi, 275–88. New York: Routledge.

Hardoy, Jorge. E., and David Satterthwaite. 1986. *Small and Intermediate Urban Centers: Their Role in National and Regional Development in the Third World.* London: Hodder and Soughton.

Hawkins, Christopher V. 2010. "Competition and Cooperation: Local Government Joint Ventures for Economic Development." *Journal of Urban Affairs* 32, no. 2 (May): 253–75. https://doi.org/10.1111/j.1467-9906.2009.00492.x.

Hopkins, David A. 2019. "The Suburbanization of the Democratic Party, 1992–2018," presented at the Annual Meetings of the American Political Science Association, Washington, DC, August 29, 2019. https://cookpolitical.com/sites/default/files/2019-09/Hopkins%20Suburbanization%20APSA%202019.pdf.

Jimenez, Benedict S., and Rebecca Hendrick. 2010. "Is Government Consolidation the Answer?" *State and Local Government Review* 42, no. 3 (December): 258–70. https://doi.org/10.1177/0160323X10386805.

Klein, Heinz K., and Michael D. Myers. 1999. "A Set of Principles for Conducting and Evaluating Interpretive Field Studies in Information Systems." *MIS Quarterly* 23, no. 1 (March): 67–93. https://doi.org/10.2307/249410.

Kneebone, Elizabeth, and Alan Berube. 2013. *Confronting Suburban Poverty in America.* Washington, DC: Brookings Institution Press. https://doi.org/10.7864/j.ctt4cg88q.

Kneebone, Elizabeth, and Carey A. Nadeau. 2015. "The Resurgence of Concentrated Poverty in America: Metropolitan Trends in the 2000s." In *The New American Suburb: Poverty, Race, and the Economic Crisis,* edited by Katrin B. Anacker, 15–38. New York: Routledge.

Lee, Sugie, and Nancey Green Leigh. 2005. "The Role of Inner Ring Suburbs in Metropolitan Smart Growth Strategies." *Journal of Planning Literature* 19, no. 3 (February): 330–46. https://doi.org/10.1177/0885412204271878.

Leitner, Helga. 2012. "Spaces of Encounters: Immigration, Race, Class, and the Politics of Belonging in Small-Town America." *Annals of the Association of American Geographers* 102, no. 4 (July): 828–46. https://doi.org/10.1080/00045608.2011.601204.

Lincoln, Yvonna S. 1995. "Emerging Criteria for Quality in Qualitative and Interpretive Research." *Qualitative Inquiry* 1, no. 3 (September): 275–89. https://doi.org/10.1177/107780049500100301.

Lucy, William. 2017. *Foreclosing the Dream: How America's Housing Crisis Is Reshaping Our Cities and Suburbs.* New York: Routledge. https://doi.org/10.4324/9781351179706.

Lynn, Laurence E., Jr., Carolyn J. Heinrich, and Carolyn J. Hill. 2000. "Studying Governance and Public Management: Challenges and Prospects." *Journal of Public Administration Research and Theory* 10, no. 2 (April): 233–62. https://doi.org/10.1093/oxfordjournals.jpart.a024269.

Madden, Janice Fanning. 2003. "The Changing Spatial Concentration of Income and Poverty Among Suburbs of Large US Metropolitan Areas." *Urban Studies* 40, no. 3 (March): 481–503. https://doi.org/10.1080/0042098032000053888.

Mandelker, Daniel R., Roger A. Cunningham, and John M. Payne. 2001. *Planning and Control of Land Development: Cases and Materials.* New York: Lexis.

Markusen, Ann R., Yong-Sook Lee, and Sean DiGiovanna. 1999. "Reflections on Comparisons Across Countries." In *Second Tier Cities: Rapid Growth Beyond the Metropolis,* edited by Ann R. Markusen, Yong-Sook Lee, and Sean DiGiovanna, 335–58 Minneapolis: University of Minnesota Press.

Massey, Douglas S., and Jonathan Tannen. 2018. "Suburbanization and Segregation in the United States: 1970–2010." *Ethnic and Racial Studies* 41, no. 9 (July): 1594–611. https://doi.org/10.1080/01419870.2017.1312010.

Matkin, David, and H. George Frederickson. 2009. "Metropolitan Governance: Institutional Roles and Interjurisdictional Cooperation." *Journal of Urban Affairs* 31 (1): 45–66. https://doi.org/10.1111/j.1467-9906.2008.00428.x.

Mikelbank, Brian A. 2004. "A Typology of US Suburban Places." *Housing Policy Debate* 15, no. 4 (January): 935–64. https://doi.org/10.1080/10511482.2004.9521527.

Miles, Steven. 2006. "Small City–Big Ideas: Culture-Led Regeneration and the Consumption of Place." In *Small Cities: Urban Experience Beyond the Metropolis,* edited by David Bell and Mark Jayne, 135–50. New York: Routledge.

Molotch, Harvey. 1976. "The City as a Growth Machine: Toward a Political Economy of Place." *American Journal of Sociology* 82, no. 2 (September): 309–32. https://doi.org/10.1086/226311.

Murphy, Alexandra K., and Danielle Wallace. 2010. "Opportunities for Making Ends Meet and Upward Mobility: Differences in Organizational Deprivation Across Urban and Suburban Poor Neighborhoods." *Social Science Quarterly* 91, no. 5 (December): 1164–86. https://doi.org/10.1111/j.1540-6237.2010.00726.x.

Newton, Kenneth. 1982. "Is Small Really So Beautiful? Is Big Really So Ugly? Size, Effectiveness, and Democracy in Local Government." *Political Studies* 30, no. 2 (June): 190–206. https://doi.org/10.1111/j.1467-9248.1982.tb00532.x.

Norman, Jon R. 2013. *Small Cities USA: Growth, Diversity, and Inequality.* New Brunswick, NJ: Rutgers University Press.

Ofori-Amoah, Benjamin, ed. 2006. *Beyond the Metropolis: Urban Geography as if Small Cities Mattered.* Lanham, MD: University Press of America.

Oguztimur, Senay, and Ulun Akturan. 2016. "Synthesis of City Branding Literature (1988–2014) as a Research Domain." *International Journal of Tourism Research* 18, no. 4 (July/August): 357–72. https://doi.org/10.1002/jtr.2054.

Oliver, J. Eric. 2001. *Democracy in Suburbia.* Princeton, NJ: Princeton University Press.

Orfield, Myron. 2002. *American Metropolitics: The New Suburban Reality.* Washington DC: Brookings Institution Press.

Paradis, Thomas W. 2000. "Conceptualizing Small Towns as Urban Places: The Process of Downtown Redevelopment in Galena, Illinois." *Urban Geography* 21, no. 1 (January): 61–82. https://doi.org/10.2747/0272-3638.21.1.61.

Paradis, Thomas W. 2002. "The Political Economy of Theme Development in Small Urban Places: The Case of Roswell, New Mexico." *Tourism Geographies* 4, no. 1 (January): 22–43. https://doi.org/10.1080/146166800110102607.

Parks, Roger B., and Ronald J. Oakerson. 2000. "Regionalism, Localism, and Metropolitan Governance: Suggestions from the Research Program on Local Public Economies." *State & Local Government Review* 32, no. 3 (Autumn): 169–79. https://doi.org/10.1177/0160323x0003200302.

Partridge, Mark D., Dan S. Rickman, Kamar Ali, and M. Rose Olfert. 2008. "Lost in Space: Population Growth in the American Hinterlands and Small Cities." *Journal of Economic Geography* 8, no. 6 (November): 727–57. https://doi.org/10.1093/jeg/lbn038.

Peters, B. Guy, and Jon Pierre. 2001. "Developments in Intergovernmental Relations: Towards Multi-Level Governance." *Policy and Politics* 29, no. 2 (April): 131–135. https://doi.org/10.1332/0305573012501251.

Post, Stephanie Shirley, and Robert M. Stein. 2000. "State Economies, Metropolitan Governance, and Urban-Suburban Economic Dependence." *Urban Affairs Review* 36, no. 1 (September): 46–60. https://doi.org/10.1177/10780870022184741.

Puentes, Robert, and David Warren. 2006. "One-Fifth of America: A Comprehensive Guide to America's First Suburbs." Washington, DC: Brookings Institution. https://www.brookings.edu/wp-content/uploads/2016/06/20060215_FirstSuburbs.pdf.

Putnam, Robert D. 2000. "Bowling Alone: America's Declining Social Capital." In *Culture and Politics*, edited by Lane Crothers and Charles Lockhart, 223–234. New York: Palgrave Macmillan. https://doi.org/10.1007/978-1-349-62397-6_12.

Raphael, Steven, and Michael A. Stoll. 2010. *Job Sprawl and the Suburbanization of Poverty.* Washington, DC: Brookings Institution. https://www.brookings.edu/wp-content/uploads/2016/06/0330_job_sprawl_stoll_raphael.pdf.

Ring, J. Kirk, Ana Maria Peredo, and James J. Chrisman. 2010. "Business Networks and Economic Development in Rural Communities in the United States." *Entrepreneurship Theory and Practice* 34, no. 1 (January): 171–95. https://doi.org/10.1111/j.1540-6520.-.00307.x.

Robertson, Kent. 2001. "Downtown Development Principles for Small Cities." In *Downtowns: Revitalizing the Centers of Small Urban Communities*, edited by Michael A. Burayidi, 9–22. New York: Routledge.

Rowlands, Bruce H. 2005. "Grounded in Practice: Using Interpretive Research to Build Theory." *The Electronic Journal of Business Research Methodology* 3, no. 1 (September): 81–92. https://issuu.com/academic-conferences.org/docs/ejbrm-volume3-issue1-article152?mode=a_p.

Sarzynski, Andrea, and Thomas J. Vicino. 2019. "Shrinking Suburbs: Analyzing the Decline of American Suburban Spaces." *Sustainability* 11, no. 19 (September): 5230. https://doi.org/10.3390/su11195230.

Savas, Emanuel S. 1977. "An Empirical Study of Competition in Municipal Service Delivery." *Public Administration Review* 37, no. 6 (November-December): 717–24. https://doi.org/10.2307/975342.

Schildt, Chris, Naomi Cytron, Elizabeth Kneebone, and Carolina Reid. 2013. "The Subprime Crisis in Suburbia: Exploring the Links Between Foreclosures and

Suburban Poverty." *Federal Reserve Bank of San Francisco Working Paper* 2013–02. https://www.frbsf.org/community-development/files/wp2013-02.pdf.

Scott, Allen John. 2014. "Beyond the Creative City: Cognitive–Cultural Capitalism and the New Urbanism." *Regional Studies* 48, no. 4 (April): 565–78. https://doi.org/10.1080/00343404.2014.891010.

Short, John Rennie, Bernadette Hanlon, and Thomas J. Vicino. 2007. "The Decline of Inner Suburbs: The New Suburban Gothic in the United States." *Geography Compass* 1, no. 3 (May): 641–56. https://doi.org/10.1111/j.1749-8198.2007.00020.x.

Smith, Christa. 2007. "Managing Downtown Revitalization Projects in Small Cities: Lessons from Kentucky's Main Street Program." In *Beyond the Metropolis: Urban Geography as if Small Cities Mattered*, edited by Benjamin Ofori-Amoah, 245–68. Lanham, MD: University Press of America.

Stone, Clarence N. 2005. "Looking Back to Look Forward: Reflections on Urban Regime Analysis." *Urban Affairs Review* 40, no. 3 (January): 309–41. https://doi.org/10.1177/1078087404270646.

Thrift, Nigel. 2000. "'Not a Straight Line but a Curve', or, Cities are Not Mirrors of Modernity." In *City Visions*, edited by David Bell and Azzedine Haddour, 245–75. New York: Routledge.

Tiebout, Charles M. 1956. "A Pure Theory of Local Expenditures." *Journal of Political Economy* 64, no. 5 (October): 416–24. https://doi.org/10.1086/257839.

Tighe, J. Rosie, and Stephanie Ryberg-Webster, eds. 2019. *Legacy Cities: Continuity and Change Amid Decline and Revival*. Pittsburgh, PA: University of Pittsburgh Press.

Timberlake, Jeffrey M., Aaron J. Howell, and Amanda J. Staight. 2011. "Trends in the Suburbanization of Racial/Ethnic Groups in US Metropolitan Areas, 1970 to 2000." *Urban Affairs Review* 47, no. 2 (March): 218–55. https://doi.org/10.1177/1078087410389531.

Tocqueville, Alexis de. (1835) 2003. *Democracy in America*. Washington, DC: Regnery.

Vicino, Thomas E. 2006. "Suburban Crossroads: An Analysis of Socioeconomic Change in Baltimore's First-Tier Suburbs, 1970 to 2000." Doctoral diss., University of Maryland.

Vicino, Thomas J. 2008. "The Spatial Transformation of First-Tier Suburbs, 1970 to 2000: The Case of Metropolitan Baltimore." *Housing Policy Debate* 19, no. 3 (January): 479–518. https://doi.org/10.1080/10511482.2008.9521644.

Waitt, Gordon. 2006. "Creative Small Cities: Cityscapes, Power and the Arts". In *Small Cities: Urban Experience Beyond the Metropolis*, edited by David Bell and Mark Jayne, 169–84. New York: Routledge.

Walker, Jack L. 1969. "The Diffusion of Innovations among the American States." *American Political Science Review* 63, no. 3 (September): 880–99. https://doi.org/10.2307/1954434.

Zavattaro, Staci M. 2010. "Municipalities as Public Relations and Marketing Firms." *Administrative Theory and Praxis* 32 (2): 191–211. https://doi.org/10.2753/ATP1084-1806320202.

8

LOCAL GOVERNMENT RESPONSES TO PROPERTY TAX CAPS

An Analysis of Indiana Municipal Governments

Dagney Faulk, Charles D. Taylor, and Pamela Schaal

This chapter investigates the impact of a state-imposed policy change, the imposition of local property tax caps in Indiana in 2008, and its effects on the state's smaller cities and towns. The cities and towns of Indiana represent an array of small communities, some of which are growing quickly while others experience a protracted decline due primarily to changes in the manufacturing sector. State policy changes, such as tax caps, often have a differential effect on growing and declining communities and test the capacity of local governments to adjust and provide services. The analysis in this chapter examines broad impacts of a state-imposed policy change on small cities and is a first step to understanding the adjustment process.

Recent research focuses on state preemption, wherein state governments act to limit local government policy actions (Blair and Starke 2017; Riverstone-Newell 2017; Swindell, Stenberg, and Svara 2017). Types of state preemption include legislative actions, executive orders, and administrative mandates (Blair and Starke 2017). Although state preemption efforts often serve to limit local government policy innovation in such areas as the minimum wage, civil rights, environmental regulations, and tobacco use (Riverstone-Newell 2017), state-imposed fiscal rules such as tax and expenditure limitations (TELs) also constitute a form of state preemption (Park 2018). Property taxes, traditionally the largest source of local government revenue, are frequently the subject of state imposed TELs (Park 2018). In Indiana, like many states, Republicans hold a majority in the state legislature and the governorship, whereas Democrats predominantly control city halls (Hicks et al. 2018), so that preemptive state policies often lead to conflict due to differences in policy and funding priorities between state and local governments.

The opening decades of the twenty-first century have been a turbulent time for local governments in Indiana. A court-ordered reassessment exposed fundamental problems with Indiana's property tax system, which ultimately led to calls for numerous property tax reforms, including an organized effort for total property tax repeal. In 2008, the Indiana General Assembly passed legislation to implement property tax rate caps. These caps dramatically reduced the revenue of some local governments while having little impact on others. For example, the small cities of Anderson, Gary, and Muncie experienced property tax revenue losses of greater than 30 percent of the certified levy, whereas Bloomington and Carmel experienced reductions of less than 3 percent. The imposition and implementation of the tax caps coincided with the Great Recession and the subsequent slow recovery. In response to declining revenue, local governments can cut spending, including personnel spending, find new revenue sources, or both. We find evidence that Indiana municipalities engaged in strategies to reduce budgets and employment and also increase revenue to some degree over the 2007–2014 period.

This study provides an analysis of small to midsized cities and towns within the same state and during the same time period. Of the twenty-eight municipalities examined, twenty-seven are part of metropolitan areas, and one is located within a nonmetropolitan county. Only Indianapolis (796,611) and Fort Wayne (253,194) have populations above 120 thousand people. This geographic and temporal focus keeps the overarching legal and economic environment constant while it allows impacts from the imposition of tax caps to vary on the basis of municipality. We examine total local government employment changes and changes in the functional areas of fire services, police services, administration, highways, and parks and recreation. These government functions were chosen because municipal governments commonly provide them. We also examine changes in municipal budgets and municipalities' reliance on local option income taxes and annexation as means to increase revenue.

We find that revenue losses from property tax caps are a significant determinant of decreases in municipal budgets and in local government employment over this period but are not associated with higher income tax rates. Functions such as fire, police, highways, and parks and recreation employment are negatively affected. The caps show no statistically significant effect on administration employment or land area.

In the next sections, we provide a brief review of the literature on cutback management and local government responses to fiscal changes followed by an overview of Indiana's property tax system and the changes since 2000. Then, using data on municipal employment and local government financial data, we examine the impact of tax caps on budgets, local government employment, and alternative revenue sources for the twenty-eight selected municipalities. The final section presents conclusions.

Literature

During economic downturns, while the federal government frequently engages in Keynesian spending through deficit financing, state constitutions often require state and local governments to balance their budgets by cutting spending (Levine 1978). Once considered anomalous in public organizations, cuts in spending due to a lack of growth have become more permanent in the current political landscape.

The literature on measuring local fiscal conditions can be divided into two branches: fiscal stress caused by local government decisions focusing on local financial management (micro level) and fiscal stress due to underlying fiscal and economic conditions (macro level) (Skidmore and Scorsone 2011; Chernick and Reschovsky 2006). We examine both types of fiscal stress.

Focusing on the micro level, the first branch of literature examines the fiscal stress precipitated by local financial management decisions. Under pressure to reduce spending, managers cut back or manage "organizational change toward lower levels of resource consumption and organizational activity," which requires "making hard decisions about who will be let go, what programs will be scaled down or terminated, and what clients will be asked to make sacrifices" (Levine 1979, 180). The organizational responses to cutback demands are driven by a variety of motives, some directed at serving public purposes, some intended to serve organizational goals, and others intended to serve organization subunits (Levine 1978).

The cutback strategy chosen by an organization might be driven by technical rationality or by internal or external political competition for resources. According to rational or political theories, managers first use approaches that are less disruptive or less likely to attract political resistance, such as broadening tax bases, drawing down reserves, or using nonrecurring revenues. If the fiscal stress becomes more severe or of a longer duration, public officials will attempt to defer or contain expenses by postponing capital improvements or by instituting hiring freezes. Under the most austere conditions, they will eventually resort to employee layoffs and service cuts (Nelson 2012; Wolman 1980; Forrester and Spindler 1990). Although these theories differ in predicting which changes will be adopted first, they agree that layoffs and service cuts tend to be the strategies of last resort.

Once an organization has decided to make cuts, there are multiple approaches for doing so. Across-the-board cuts attempt to spread the pain by imposing equal or similar cuts across all functions. Alternatively, budget reductions may be targeted to certain departments or functions either rationally by taking resources from less essential or low priority services or politically by directing resources away from departments or beneficiaries with little political power and toward those with greater influence (Levine 1978; Jick and Murray 1982; Skidmore and Scorsone 2011; Bartle 1996). Other scholars argue that strategies may be less structured or predictable, having the appearance of a garbage-can approach (Downs and Rocke 1984; Jick and Murray 1982; Pammer 1990; Bartle 1996). Due to the wide variety of differences in state and local political and economic environments, cutback strategies lack a discernible pattern (Nelson 2012). This approach predicts variation among municipalities in their responses to fiscal stress.

Underlying fiscal and economic (macro level) conditions also impact local government budgets and employment levels. Few studies have examined local government fiscal stabilization strategies (Wang and Hou 2012). Ross, Yan, and Johnson (2015) examined fiscal responses to the Great Recession of America's thirty-five largest cities and found that these cities increased property taxes and engaged in deficit spending to stabilize revenue. Kopelman and Rosen (2016) estimated that the probability of job loss during the Great Recession was lowest for local government workers in comparison with federal and state government workers and private-sector workers. In their analysis of Florida city and county governments, Cromwell and Ihlanfeldt (2015) found that fiscal stress resulted in higher property tax millage rates and cuts in capital expenditures and less essential services.

Finally, the literature on tax and expenditure limits (TELs) that states impose on local governments is particularly relevant here. Property tax limits are one source of fiscal stress. A variety of studies have examined the fiscal effects of property tax limits on local governments. Dye and McGuire (1997) found evidence that TELs reduce local government revenue and spending, and Maher and Deller (2012) found that TELs weaken municipal financial conditions. Similarly, McCubbins and Moule (2010) showed that tax and expenditure limits had extreme cyclical effects on state and local revenues. For example, TELs reduced reliance on local property taxes and increased reliance on income-elastic revenue sources such as sales and income taxes, so that revenue declines were more extreme during recessions. St. Clair (2012) showed that Colorado TELs increased local government revenue and expenditure volatility. Sexton, Sheffrin, and O'Sullivan (1999) found that local governments increased reliance on other sources of revenue such as fees, special assessment-districts, tax increment financing, and lease purchase plans. Mullins (2004) showed that TELs had differential effects among general-purpose governments in which communities with disadvantaged populations experienced the largest decreases in revenue and expenditures after the limits were imposed. Joyce and Mullins (1991) and Sharp and Elkins (1987) found that local TELs resulted in greater reliance on nontax revenue sources such as user fees. Results of these studies suggest that property tax limits will have differential effects on local governments, with the largest impacts occurring in communities with disadvantaged populations (typically older urban areas), and that local government will turn to other, more volatile revenue sources to close budget gaps. These studies have examined the impact of TELs on the sources of local government revenue and the level and growth of revenue or expenditures, but we know of no study that directly examines the impacts of these policies on municipal employment and differential impacts on employment across functional areas.

Overview of Property Tax Reform in Indiana

The 2008 property tax restructuring is the most recent in a long line of both legislated and court-ordered property tax changes implemented in Indiana. Property tax limits were first implemented in the state in the 1970s. These initial limits focused on constraining local government revenue. According to Anderson (2006), Indiana was one of forty-three states in the continental United States that imposed some form of property tax limit and one of four states that imposed only revenue limits at that time. Indiana was also one of twenty-six states that did not have mandatory annual assessments.

Major changes to Indiana's property tax system over the prior decade included a 1998 Indiana Supreme Court ruling that led to the implementation of a new assessment system and a mass reappraisal of properties in the state, which exposed severe problems with property tax administration and uniformity of assessment (Brown 2005). In 2002, the General Assembly approved a measure to remove inventories from the business personal property tax by 2006. The 2008 property tax restructuring effort imposed stringent limits on local government property tax rates in addition to reforming the assessment process.

The 2008 restructuring was driven by taxpayer dissatisfaction resulting from dramatic increases in taxes for some taxpayers during 2007. Reassessment had caused some Indiana taxpayers to experience large increases in their property tax payments. In addition, inconsistent assessment practices caused some taxpayers to experience higher assessed values than owners of similar nearby properties. These assessment-related horizontal inequities led taxpayers to march on the state capital and organize a campaign to abolish property taxes.

The Indiana General Assembly responded by imposing property tax rate caps which significantly limited the ability of local governments to raise revenue through property taxes. For tax cap purposes, property was divided into three categories: homestead residential, nonhomestead residential, and nonresidential. For tax bills payable in 2009, the property tax liability for homestead residential property was capped at a maximum of 1.5 percent of its gross assessed value. For 2010 and beyond, the cap was set at 1 percent. Nonhomestead residential property was capped at 2.5 percent in 2009 and 2 percent for 2010 and beyond. The caps for nonresidential and personal property were 3.5 percent in 2009 and 3 percent for 2010 and beyond.

The caps place a ceiling on a parcel owner's total property tax liability. Therefore, in 2010 and beyond, an owner-occupied home with a gross assessed value of $100,000 would be subject to a maximum total annual property tax bill of $1,000 split between the county, township, city, school district, and any special districts within which the property is located (Ottensmann, Payton, and Klacik 2008). The legislation also provided an additional circuit breaker to provide further tax relief for senior citizens. If the tax rate is initially above the rate cap, the rate is reduced, and associated revenue is refunded to the taxpayer as a credit. The cost of funding the credits is shared by local government units in proportion to their shares of the precredit property tax bill. In 2009, the initial year in which the tax caps were partially implemented, property owners received a total of $163 million in tax credits or approximately 2.7 percent of the statewide gross property tax levy. In 2010, after the caps were fully phased in, total tax credits increased to $430 million, amounting to about 7 percent of the gross levy (Nagle 2011).

Because this provision substantially lowered local government revenue, the state assumed responsibility for funding some local property tax levies. Most notably, the general fund property tax levy for local school corporations was abolished. School corporations still levy property taxes for debt service, capital projects, and transportation, but the state now funds instructional costs through a funding formula. Other levies taken over by the state include child welfare levies, juvenile incarceration, indigent health care, state fair and forestry levies, preschool special education levies, and police and fire pensions. To further limit local spending, the statute requires that referenda be held for new school and local government capital projects.

The property tax reform bill also increased the state sales and use tax rate by 1 percentage point, from 6 percent to 7 percent. The additional revenue generated by this tax increase was committed to pay for the local levies assumed by the state (Ottensmann, Payton, and Klacik 2008).

The impacts of the property tax caps vary widely across Indiana, and within a given county the impact of the tax caps can vary greatly among taxing units.

Property parcels within cities and towns are subject to taxation by the greatest number of taxing units and therefore tend to have more parcels subject to the tax caps. Consequently, cities and towns (compared with townships, school districts, special districts, and the county units of government) often experience the largest impacts among taxing units within their counties (Nagle 2011). For example, while the overall impacts of tax caps in Delaware and Madison Counties for 2011 were 25 and 22.6 percent reductions of their gross levies, the impacts on their county seats, the cities of Muncie and Anderson, were equal to 34.5 and 34.2 percent declines in their gross levies (Indiana Legislative Services Agency 2011).

In 2007, the General Assembly authorized three new local option income taxes (LOITs) to provide local governments with additional ways to raise revenue while reducing property tax burdens. The LOIT to Freeze the Property Tax Levy provides a means to raise revenue, replacing normal property tax increases. The LOIT for Property Tax Relief can be used to reduce property taxes. The LOIT for Public Safety can be used to fund public safety programs, thus reducing the amount of property taxes needed to fund these services. Faulk et al. (2010) have provided details on these LOITs. As of 2014, thirty-seven of Indiana's ninety-two counties had adopted at least one of the new LOITs related to property taxes.

Municipal Responses to Property Tax Caps

Drawing on the prior literature, we develop a theory explaining how Indiana municipalities respond to fiscal stress due to tax caps. Scorsone and Plerhoples (2010) discuss changes in local government responses to fiscal stress. Prior to the 2000s, state and local governments responded to fiscal stress by both increasing taxes and cutting services, but beginning with the 2001 recession, government strategies shifted away from tax increases and toward service cuts.

In this study, we begin from the obvious premise that the property tax caps imposed in 2009 not only cause fiscal stress but also limit the response strategies available to cities. Because the purpose of the property tax caps is to limit the ability of local governments to increase tax rates, cities impacted by the tax caps will necessarily need to adopt strategies that do not involve increasing property tax rates. Although a city has other revenue-increasing strategies available to it, such as adopting or increasing local option income taxes (LOITs) or annexing territory to increase its tax base, these strategies take time to implement and, in the case of LOIT rate increases, often require the cooperation of other local governments within the county. Spending cuts, on the other hand, can be implemented immediately and unilaterally. For this reason, we expect that the property tax caps will result in reductions in municipal budgets, leading to the first in our series of testable hypotheses:

> Hypothesis 1: Municipalities that experience large reductions in revenue from tax caps will reduce their budgets more than municipalities in which the tax cap impacts are smaller.

Because wages and salaries constitute a large portion of city expenditures, spending cuts eventually lead to decreases in local government employment. A variety of studies have shown that fiscal stress is associated with decreases in public employment as well as spending (Bartle 1996; Lewis 1988). Therefore,

> Hypothesis 2: Municipalities that experience large reductions in revenue from tax caps will reduce their staffing levels more than municipalities in which the tax cap impacts are smaller.

Municipal officials may choose to target budget and staff reductions to preserve services perceived as essential, such as public safety, at the expense of services perceived as less essential, such as parks and recreation. In their study of fiscal stress among Michigan cities, Skidmore and Scorsone (2011) found that general government and recreation were particularly vulnerable to cuts, whereas public safety services tended to be protected. Unions may also play a role here. Based on these findings we suggest the following hypothesis:

> Hypothesis 3a: The impact of tax cap–related revenue losses on staffing reductions will be larger in the administrative and recreation functions than in the police and fire functions.

Not all local government services are funded with property taxes, however. In Indiana, local highways are funded from shared state gasoline tax revenue rather than property taxes. We expect that local highway funding and associated staffing will not be affected by property tax caps. We include hypothesis 3b to test this relationship:

> Hypothesis 3b: Revenue reductions from property tax caps will not affect highway staffing.

Municipalities may also deal with fiscal stress by finding alternative sources of revenue. In Indiana, revenue options are limited. A variety of studies have shown that under property tax limits, local governments adopt alternative revenue sources such as local option taxes, fees, and surcharges (Joyce and Mullins 1991; Mullins and Joyce 1996; Shadbegian 1999; Bartle, Ebdon, and Krane 2003). Kim, Bae, and Eger (2009) and Zhao (2005) found that fiscal stress does not influence local sales tax adoption in Georgia.

There are no general-purpose local option sales taxes in Indiana, but six local option income taxes (LOIT) exist. LOIT adoption in Indiana is done on a county level, with revenues shared among all local governments in the county. Some of the LOITs may be adopted by a vote of the county council. Others are adopted by a vote of the county income tax council, a body in which each local government in the county gets a vote weighted on the basis of its population. Municipalities are not authorized to adopt LOITs unilaterally, although cities with large populations relative to other local governments within the county and to the county as a whole have a large influence on adoption of LOITs by county income tax councils. We expect that cities with large tax cap impacts will attempt to influence the LOIT process to adopt or increase LOIT rates. Furthermore, in counties where the tax cap impacts are large, both the county and municipal governments are likely to experience similar impacts, making it likely that local governments will cooperate to adopt or increase LOITs. Consequently, we expect LOIT rates to increase for cities with large tax cap impacts:

> Hypothesis 4: Municipalities that experience large reductions in revenue from tax caps will increases LOIT rates.

Finally, annexation is another way that municipalities can potentially raise additional revenue. Annexing properties adjacent to existing boundaries increases the property tax base but also increases a municipality's service area. If economies of scale are present, tax revenue should increase more than service costs after annexation so that per capita taxes and spending decrease after annexation. A contrasting view is that municipalities that annex land may reduce local government competition and exert monopoly power, increasing taxes and spending. Older studies using data from the 1960s and 1970s to examine the relationship between taxes or spending and annexation have found mixed results (Mehay 1981; Gonzalez and Mehay 1987; Liner 1992, 1994; Liner and McGregor 2002). More recent studies (Edwards and Xiao 2009) have found that per capita local government expenditures decrease with annexation, indicating that economies of scale exist, with population density hampering the impact of scale. If economies of scale are present, expanding the property tax base through annexation can improve the fiscal situation.

An Indiana city greatly affected by tax caps can also benefit by annexing undeveloped land to capture the value of subsequent development in its tax base. As the tax base increases, the city is able to reduce its tax rate, which reduces the amount of revenue lost to tax caps and thus generates net revenue. We hypothesize that the potential to generate net revenue via annexation will encourage fiscally stressed cities to pursue annexation, leading to our final hypothesis:

Hypothesis 5: Municipalities that experience large reductions in revenue from tax caps will experience larger increases in land area than municipalities with smaller tax cap impacts.

Data and Method

This study uses data from Indiana cities and towns to examine their responses to fiscal stress caused by property tax rate caps. Using the US Census Bureau's annual individual unit files for municipalities, we assembled data for total full-time equivalent (FTE) local government employees in six functional areas: financial administration, general administration, fire, police, highways, and recreation. As noted, the municipalities included in this analysis consist of the twenty-eight municipalities sampled annually by the Census Bureau from 2007 through 2014, matched with municipal or county-level data from various other sources. The 2007–2014 period provides an opportunity to examine how Indiana municipalities respond to fiscal stress. Because 2014 was the fifth year after the property tax caps were implemented, and also five years into recovery from the Great Recession, local governments had time to respond to the new fiscal environment.

Table 8.1 provides basic socioeconomic, demographic, and fiscal characteristics for these municipalities. There is great variation in population growth and income among municipalities. Those in the Indianapolis suburbs (Carmel, Fishers, and Noblesville) tend to have the highest income levels and population growth rates, whereas former industrial powerhouses (Richmond, Muncie, and Marion) tend to have the lowest income levels and population growth. While there is much variation in the size of the cities and towns included in this analysis, they are all considered small or midsized cities in comparison with the major metropolitan centers that are the focus of much analysis.

Our approach is to use panel regression models to estimate the impact of tax caps on municipal budgets, staffing levels, LOIT rates, and land area (as a proxy for annexation). We compute standard errors clustered by municipality to control for heteroskedasticity and serial correlation within each cluster. The model takes the following form:

$$Y_{it} = \beta_0 + \beta_1 D_{it} + \beta_2 C_{it} + \beta_3 F_{it} + \beta_4 R_t + \varphi_t + \delta_i + \varepsilon_{it}.$$

Our model specifies an outcome measure, Y (certified budget, staffing level, local income tax rate, or land area) in municipality i and year t, as a function of an intercept, β_0, demographic characteristics (D) of the municipality, the revenue loss due to tax caps (C), other fiscal characteristics (F), and a recession indicator

TABLE 8.1. Characteristics of municipalities

	2014 REVENUE LOSS OUT OF CERTIFIED LEVY DUE TO TAX CAPS (%)	2007 POPULATION	2014 POPULATION	POPULATION CHANGE (%)	2007 LOCAL GOVERNMENT EMPLOYMENT	2014 LOCAL GOVERNMENT EMPLOYMENT	LOCAL GOVERNMENT EMPLOYMENT CHANGE (%)	2014 MEDIAN HOUSEHOLD INCOME BY COUNTY ($)
Bloomington	0.7	71,044	83,460	17.48	731	804	9.99	43,841
Lawrenceburg	1.1	4,781	4,968	3.91	120	135	12.50	59,280
Carmel	2.5	65,087	86,588	33.03	417	518	24.22	89,861
Fishers	5.3	65,819	87,022	32.21	352	432	22.73	89,861
Lafayette	5.4	63,905	70,813	10.81	712	701	-1.54	46,276
Greenwood	6.8	46,528	54,615	17.38	253	299	18.18	58,833
Columbus	7.2	39,810	46,112	15.83	472	444	-5.93	54,101
Shelbyville	8.6	18,375	19,069	3.78	753	791	5.05	54,831
New Albany	9.4	36,924	36,627	-0.80	254	260	2.36	53,186
Danville	10.8	8,185	9,590	17.17	64	81	26.56	70,358
Marion	11.0	30,358	29,218	-3.76	260	224	-13.85	40,234
Evansville	13.1	116,445	120,441	3.43	1,265	1,246	-1.50	42,622
Hammond	13.3	77,136	78,489	1.75	931	859	-7.73	50,774
Fort Wayne	14.3	253,194	260,893	3.04	2,026	1,997	-1.43	48,651
Indianapolis	15.7	796,611	848,762	6.55	15,901	14,462	-9.05	42,700
Mishawaka	16.1	49,549	48,189	-2.74	570	527	-7.54	46,388
Richmond	16.4	36,884	36,032	-2.31	545	512	-6.06	40,929
Kokomo	16.8	45,866	58,112	26.70	545	454	-16.70	47,433
Jeffersonville	17.7	31,649	46,330	46.39	254	352	38.58	52,050

(continued)

TABLE 8.1. (continued)

	2014 REVENUE LOSS OUT OF CERTIFIED LEVY DUE TO TAX CAPS (%)	2007 POPULATION	2014 POPULATION	POPULATION CHANGE (%)	2007 LOCAL GOVERNMENT EMPLOYMENT	2014 LOCAL GOVERNMENT EMPLOYMENT	LOCAL GOVERNMENT EMPLOYMENT CHANGE (%)	2014 MEDIAN HOUSEHOLD INCOME BY COUNTY ($)
Noblesville	18.0	41,504	57,523	38.60	383	361	−5.74	89,861
East Chicago	20.9	30,137	29,007	−3.75	875	706	−19.31	50,774
Logansport	25.4	18,657	17,990	−3.58	257	239	−7.00	44,430
Elkhart	29.4	52,805	52,049	−1.43	588	570	−3.06	50,192
Terre Haute	31.7	59,716	60,948	2.06	609	567	−6.90	41,260
Anderson	34.8	57,003	55,450	−2.72	777	631	−18.79	44,730
Gary	38.1	96,383	77,955	−19.12	1,444	1,148	−20.50	50,774
South Bend	38.8	104,357	101,266	−2.96	1,288	1,259	−2.25	46,388
Muncie	42.4	67,899	69,700	2.65	592	533	−9.97	39,449
Mean	16.8	85,236	90,972	8.56	1,187	1,111	−0.17	53,217
Std Deviation	0.12	146,974	155,937	15.21	2,917	2,648	14.97	14,568
Min	0.7	4,781	4,968	−19.12	64	81	−20.50	39,449
Max	42.4	796,611	848,762	46.39	15,901	14,462	38.58	89,861

(R). We also control for the presence of municipal (cross-section) fixed effects which take into account differences among municipalities that do not vary over time, period fixed effects to control for difference among municipalities that vary over time, and a white-noise error term, ε. All dollar values have been converted to real values (2014 purchasing power) using the national consumer price index (CPI). Variable definitions and sources are shown in table 8.2 along with descriptive statistics for the total sample. We include both the levels and scaled (per capita or per thousand) versions of each variable. The scaled (per capita) variables are used in the regression models.

The Impact of Fiscal Stress (C_{it})

The tax cap revenue loss variable is the reduction in municipal property tax revenue due to tax caps in a particular year. It is the amount of amount of revenue refunded to property taxpayers after the rate cap is imposed. The mean value is $57 per capita, approximately 6.2 percent of mean certified budget per capita. According to hypotheses 1, 2, 4, and 5, we expect cities with greater revenue reductions from tax caps to experience greater decreases in local government budgets and employment, higher local income tax rates, and more annexation than cities with lower tax cap impacts.

Fiscal Variables and Recession (F_{it} and R_t)

Property assessed value is the measure of fiscal capacity. We expect there to be a positive relationship between assessed value and the municipal budget and employment. We have no a priori expectation about the relationship between the assessed value and LOIT rates or annexation. Federal and state intergovernmental aid are other revenue sources used to fund local government functions and programs. In the case of police and fire services, for example, federal intergovernmental aid has been granted explicitly to maintain staffing levels. Communities receiving more intergovernmental aid may be able to better withstand budget cuts due to property tax caps. We expect a positive relationship between intergovernmental aid and staffing levels.

The recession dummy variable captures the impact of the Great Recession (December 2007 through June 2009) on local governments. We expect the recession to be associated with decreases in budgets and local government employment. We have no a priori expectation about the relationship between the recession and local income tax rates or annexation.

TABLE 8.2. Variable definitions, sources, and descriptive statistics

VARIABLE (SOURCE)	MEAN	MEDIAN	STD. DEV.	MIN	MAX	OBS.
Certified Budget ($real thousands) (DLGF)	54,164	48,195	37,281	5,479	183,376	215
Certified Budget per capita ($real)	914.82	901.60	383.21	41.61	2662.30	215
Total full-time equivalent employment (ASPEP)	1,132	568	2,518	64	15,901	217
Total full-time equivalent employment per thousand population[a]	12.42	10.65	7.38	4.50	42.16	217
Financial administration full-time equivalent employment (ASPEP)	21.82	11.00	59.59	3.00	545.00	217
Financial administration full-time equivalent employment per thousand population[a]	0.25	0.21	0.16	0.06	1.17	217
Other government administration full-time equivalent employment (ASPEP)	36.61	24.00	62.05	0	499.00	217
Other government administration full-time equivalent employment per thousand population[a]	0.55	0.42	0.46	0	3.14	217
Fire full-time equivalent employment (ASPEP)	161.74	110.00	200.55	8.00	1276.00	217
Fire full-time equivalent employment per thousand population[a]	2.15	2.18	0.62	0.71	4.57	217
Police full-time equivalent employment (ASPEP)	233.22	123.00	467.77	17.00	3276.00	217
Police full-time equivalent employment per thousand population[a]	2.54	2.36	0.96	1.08	6.14	217
Highway full-time equivalent employment (ASPEP)	48.18	34.00	56.94	4.00	430.00	217
Highway full-time equivalent employment per thousand population[a]	0.71	0.69	0.35	0.09	3.02	217
Parks and recreation full-time equivalent employment (ASPEP)	60.80	30.00	87.52	0	641.00	217
Parks and recreation full-time equivalent employment per thousand population[a]	0.75	0.66	0.53	0	2.92	217

Variable					
Local option income tax rate (LSA)	1.21	1.15	0.53	0	2.50	217
Land area[b] (sq. miles) (ACS)	43.96	27.45	67.50	8.68	361.61	202
Land area per thousand population[a]	0.49	0.46	0.13	0.28	0.93	202
Tax cap revenue loss ($real thousands) (DLGF)	3,639	740	6,407	0	34,739	217
Tax cap revenue loss per capita	57.18	17.17	99.03	0	545.98	217
Population (ACS)	89,984	55,554	151,032	4,769	848,762	217
Certified net assessed value ($real millions) (DLGF)	3,938	2,117	7,272	335	47,525	217
Certified net assessed value per capita ($real)	44,925	39,737	27,111	19,491	313,584	217
Federal intergovernmental revenue, $real thousands (COG-F)	6,872	1,796	16,223	0	116,466	217
Federal intergovernmental revenue per capita ($real)	70	32	142	0	1,141	217
State intergovernmental revenue ($real thousands) (COG-F)	38,267	12,216	112,994	658	804,002	217
State intergovernmental revenue per capita ($real)	441	216	1,009	61	10,587	217
Median household income, county ($real) (SAIPE)	53,688	49,501	14,414	36,310	94,820	217
Poverty rate, county (SAIPE)	14.49	15.20	5.33	3.90	24.70	217
Recession dummy=1 if at least two quarters of the year were in recession (NBER)	0.23	0.00	0.42	0	1.00	217

Sources: Data drawn from ASPEP (US Census Bureau 2014a); COG-F (US Census Bureau 2014b); DLGF (Indiana Department of Local Government Finance); ACS (US Census Bureau's American Community Survey); LSA (Indiana Legislative Services Agency 2015); SAIPE (US Census Bureau 2014c); and NBER (National Bureau of Economic Research n.d.).

Notes: All dollar values were adjusted for inflation (to 2014 purchasing power) using the CPI.

[a] Per capita values were used in regression models.

[b] Land area was not available for the smallest municipalities (Lawrenceburg and Danville).

Demographic and Socioeconomic Variables (D_{it})

We expect that local government employment will rise with the demand for government services. We include several measures of service demand. Municipalities with larger populations tend to offer a wider array of government services and infrastructure, cover a larger geographic area, and may be better able to take advantage of economies of scale. We expect a negative relationship between population and each of the outcome variables.

We control for demographic and socioeconomic characteristics that reflect tastes for public goods and therefore the level and types of local government employment. The state of the local economy may influence local government employment. We include the county poverty rate as a measure of economic distress. Distressed areas may have higher local government staffing to provide services to this population or lower staffing due to fiscal stress, so the sign is indeterminate. Wagner's "law" predicts that the demand for government services will increase with income. Median household income is included to capture this effect. Places with higher incomes may demand more public services and associated higher local government employment and budgets. We expect a positive relationship between local government employment and income and a positive relationship between local government budgets and income. We have no a priori expectations about the relationship between the poverty rate or median household income and local income tax rates or annexation.

Results

Property Tax Caps and Local Government Spending

Under state law, local governments are required to balance their budgets annually. Table 8.3 reports estimation results for the budget model. After controlling for demographic and fiscal influences, property tax caps negatively and significantly impact municipal budgets. Using the revenue loss coefficient to calculate the impact, a revenue loss of $57.18 per capita (the mean value) is associated with an approximately $3.67 million (6.79 percent) decrease in the certified budget for a city with mean population of 89,984 (table 8.4). These results support our first hypothesis: municipalities experiencing large tax cap impacts reduce spending.

Property Tax Caps and Local Government Staffing

Model results examining the relationship between revenue losses and local government staffing are presented in table 8.5. Model results in column 1 show the

TABLE 8.3. Budget model results

	BUDGET PER CAPITA
	COEFFICIENT [P-VALUE]
Constant	5797.1020
	[0.1054]
Population (ln)	−455.0798
	[0.1419]
Tax cap revenue loss per capita	−0.7143***
	[0.0056]
Net assessed value per capita	0.0002
	[0.2671]
Federal intergovernmental revenue per capita	−0.0032
	[0.9287]
State intergovernmental revenue per capita	−0.0178***
	[0.0000]
Median household income (County)	0.0015
	[0.7855]
Poverty rate (County)	0.6595
	[0.8279]
Recession dummy	69.0892***
	[0.0032]
Period fixed effects	Yes
Cross-section fixed effects	Yes
Adj. R sq.	0.9111
F-statistic	53.191***
Durbin-Watson statistic	1.4882
N	215

Notes: All dollar values are adjusted for inflation. Standard errors are clustered by municipality.
* $p < .1$; ** $p < .05$; *** $p < .01$

TABLE 8.4. Impact of property tax revenue loss due to tax caps in the typical municipality

FUNCTION	IMPACT	PERCENTAGE (%)
Certified budget ($ millions)	−3.7	−6.8
Municipal government employment (FTE)	−36.4	−3.2
Fire (FTE)	−6.1	−3.8
Police (FTE)	−7.9	−3.4
Highway (FTE)	−2.3	−4.8
Parks and recreation (FTE)	−4.9	−8.2

Notes: Mean population = 89,984; mean circuit breaker credit per capita = $57.18.

TABLE 8.5. Employment model results

	TOTAL		FINANCIAL ADMINISTRATION		OTHER GOVERNMENT ADMINISTRATION		FIRE		POLICE		HIGHWAY		PARKS AND RECREATION	
	COEFFICIENT [P-VALUE]		COEFFICIENT [P-VALUE]		COEFFICIENT [P-VALUE]		COEFFICIENT [P-VALUE]		COEFFICIENT [P-VALUE]		COEFFICIENT [P-VALUE]		COEFFICIENT [P-VALUE]	
Constant	0.0779*** [0.0000]		0.0029* [0.0072]		-0.0033 [0.2941]		0.0162*** [0.0000]		0.0159*** [0.0000]		0.0159*** [0.0000]		-0.0013 [0.5233]	
Population (ln)	-0.0059*** [0.0000]		-0.0002** [0.0118]		0.0003 [0.3051]		-0.0013*** [0.0000]		-0.0014*** [0.0000]		-0.0013*** [0.0000]		0.0001 [0.4568]	
Tax cap revenue loss per capita	-7.08E-06*** [0.0000]		-7.30E-09 [0.8985]		-1.12E-07 [0.5519]		-1.19E-06*** [0.0000]		-1.55E-06*** [0.0000]		-4.52E-07*** [0.0000]		-9.69E-07*** [0.0058]	
Net assessed value per capita	3.54E-09** [0.0300]		-1.24E-11 [0.8503]		3.48E-10* [0.0751]		5.72E-10*** [0.0025]		-3.02E-10 [0.1219]		4.13E-10 [0.4097]		-2.52E-11 [0.9430]	
Federal intergovernmental revenue per capita	-1.94E-06** [0.0257]		3.21E-08* [0.0544]		1.06E-07 [0.3932]		-4.45E-07*** [0.0057]		2.54E-07 [0.1116]		6.48E-09 [0.9059]		1.17E-07* [0.0779]	
State intergovernmental revenue per capita	-3.77E-07 [0.1119]		-4.92E-11 [0.9930]		-1.39E-07*** [0.0000]		1.63E-07*** [0.0045]		-2.13E-08 [0.3352]		-2.02E-08 [0.6275]		-1.73E-08 [0.3266]	
Median household income (county)	8.90E-09 [0.8569]		2.81E-09 [0.2269]		8.42E-09 [0.2654]		-3.60E-09 [0.4902]		2.91E-08*** [0.0269]		-7.33E-09** [0.0418]		1.52E-08 [0.1312]	
Poverty rate (county)	-5.07E-05** [0.0433]		-1.20E-05*** [0.0000]		1.25E-05*** [0.0004]		-2.26E-06 [0.7464]		-1.57E-07 [0.9567]		-8.36E-06 [0.1788]		-3.65E-06 [0.4123]	
Recession dummy	0.0002** [0.0288]		-0.0001*** [0.0000]		-0.0002*** [0.0049]		0.0003*** [0.0003]		-6.04E-05* [0.0750]		-1.74E-05 [0.4147]		0.0003*** [0.0025]	

Period fixed effects	Yes	Yes	Yes	Yes	Yes	Yes	Yes
Cross-section fixed effects	Yes	Yes	Yes	Yes	Yes	Yes	Yes
Adj. R sq.	0.975	0.676	0.819	0.797	0.919	0.679	0.834
F-statistic	202.666***	11.733***	24.389***	21.209***	59.445***	14.069***	26.902***
Durbin Watson statistic	1.643	1.191	1.488	1.153	1.521	1.448	2.404
Obs.	217	217	217	217	217	217	217

Notes: All dollar values are adjusted for inflation. Standard errors are clustered by municipality.

* $p < .1$; ** $p < .05$; *** $p < .01$

expected pattern and provide support for hypothesis 2. As the revenue loss from tax caps increase, total full-time equivalent staffing decreases. Using the staffing change coefficient to calculate the impact of a mean revenue loss on a city of mean population results in an estimated reduction in full-time equivalent staffing of approximately thirty-six workers or 3.2 percent of mean total staffing (table 8.4).

The remaining columns (table 8.5) show results of FTE employment models for various government functions. These model results provide limited evidence that municipalities tend to protect the fire and police functions at the expense of administration and recreation (hypothesis 3a). The model results show that municipalities tend to decrease fire and police employment along with parks and recreation employment. The estimated mean decrease in fire staffing is 6.12 workers (3.79 percent), in police staffing it is almost 8 workers (3.42 percent), and in parks and recreation employment it is about 5 workers (8.2 percent) (table 8.4). The larger proportional decrease in parks and recreation employment suggests that these positions are viewed as more expendable than public safety employment.

Intergovernmental grants also play a role in fire employment. Fire staffing is negatively related to federal intergovernmental revenue and positively related to state intergovernmental revenue, indicating that this type of revenue is a significant contributor to employment levels for fire services either directly or through the fungibility of spending categories.

In contrast to expectations, revenue reductions due to property tax caps do not significantly affect staffing in financial administration and other government administration. Average employment levels for these government functions are the lowest of any of the functions examined, at 21.8 employees and 36.6 employees, respectively. Local governments that need to substantially decrease expenditures would need to consider decreasing fire and police employment, which comprise the largest share of local government employment.

Highway staffing is lower in municipalities experiencing property tax revenue losses due to tax caps. The typical city decreased highway employment by 2.3 workers (4.8 percent) (table 8.4). We did not expect tax caps to affect highway employment, but the fungibility of spending categories may contribute to this effect.

Property Tax Caps and Local Income Taxes and Annexation

Finally, we investigate changes in two other revenue sources: local option income taxes and annexation (table 8.6). The model results provide no support for hypothesis 4 over the period examined; municipalities with large tax cap impacts

TABLE 8.6. Local option income tax model and land area model results

	LOCAL OPTION INCOME TAX RATE	LAND AREA (PER CAPITA)
	COEFFICIENT [P-VALUE]	COEFFICIENT [P-VALUE]
Constant	11.778*	0.0027***
	[0.0506]	[0.0099]
Population (ln)	−1.023*	−0.0002**
	[0.0779]	[0.0226]
Tax cap revenue loss per capita	7.48E-05	6.14E-08
	[0.8999]	[0.1791]
Net assessed value per capita	−7.15E-07	8.41E-11*
	[0.1618]	[0.0691]
Federal intergovernmental revenue per capita	4.57E-05	−6.33E-09
	[0.7441]	[0.5498]
State intergovernmental revenue per capita	−2.56E-05**	−7.00E-10
	[0.0263]	[0.9216]
Median household income (county)	9.27E-06	9.25E-10
	[0.3311]	[0.5794]
Poverty rate (county)	0.0022	8.29E-07
	[0.8643]	[0.2604]
Recession dummy	0.3216***	1.27E-05*
	[0.0004]	[0.0743]
Period fixed effects	Yes	Yes
Cross-section fixed effects	Yes	Yes
Adj. R sq.	0.729	0.942
F-statistic	14.816***	82.313***
Durbin Watson statistic	1.189	1.154
Obs.	217	202[a]

Notes: All dollar values are adjusted for inflation. Standard errors are clustered by municipality.

[a] Land area is not available annually for Lawrenceburg and Danville.

$*p<.1;$ $**p<.05;$ $***p<.01$

do not have significantly higher LOIT rate increases. The data set includes only the first five years after the tax caps were implemented. Because cities cannot increase income tax rates unilaterally and negotiating with other local governments in the county may take time, these results may change as additional years of data become available. We use land area as a proxy for annexation and find no significant relationship between tax cap revenue losses and land area, which suggests that municipalities experiencing greater property tax revenue reductions do not annex more land.

Other Influences on Local Budgets, Employment, Tax Rates, and Annexation

Other control variables generally have the expected relationships. The impact of population on total FTE staffing is negative and significant (table 8.5), indicating that employment per capita decreases as the population increases and suggesting that economies of scale are present. Financial administration, fire, police, and highway staffing are negatively related to population, indicating the presence of economies of scale for each of these functions. Assessed value is positively related to total staffing, other government administration staffing, fire staffing, budgets, and land area, which indicates that places with more property wealth have larger local governments, budgets, and land area.

Land area per capita is negatively related to population (table 8.6), indicating that as population increases land area per capita decreases, which likely reflects that larger cities are more densely developed. Local income taxes are negatively related to population, which indicates that more populous municipalities have lower income tax rates.

The federal and state intergovernmental revenue variables measure the aggregate amount of intergovernmental transfers from the state and federal government that the municipality received. The certified budget is negatively related to state intergovernmental revenue (table 8.3), indicating that per capita budgets are lower in municipalities that receive less state aid. The impact of intergovernmental aid on employment (table 8.5) varies by type of aid and employment function. Federal intergovernmental revenue is negatively related to total and fire staffing but positively related to financial administration staffing and parks and recreation staffing, whereas state intergovernmental revenue is negatively related to other government administration and positively related to fire staffing.

Median household income is a positive and significant determinant of police staff levels, indicating that demand for these services increases with income. Thus households with higher incomes are more likely to value this service. For parks and recreation staffing, the coefficient on median household income is positive, as expected, but does not meet the threshold of statistical significance. Highway staffing is negatively related to median household income, indicating that staff levels decreases as income increases. These income effects are substantively large. For a city of mean population (89,984), an increase in median household income by one standard deviation ($14,414) is associated with an increase in police staffing of about 37 FTE (16.2 percent) and a decrease in highway staffing of about 9 FTE (19.7 percent) (table 8.7).

The poverty rate is negatively associated with total local government employment and financial administration employment, which indicates that munici-

TABLE 8.7. Impact of a one standard deviation increase in median household income or the poverty rate on municipal staffing

	IMPACT	PERCENTAGE (%)
Median household income		
Police (FTE)	37.7	16.2
Highway (FTE)	−9.5	−19.7
Poverty rate		
Municipal government employment (FTE)	−24.3	−2.2
Financial administration (FTE)	−5.8	−26.4
Other government administration (FTE)	6.0	16.4

palities in distressed counties have fewer local government employees overall and fewer working in financial administration specifically. Other government administration is positively related to the poverty rate, indicating that more poverty leads to more people working in administrative roles. Like the income effects, these poverty effects are substantively large. For a city of mean population, an increase in the poverty rate by one standard deviation (5.33 percent) is associated with a total staffing decrease of 24 FTE (2.15 percent), a financial administration staffing decrease of about 6 FTE (26.4 percent), and an increase in other administrative staffing of about 6 FTE (16.4 percent) (table 8.7).

The recession indicator is positive and significant for municipal budgets, and for total, fire, and parks and recreation staffing. These findings indicate that budgets and staff levels for these functions increased during the recession, which is not the expected relationship. One possible explanation is the role of federal stimulus spending. In contrast, financial administration, other administration, and police staffing were negatively related to the recession. The significance of the recession dummy variable and the variable measuring revenue losses due to tax caps suggest that both these factors affected municipal spending and employment decisions over this period. The LOIT and land area model results show a positive relationship between LOIT rates and the recession and between land area and the recession, suggesting that municipal officials were willing to raise income tax rates and expand borders during the recession.

Conclusion and Extensions

The cities and towns considered here are small to midsized when in comparison to cities located in the nation's largest metro areas, and they provide a first step to understanding how small cities respond to fiscal stress caused by state-imposed policies. The analysis presented in this article shows that Indiana's smaller cities and towns have adapted to fiscal stress, in this case caused by state-imposed property tax rate caps, by cutting spending and employment. As revenue losses due to tax caps increased, municipal budgets and staffing levels decreased over the research period, 2007 to 2014. There is evidence that public safety is protected from cuts, in that fire and police employment experienced lower proportional decreases than parks and recreation employment. There was no change in financial administration or other government administration related to tax caps.

Highway employment was negatively affected by tax caps, which was not the expected result. The model results suggest that state grants (intergovernmental revenue) likely enhanced municipalities' ability to maintain fire employment so that public safety cuts were not more extreme.

Although studies examining the longer-term impact of property tax limits showed that US local governments increased reliance on local option taxes, there is not sufficient evidence to conclude that Indiana municipalities experiencing the most stress were more likely to increase local income tax rates over this eight-year period. The coefficient on that variable was not significant, indicating that local income tax rates were not influenced by revenue losses from tax caps up to five years after the caps were implemented.

Another option for increasing revenue is to annex land. In addition to increasing the number of properties on the municipal property tax rolls, municipal annexation allows the municipality to expand its customer base and potentially take advantage of economies of scale, which may serve to decrease the average cost of providing services (Carr 2004). Our results suggest that municipalities did not annex more land after property tax caps were implemented.

The analysis presented here spans an eight-year period corresponding to the Great Recession, slow recovery, and implementation of property tax rate caps in Indiana. Bozeman (2010) calls for life cycle–oriented studies of public organizations. Many communities in the Rust Belt have experienced decades of decline due to changes in the structure of local economies that have impacted local government. An examination of a longer time period to categorize types of cutbacks and revenue options might reveal clearer patterns or different local government choices.

References

Anderson, Nathan B. 2006. "Property Tax Limitations: An Interpretive Review." *National Tax Journal* 59, no. 3 (September): 685–94. https://doi.org/10.17310/ntj.2r006.3.18.

Bartle, John. R. 1996. "Coping with Cutbacks: City Response to Aid Cuts in New York State." *State and Local Government Review* 28, no. 1 (Winter): 38–48. https://www-jstor-org.proxy.bsu.edu/stable/4355141.

Bartle, John. R., Carol Ebdon, and Dale Krane. (2003) "Beyond the Property Tax: Local Government Revenue Diversification." *Journal of Public Budgeting, Accounting & Financial Management* 15, no. 4 (March): 622–48. https://doi.org/10.1108/JPBAFM -15-04-2003-B006.

Blair, Robert F., and Anthony M. Starke. 2017. "The Emergence of Local Government Policy Leadership: A Roaring Torch or a Flickering Flame?" *State & Local Government Review* 49, no. 4 (December): 275–284. https://doi.org/10.1177/0160323X17 754237.

Bozeman, Barry. 2010. "Hard Lessons from Hard Times: Reconsidering and Reorienting the 'Managing Decline' Literature." *Public Administration Review* 70, no. 4 (July/ August): 557–563. https://doi.org/10.1111/j.1540-6210.2010.02176.x.

Brown, Mark D. 2005. *Statewide Property Tax Equalization Study Policy Report.* Indiana Fiscal Policy Institute.

Carr, Jared B. 2004. "Perspectives on City-County Consolidation and its Alternatives." In *City-County Consolidation and Its Alternatives,* edited by Jared B. Carr and Richard C. Feiock, Armonk, NY: M. E. Sharpe.

Chernick, Howard, and Andrew Reschovsky. 2006. "Fiscal Disparities in Selected Metropolitan Areas." *National Tax Association - Tax Institute of America. Proceedings of the 99*$_{th}$ *Annual Conference on Taxation* (January): 76–84.

Cromwell, Erich, and Keith Ihlanfeldt. 2015. "Local Government Responses to Exogenous Shocks in Revenue Sources: Evidence from Florida." *National Tax Journal* 68, no. 2 (January): 339–76. https://doi.org/10.17310/ntj.2015.2.05.

Downs, George W., and David M. Rocke. 1984. "Theories of Budgetary Decisionmaking and Revenue Decline." *Policy Sciences* 16, no. 4 (March): 329–47. https://doi.org/10 .1007/BF00135953.

Dye, Richard F., and Therese J. McGuire. 1997. "The Effect of Property Tax Limitation Measures on Local Government Fiscal Behavior." *Journal of Public Economics* 66, no. 3 (December): 469–87. https://doi.org/10.1016/S0047-2727(97)00047-9.

Edwards, Mary M., and Yu Xiao. 2009. "Annexation, Local Government Spending, and the Complicating Role of Density." *Urban Affairs Review* 45, no. 2 (July): 147–65. https://doi.org/10.1177/1078087409341036.

Faulk, Dagney, Kevin Kuhlman, Hikoyat Salimova, and Srikant Devaraj. 2010. *Local Option Income Taxes in Indiana An Overview.* Ball State University: Center for Business and Economic Research. http://projects.cberdata.org/reports/LOIT03.18.pdf.

Forrester, John P., and Charles J. Spindler. 1990. "Assessing the Impact on Municipal Revenues of the Elimination of General Revenue Sharing." *State & Local Government Review* 22, no. 2 (Spring): 73–83. https://www-jstor-org.proxy.bsu.edu/stable /4354983.

Gonzalez, Rodolfo A., and Stephen L. Mehay. 1987. "Municipal Annexation and Local Monopoly Power." *Public Choice* 52, no. 3 (January): 245–55. https://doi.org/10 .1007/BF00116707.

Hicks, William D., Carol Weissert, Jeffrey Swanson, Jessica Bulman-Pozen, Vladimir Kogan, Lori Riverstone-Newell, Jaclyn Bunch, et al. 2018. "Home Rule be Damned: Exploring Policy Conflicts between the Statehouse and City Hall." *PS, Political Science & Politics* 51, no. 1 (January): 26–38. https://doi.org/10.1017/S1049096517001421.

Indiana Department of Local Government Finance (DLGF). 2014. *Certified Budget, Levy, CNAV, Tax Rate by Fund.* Indianapolis, IN: DLGF. https://www.in.gov/dlgf/8379 .htm.

Indiana Legislative Services Agency (LSA). 2011. *Circuit Breaker Report (December 2011).* Indianapolis, IN: Office of Fiscal Analysis and Management. http://iga.in.gov /legislative/2020/publications/property_tax/#document-50058b0a.

Indiana Legislative Services Agency (LSA). 2015. *Handbook of Taxes, Revenue and Appropriations*. Indianapolis, IN: Office of Fiscal Analysis and Management. http://iga.in.gov/static-documents/f/9/4/0/f9407ace/2015%20Tax%20Handbook%20WEBPAGE.pdf.

Jick, Todd D., and Victor V. Murray. 1982. "The Management of Hard Times: Budget Cutbacks in Public Sector Organizations." *Organization Studies* 3, no. 2 (April): 141–69.

Joyce, Philip G., and Daniel R. Mullins. 1991. "The Changing Fiscal Structure of the State and Local Public Sector: The Impact of Tax and Expenditure Limitations." *Public Administration Review* 51, no. 3 (May-June): 240–53. https://doi.org/10.2307/976948.

Kim, DaeJin, Sang Seok Bae, and Robert J. Eger. 2009. "Is Local Discretionary Sales Tax Adopted to Counteract Fiscal Stress? The Case of Florida Counties." *Economic Development Quarterly* 23, no. 2 (May): 150–66. https://doi.org/10.1177/0891242408327708.

Kopelman, Jason L., and Harvey S. Rosen. 2016. "Are Public Sector Jobs Recession-Proof? Were They Ever?" *Public Finance Review* 44, no. 3 (May): 370–96. https://doi.org/10.1177/1091142114565042.

Levine, Charles H. 1978. "Organizational Decline and Cutback Management." *Public Administration Review* 38, no. 4 (July-August): 316–25. https://doi.org/10.2307/975813.

Levine, Charles H. 1979. "More on Cutback Management: Hard Questions for Hard Times." *Public Administration Review* 39, no. 2 (March-April): 179–83. https://doi.org/10.2307/3110475.

Lewis, Gregory B. 1988. "The Consequences of Fiscal Stress: Cutback Management and Municipal Employment." *State & Local Government Review* 20, no. 2 (Spring): 64–71. https://www-jstor-org.proxy.bsu.edu/stable/4354931.

Liner, Gaines H. 1992. "Annexation impact on municipal efficiency." *Review of Regional Studies* 22, no. 1 (January): 75–87. https://rrs.scholasticahq.com/article/9133-annexation-impact-on-municipal-efficiency.

Liner, Gaines H. 1994. "Institutional Constraints, Annexation and Municipal Efficiency in the 1960s." *Public Choice* 79, no. 3/4 (January): 305–23. https://doi.org/10.1007/BF01047775.

Liner, Gaines H., and Rob Roy McGregor. 2002. "Optimal Annexation." *Applied Economics* 34, no. 12 (August): 1477–85. https://doi.org/10.1080/00036840110108035.

Maher, Craig S., and Steven C. Deller. 2012. "Measuring the Impacts of TELs on Municipal Financial Conditions." In *Handbook of Local Government Fiscal Health*, edited by Helisse Levine, Jonathan B. Justice, and Eric A. Scorsone, 405–26. Burlington, MA: Jones & Bartlett Learning.

McCubbins, Mathew D., and Ellen Moule. 2010. "Making Mountains of Debt Out of Molehills: The Pro-Cyclical Implications of Tax and Expenditure Limitations." *National Tax Journal* 63, no. 3 (September): 603–21. https://doi.org/10.17310/ntj.2010.3.09.

Mehay, Stephen L. 1981. "The Expenditure Effects of Municipal Annexation." *Public Choice* 36, no. 1 (January): 53–62. https://doi.org/10.1007/BF00163770.

Mullins, Daniel R. 2004. "Tax and Expenditure Limitations and the Fiscal Response of Local Government: Asymmetric Intra-Local Fiscal Effects." *Public Budgeting & Finance* 24, no. 4 (Winter): 111–47. https://doi.org/10.1111/j.0275-1100.2004.00350.x.

Mullins, Daniel R., and Philip G. Joyce. 1996. "Tax and Expenditure Limitations and State and Local Fiscal Structure: An Empirical Assessment." *Public Budgeting & Finance* 16, no. 1 (Spring): 75–101. https://doi.org/10.1111/1540-5850.01061.

Nagle, Matt. 2011. *Assessing Indiana's Tax, Fiscal, and Economic Conditions*. Indianapolis, IN: IU Public Policy Institute. http://ppidb.iu.edu/publication/details/567.

National Bureau of Economic Research (NBER). n.d. *US Business Cycles Expansions and Contractions*. Cambridge, MA. Accessed March 4, 2021. http://www.nber.org/cycles/cyclesmain.html.

Nelson, Kimberly L. 2012. "Municipal Choices during a Recession: Bounded Rationality and Innovation." *State & Local Government Review* 44, 1_suppl (August): 44S–63S. https://doi.org/10.1177/0160323X12452888.

O'Sullivan, Arthur. 2001. "Limits on Local Property Taxation the United States Experience." In *Property Taxation and Local Government Finance*, edited by Wallace E. Oates, 177–200. Cambridge, MA: Lincoln Institute of Land Policy.

Ottensmann, John R., Seth Payton, and Drew Klacik. 2008. *Impacts of Property Tax Reform*. Indianapolis, IN: Center for Urban Policy and the Environment. (August). https://archives.iupui.edu/handle/2450/4637.

Pammer, William J. 1990. *Managing Fiscal Strain in Major American Cities: Understanding Retrenchment in the Public Sector*. New York: Greenwood Press.

Park, Sungho. 2018. "The Impact of State-Imposed Fiscal Rules on Municipal Government Fiscal Outcomes: Does Institutional Configuration Matter?" *State and Local Government Review* 50, no. 4 (December): 230–43. https://doi.org/10.1177/0160323X18823245.

Riverstone-Newell, Lori. 2017. "The Rise of State Preemption Laws in Response to Local Policy Innovation." *Publius* 47, no. 3 (May): 403–25. https://doi.org/10.1093/publius/pjx037.

Ross, Justin, Wenli Yan, and Craig Johnson. 2015. "The Public Financing of America's Largest Cities: A Study of City Financial Records in the Wake of the Great Recession." *Journal of Regional Science* 55, no. 1 (January): 113–38. https://doi.org/10.1111/jors.12117.

Scorsone, Eric A., and Christina Plerhoples. 2010. "Fiscal Stress and Cutback Management Amongst State and Local Governments: What Have We Learned and What Remains To Be Learned?" *State & Local Government Review* 42, no. 2 (August): 176–87. https://doi.org/10.1177/0160323X10378826.

Sexton, Terri A., Steven M. Sheffrin, and Arthur O'Sullivan. 1999. "Proposition 13: Unintended Effects and Feasible Reforms." *National Tax Journal* 52, no. 1 (March): 99–111. https://doi.org/10.1086/NTJ41789379.

Shadbegian, Ronald J. 1999. "The Effect of Tax and Expenditure Limitations on the Revenue Structure of Local Government, 1962–87." *National Tax Journal* 52, no. 2 (June): 221–37. https://doi.org/10.1086/NTJ41789391.

Sharp, Elaine B., and David Elkins. 1987. "The Impact of Fiscal Limitation: A Tale of Seven Cities." *Public Administration Review* 47, no. 5 (September-October): 385–92. https://doi.org/10.2307/976063.

Skidmore, Mark, and Eric Scorsone. 2011. "Causes and Consequences of Fiscal Stress in Michigan Cities." *Regional Science and Urban Economics* 41, no. 4 (July): 360–71. https://doi.org/10.1016/j.regsciurbeco.2011.02.007.

St. Clair, Travis. 2012. "The Effects of Tax and Expenditure Limitations on Revenue Volatility: Evidence from Colorado." *Public Budgeting and Finance* 32, no. 3 (Fall): 61–78. https://doi.org/10.1111/j.1540-5850.2012.01016.x.

Swindell, David, Carl Stenberg, and James Svara. 2017. *Navigating the Waters between Local Autonomy and State Preemption*. The Big Ideas Work Paper. (October). Phoenix, AZ: Alliance for Innovation. https://urbaninnovation.asu.edu/sites/default/files/2017_big_ideas_work_paper_0.pdf.

US Census Bureau. 2014a. *Annual Survey of Public Employment and Payroll* (ASPEP). Accessed July 16, 2020. https://www.census.gov/data/datasets/2014/econ/apes/annual-apes.html.

US Census Bureau. 2014b. *Annual Survey of State and Local Government Finances.* Accessed July 16, 2020. https://www.census.gov/data/datasets/2014/econ/local/public-use-datasets.html.

US Census Bureau. 2014c. *Small Area Income and Poverty Estimates* (SAIPE). Accessed March 4, 2016. https://www.census.gov/programs-surveys/saipe.html.

Wang, Wen, and Yilin Hou. 2012. "Do Local Governments Save and Spend Across Budget Cycles? Evidence from North Carolina." *The American Review of Public Administration.* 42, no. 2 (March): 152–69. https://doi.org/10.1177/0275074011398387.

Wolman, Harold. 1980. "Local Government Strategies to Cope with Fiscal Pressure" In *Fiscal Stress and Public Policy,* edited by Charles H. Levine and Irene Rubin, (January): 231–48. Beverly Hills: Sage.

Zhao, Zhirong. 2005. "Motivations, Obstacles, and Resources: The Adoption of the General-Purpose Local Option Sales Tax in Georgia Counties." *Public Finance Review.* 33, no. 6 (January): 721–46. doi:10.1111/j.1540-5850.2012.01016.x10.1177/1091142105279555.

9

ASYMMETRIC LOCAL EMPLOYMENT MULTIPLIERS, AGGLOMERATION, AND THE DISAPPEARANCE OF FOOTLOOSE JOBS

Michael J. Hicks

Employment multipliers are among the most frequently used concepts in the development of state or local policies toward business. Multipliers are applied to estimate the impact of firm relocation, expansion, or contraction. Hospitals, universities, manufacturing firms, restaurants, and agricultural, mining, and logistics firms use multipliers to tout the putative benefits of their expansion or relocation to a region. Often these estimates constitute the underlying argument for tax incentives, infrastructure support, or the easing of regulatory burdens on firms.

The idea of the economic multiplier forms the foundation for local economic development efforts in the vast majority of county or municipal governments in the United States. Local government or quasi-nongovernmental organizations attempt to lure firms to regions in the expectation that their presence will boost overall economic activity. Estimated economic multipliers quantify this hope and thereby justify tax incentives, discrete infrastructure spending, the deployment of workforce training funds, and other support for new businesses. Local economic development officials also use multipliers to justify spending on failing firms to prevent a negative impact on their community.

Economists rarely estimate multipliers from historical data in a stochastic framework. A stochastic model analyzes historical data that allows for regional and temporal variation and a confidence interval. Those used for policy purposes are derived from nonstochastic input-output models. The use of multipliers in academic research rarely enters local policymaking. Thus, it is fair to say that most multipliers used for economic policy rely on concepts and multipliers that are decades old and lack nuance about local labor conditions. Multipliers from input-output models make no allowance for labor supply conditions, commuting zones, or other factors that would alter their size. Moreover, there is almost no treatment of asymmetry in the estimation of multipliers.

To address some but not all of these shortcomings, this chapter seeks to extend the stochastic multiplier tests, focusing on asymmetric labor market shocks over time and geography. The chapter is organized as follows: the next section provides a brief review of the literature. The following section includes a discussion of the method and data, focusing on an identification strategy that seeks to distinguish local from national labor market shocks. To isolate agglomeration effects on multiplier estimates, I use asymmetric labor market shocks and control for population size. The next section describes the choice of time periods to analyze and geographic categories to use in these estimates. Multipliers change over time and across geographies, so to isolate these effects, I control for size in the regression but estimate across smaller categories of county size. The penultimate section includes a discussion of the estimates, their strengths and weaknesses, and their use in policy development, especially with regard to traditional economic development policies. I also offer theoretical interpretation and describe limitations of this research that can be evaluated in later studies. I begin with a summary of key findings.

First, I found that the size of economic multipliers has declined significantly over time. From 1969 through 1985, county level multipliers ranged from 3.58 to 5.18. From 2000 to 2015 they declined to 1.28 and 1.21, respectively. I attribute this decline to the reduction of job-related migration and expansion of nonfootloose employment across the United States.

Footloose employment comprises those jobs that may conceptually locate anywhere because they do not depend on local demand for goods or services. Examples of these include manufacturing, back-office financial services, and some logistics. In contrast, nonfootloose firms depend on local demand for services. Employment in these firms includes occupations as pediatricians, fire fighters, and wait-staff.

Second, I find significant asymmetry in multipliers. Job losses cause much larger multiplier effects than do job gains. This implies significant downside risk to the most common types of economic development activities designed to attract new jobs to a community. Finally, I find that multipliers are larger in more urban communities. This is consistent with both economic theory and the findings from other studies on size and multiplier effect.

Literature

Despite well-known problems with economic base theory in general (Krugman 1991, 2011), the use of employment multipliers derived from economic base theory is a low-cost, easily interpreted tool for explaining the potential effects of changes to firm size or location on a local economy. The general approach to interpreting multipliers assumes symmetric effects and nearly perfect labor supply elasticity. Thus, a labor demand shock in tradable sector (footloose) employment will generate an employment multiplier value that is insensitive to the direction of the impact and highly elastic.

These modeling assumptions are highly restrictive. This alone casts some doubt on their use for major policy development or analysis. In support of more policy-oriented use of multipliers, empirical research has long attempted to isolate local variation to make them more appropriate for specific regions. Richardson and Gordon (1978) and Richardson (1985) provide a lengthy review of the modeling approaches for determining multipliers. National multiplier modeling efforts, such as the US Bureau of Economic Analysis, Regional Input Multipliers (RIMS II) are derived from input-output (I-O) tables. These are necessarily symmetrical because the I-O tables require deterministic computation to derive multipliers. Evaluating either the symmetry or other dynamic properties of multipliers requires some use of stochastic modeling.

Stochastic estimates of multipliers have also been used extensively, beginning with Polak's (1939) effort to estimate the propagation of business cycles. Braschler (1972) offered a compelling overview of the relationship between deterministic and stochastic multiplier estimates. McNulty (1977) estimated the dynamic effects of labor market shocks in a multiplier framework. Thompson (1983) estimated employment multipliers across different city sizes and critically reviewed empirical studies of employment multipliers focusing on region size.

More recently Moretti (2010) estimated employment multipliers for tradable and nontradable goods, spawning an extended literature that includes van Dijk (2017) and Rickman and Guettabi's (2013) evaluation of asymmetric labor demand shocks on housing. This literature is distinctive because it better identifies the local demand shock, using an instrumentation strategy (Bartik 1993) that has gained broad acceptance.

Despite the research on these issues, there is very little direct analysis of asymmetry in multipliers; indeed, I find few examples in the literature of direct estimates of asymmetry on employment multipliers. Brownrigg (1980) acknowledged the poor use of the symmetry assumption in his analysis of plant closures in Scotland. He finds that plant closures have smaller employment propagation effects than do the estimated symmetric multipliers derived from I-O tables. He does not directly evaluate the symmetry of multipliers, but provides an excellent review of the limitations of I-O derived multipliers.

Richardson and Gordon (1978) mentioned an absence of research on symmetry in a survey article on regional science. Shaffer (1983) examined the symmetry of export base multipliers. In his estimates, he compares the I-O assumption of symmetry with a relaxed empirical specification that permits asymmetry in estimated multipliers. He finds that positive demand shocks cause smaller multipliers than do negative shocks. Shahidsaless, Gillis, and Shaffer (1983) estimated county level manufacturing employment shocks. They found that periods of increasing employment were associated with smaller multipliers than periods of declining employment during the 1950–1960 period, but during the 1960–1970 period there was no meaningful difference.

Likewise, there has been very little review of changes to multipliers over time. Whereas regional multipliers are commonly estimated each year, compilation of changes over time are uncommon. The US Bureau of Economic Analysis does not systematically retain I-O multipliers over time, although they have at least one study comparing output and export multipliers over a two-decade period (Guo and Planting 2000). The limited analysis of this issue is surprising, given the enormous resources spent on data collection and the computational challenges in deriving employment multipliers for any given time period.

The multiplier literature is well developed, based upon a lengthy history of input-output modeling as well as more modern stochastic modeling approaches. For this reason, I will not undertake a detailed explanation of the economic base theory, the I-O tables, or the stochastic models used to estimate empirically observed multipliers. What remains elusive in this literature is a comparison of these multipliers over a lengthy period of time, along with an evaluation of the symmetry of the effects of positive and negative labor demand shocks upon the estimated multiplier.

This study seeks to evaluate these two issues as well as the role of urbanization on the symmetry and effect over time of these multipliers. From that, I will draw policy conclusions focused mostly on the shift from traditional economic development policies toward local, place[\-based development efforts.

Method

The employment shocks used to estimate the multiplier are changes in footloose (tradable) employment on nonfootloose (nontradable) employment. This is estimated in a simple cross-sectional model:

$$N^{NF} = MN^F + u,$$

where N is employment in nontradable and tradable industries, u the error term, and M is the traditional employment multiplier estimated as

$$M = \frac{dN^{NF}}{dN^F}.$$

To exploit the panel nature of the data in order to construct multipliers across time and geography, the base multiplier specification changes to

$$N_{i,t}^{NF} = MN_{i,t}^F + e_{i,t},$$

where i denotes county and t denotes year.

It is well known that the multiplier is affected by the population size of each geography. Larger regions possess more of the forward and backward economic linkages that create the observed local multiplier effect. In the empirical specification, I control for population, and its square, to create a multiplier estimate that is orthogonal to population distribution. I treat the role of geography in the size and symmetry of the multiplier in subsequent sections as I seek to isolate size effects on multipliers by isolating the sample to counties of different sizes.

Manufacturing employment changes in the United States are highly idiosyncratic at the county level, but aggregate values trend with the declining level of factory jobs nationwide. For this reason, identification of county level changes requires careful treatment of local impacts.

Among the most commonly deployed instruments for this identification is the Bartik (1993) shift share instrument. The specification used here is

$$\left(\frac{N_i^F}{\sum_{i=1}^n N_i^F} \right) d \sum_{i=1}^n N_i^F$$

which is the share of local manufacturing employment, times the one-period change in national manufacturing employment.

A method developed by Jones, Olson, and Wohar (2015) in their treatment of asymmetric tax multipliers is used to examine the symmetry of multiplier effects. In this approach, I calculate changes in annual footloose employment as either nonnegative or nonpositive and create two different time series representing zero or positive shocks and zero or negative shocks for each county and year. For convenience of exposition, these are referred to as either positive or negative labor market shocks, though correctly they include zero values, so are nonnegative and nonpositive, respectively. The following figures depict the mean and median of each of the data panels.

The following specification is used to estimate county level employment multipliers:

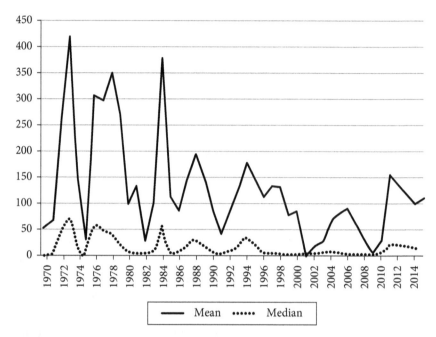

FIGURE 9.1. Positive (nonnegative) employment shocks, 1970–2014.
The 2000 NAICS transition is suppressed to zero in this graphic

Source: Data from US Bureau of Economic Analysis, Regional Economic Information Systems, both SIC and NAICS components.

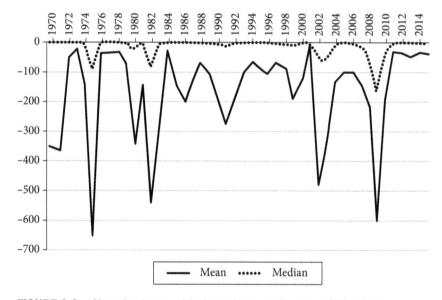

FIGURE 9.2. Negative (nonpositive) employment shocks, 1970–2015.
The 2000 NAICS transition is suppressed to zero in this graphic

Source: Data from US Bureau of Economic Analysis, Regional Economic Information Systems, both SIC and NAICS components.

$$\widetilde{E}_{i,t}^{NF} = \alpha + \theta_1 Pos\,\Delta E_{i,t}^F + \theta_2 Neg\,\Delta E_{i,t}^F + \beta_1 Pop_{i,t} + \beta_2 Pop_{i,t}^2 + \gamma NAICS_t + \delta\theta_{i,t} + e_{i,t}$$

where $\widetilde{E}_{i,t}^{NF}$ is the first differenced level of predicted employment using the Bartik instrument given previously. The coefficients θ are the values on the positive and negative changes to tradable (footloose) employment, the coefficients β are population and population squared controls, and the following terms are an annual NAICS dummy denoting the change from SIC, a first order autoregressive value, and a white-noise error term.

To create county-level employment multipliers in the United States I use data from the Department of Commerce's Bureau of Economic Analysis, Regional Economic Information System on total and manufacturing employment in each county. The dependent variable is nonmanufacturing employment, which is a proxy for nonfootloose (nontradable) employment, and the positive and negative series are constructed from manufacturing employment. Summary statistics appear in table 9.1.

This specification provides an estimate of the manufacturing multiplier on nonmanufacturing employment, represented asymmetrically with population and autocorrelation controls. As part of the strategy to examine the temporal and size as well as symmetric dimensions of multipliers, I estimate multipliers across three roughly coequal time series. Several considerations motivate the choice of time periods under analysis. The start date of 1969 bounds the earliest available annual county employment data, and 2000 involves a clear structural break between NAICS and SIC classifications. That break is confirmed in a Dickey-Fuller test, which confirms a break that is both visible and abides by common sense.

The choice of 1985 as a dividing line is less empirically justifiable from the data. There is no series breakpoint in 1985, but there are other reasons for choosing this year. This roughly balances the number of observations in the three time periods. There is no strict purpose in this choice, as it would appear labor market

TABLE 9.1. Summary statistics

	MEAN	MEDIAN	MAX	MIN	STD. DEV.
Positive labor demand changes (footloose employment)	122	1	59,854	0	634
Negative labor demand shocks (footloose employment)	−309	0	0	−93,291	3,730
Population	91,298	25,696	10,170,292	65	301,543
Nonfootloose employment	43,183	9,353	5,816,108	65	159,544

Note: This table does not include the 2000 NAICS changeover year (2000–2001).

adjustments in nonfootloose sectors would adjust in fewer than fifteen years. However, longer time series are surely a superior choice to shorter periods.

A more relevant argument for choosing 1985 as a period delineation is the 1981–2 recession and its aftermath. This recession was significant, and the Federal Reserve's historical series describes it as ". . . widespread, but manufacturing, construction and the auto industries were particularly affected" (Sablik 2013). This recession was followed by a lengthy recovery, but growth rates flattened in 1985, allowing for an appealing choice of a solid economic expansion year in which to separate periods of analysis. Three periods—from 1969 through 1985, 1985 to 1999, and 2000 through 2015—are used to compare temporal changes in multipliers.

The choices of geographic variation were simpler, relying wholly on the USDA's rural urban continuum codes. These codes range from one to nine and range from counties in metropolitan areas of one million or more, to rural counties with fewer than 2,500 residents in urban environments and not adjacent to metropolitan areas. I aggregated these codes into three groups. The largest group comprises counties in metro areas with 250 thousand or more residents (783 counties); the middle category comprises counties in metropolitan areas of fewer than 250 thousand persons to counties with urban places of twenty thousand or more residents (342 counties); and the third category comprises counties with fewer than twenty urban residents (1,746 counties). These latter are the rural areas of the sample.

Thus, I model employment multipliers across a long time period and three shorter periods, and across three geographies, allowing for asymmetry in the shocks. In the following section, I report the results of these models.

Results

Across the separate tests, three stylized results emerge. First, employment multipliers (effect of footloose demand shocks on nonfootloose jobs) were very large in the early sample period but declined in later periods. Second, multipliers are larger in urban than in rural places. Third, in most instances negative shocks yielded larger multipliers than positive shocks. See tables 9.2 through 9.4 for a summary of multiplier results.

Importantly, in every model estimated, the positive and negative shocks were statistically significant to the 0.05 or better level. However, an important question is whether the point estimates of each of these yielded results that were statistically different across the types of shocks, either positive or negative. To determine this, I conducted a series of Wald tests that test the equality of the positive and negative labor demand shocks. Again, among the base model all

TABLE 9.2. Estimated change in nonfootloose jobs of a change in one footloose job

	POSITIVE SHOCK[a]	NEGATIVE SHOCK[a]	N (I/T)
Full sample (1969–2015)	1.33	0.10*	125,146 (3,071/44)
Early (1969–1985)	3.58	5.18*	41,278 (3,021/16)
Middle (1985–1999)	0.87	2.16*	46,175 (3,051/15)
Late (2000–2015)	1.28	1.21	42,809 (2,946/16)
Large urban sample (1969–2015)	3.53	1.27*	33,677 (783/44)
Early (1969–1985)	4.21	6.46*	10,825 (779, 16)
Middle (1985–1999)	1.66	3.13*	11,615 (780/15)
Late (2000–2015)	2.38	1.22*	12,009 (777/16)
Small urban sample (1969–2015)	2.65	1.44*	14,457 (342/44)
Early (1969–1985)	3.93	4.57*	4,704 (339/16)
Middle (1985–1999)	0.52	1.62*	4,979 (341/15)
Late (2000–2015)	0.86	1.17*	5,107 (334/16)
Rural sample (1969–2015)	1.66	1.16*	69,230 (1,746/44)
Early (1969–1985)	2.99	3.63*	23,086 (1,708/16)
Middle (1985–1999)	0.39	1.08*	24,588 (1,729/15)
Late (2000–2015)	0.27	1.12*	23,206 (1,650/16)

Note: The full and early periods are truncated due to the inclusion of an autoregressive lag.

[a] The change in the number of footloose jobs was a statistically significant determinant of the change in nonfootloose jobs in each model, geography, and time period for both positive and negative shocks at the 0.05 level of significance or better using a t-test.

* Positive shocks are statistically, significantly different from negative shocks at the 0.01 level of significance using a Wald test.

coefficients were statistically different from zero, and in all but one case (late, full model) the negative and positive labor demand shock coefficients differed from one another at the 0.01 level in the Wald test.

In the spatially corrected model, all coefficients were statistically different from zero at the 0.05 level or better, and from one another at the 0.01 level, using the traditional t-statistic and Wald statistic, respectively.

The multipliers presented in tables 9.2 through 9.3 show how a change in manufacturing employment (footloose jobs) affects nonmanufacturing (nonfootloose) employment. For example, a decrease of one manufacturing job during the early period is associated with a 5.18 job decrease in nonmanufacturing employment (table 9.2). Table 9.4 illustrates the symmetric shocks for the full sample, comparing the Bartik instrument and OLS. This is for illustrative purposes only.

TABLE 9.3. Estimated change in non-footloose jobs of a change in one footloose job, spatially corrected

	POSITIVE SHOCK[A]	NEGATIVE SHOCK[A]	N (I/T)
Full sample (1969–2015)	3.35	1.18 *	125,146 (3,071/44)
Early (1969–1985)	4.40	6.28*	41,278 (3,021/16)
Middle (1985–1999)	1.57	3.09*	46,175 (3,051/15)
Late (2000–2015)	3.02	1.01*	42,809 (2,946/16)
Large urban sample (1969–2015)	5.31	1.34*	33,677 (783/44)
Early (1969–1985)	5.36	8.76*	10,825 (779, 16)
Middle (1985–1999)	2.55	4.46*	11,615 (780/15)
Late (2000–2015)	4.82	1.22*	12,009 (777/16)
Small urban sample (1969–2015)	3.47	1.31 *	14,457 (342/44)
Early (1969–1985)	4.81	5.30*	4,704 (339/16)
Middle (1985–1999)	0.68	2.10*	4,979 (341/15)
Late (2000–2015)	1.51	1.26*	5,107 (334/16)
Rural sample (1969–2015)	1.90	1.13*	69,230 (1,746/44)
Early (1969–1985)	3.18	3.95*	23,086 (1,708/16)
Middle (1985–1999)	0.25	1.32*	24,588 (1,729/15)
Late (2000–2015)	0.65	1.01*	23,206 (1,650/16)

Notes: The full and early periods are truncated due to the inclusion of an autoregressive lag. The estimates were spatially corrected using Pesaran 2006.

[a] The change in the number of footloose jobs was a statistically significant determinant of the change in nonfootloose jobs in each model, geography, and time period for both positive and negative shocks at the 0.05 level of significance or better using a t-test.

* Positive shocks are statistically, significantly different from negative shocks at the 0.01 level of significance using a Wald test.

TABLE 9.4. Symmetric shocks (full sample only)

	IV (BARTIK INSTRUMENT)	OLS
Full sample (1969–2015)	1.28	1.59
Early (1969–1985)	4.24	6.83
Middle (1985–1999)	1.72	2.95
Late (2000–2015)	1.17	1.28

Across the full sample, the size of the calculated multiplier was large in the early periods and declining in the later periods (figure 9.3). This finding occurred across all three sample groups (large urban, small urban, and rural). There is little in the literature to compare stochastic multipliers during this period, and

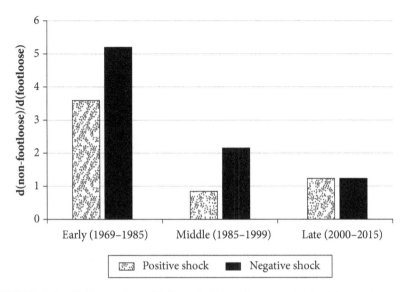

FIGURE 9.3. Full sample multipliers for labor demand shocks (change in nonfootloose jobs due to a change in footloose employment)

there is to my knowledge no systematic literature comparing the size of employment multipliers across time. However, Guo, and Planting (2000) reported output multipliers over a two-decade period (1972–1996) declining from 2.037 to 1.981. Given productivity growth in manufacturing, it seems plausible that the decline in manufacturing employment multipliers would be more pronounced than the decline in output multipliers.

There are several plausible explanations for this. First, multipliers are likely to be larger in markets where there is a denser set of backward and forward linkages among firms. That is a central finding of the I-O model multipliers. The decline in manufacturing employment as a share of total employment during this period was very steep, shrinking from 26.3 to 8.5 percent from 1969 through 2015 (figure 9.4). Also, the mean, median, standard deviation, and maximum percent of manufacturing in the observed 3,074 US counties have all declined. The mean manufacturing share decline over this time from 17.6 to 9.2 percent, while the estimated symmetric change in nonfootloose jobs to footloose jobs declined from 4.24 to 1.17 over the same time period.

Hefner and Guimaraes (1994) estimated very strong backward linkage effects of new footloose firm location decisions. Their model estimated that a 1 percent increase in backward linkages (backward multiplier) increased the probability of new firm location by 1.46 percent. They also found higher incomes, and that larger shares of manufacturing workers resulted in higher probabilities of firm

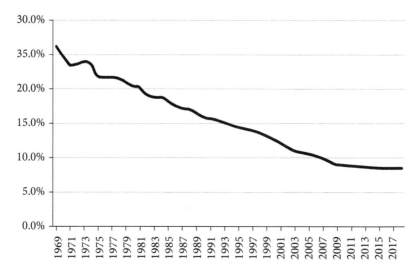

FIGURE 9.4.   Manufacturing employment share in the US, 1969–2015

entrance. Their estimates of forward linkages were roughly 0.22 percent, suggesting that suppliers, far more than customers, dictated firm location decisions in South Carolina from 1985 to 1988.

As a rough comparison over these three periods, the ratio of change between the estimated multipliers and the share of manufacturing employment (*dMultiplier/d%man*) ranged from a 1.16 for the base model to 1.72 in the spatially adjusted model. This would suggest that the theoretical connection of multipliers sizes to forward and backward linkages enjoys some empirical support across these data. Appealing briefly to the very broad theoretical literature is helpful. The link between the declining manufacturing employment shares would hypothetically play a role in the shrinking average employment multiplier in the United States. Simply, with smaller backward linkages, firms relocating or expanding in a county would draw suppliers from a larger geography, thus generating smaller employment propagation on the average county.

These estimates, across the entire geography and the three smaller geographic regions and across both the symmetric and asymmetric assumption, generate the same result. Employment multipliers are declining across time. This effect is much more pronounced than reported by Guo and Planting (2000) on output and export multipliers. The estimates illustrate a clear pattern of more modest employment multipliers across time.

The asymmetry of shocks is the focus of this section. The model results, across all four samples, show that positive shocks yielded smaller multipliers in the early (1969–1985) and middle (1985–1999) periods. In two of three geographic samples,

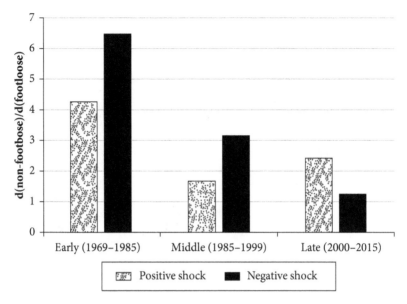

FIGURE 9.5. Asymmetric labor demand shocks in large urban places. Rural-Urban Continuum Codes 1 and 2

Source: Data from US Department of Agriculture.

this pattern continued through the latest period (2000–2015). Across these esti-mates, there were only two circumstances in which this pattern was not repeated. In the full sample in the most recent period, there was no statistical difference be-tween the positive and negative shocks. In the urban sample in the most recent period, positive shocks yielded larger multipliers than did negative shocks.

In the early period (1969–1985), the positive footloose employment shock yielded between 65 percent and 85 percent of the impact on non-footloose jobs that a negative employment shock did. In the middle period (1985–1999), this ranged from 32 percent to 53 percent, and in the latest period from 24 percent to 73 percent. See figures 9.3, 9.5, 9.6, and 9.7.

These results mimic Shaffer (1983), who compared the manufacturing multi-plier in growing and contracting nonmetropolitan US counties between 1960 and 1970. He reported that positive labor demand shocks generated a nonfootloose job impact of 1.59 jobs and that a negative labor demand shocks led to a 2.25 job im-pact. These estimates were only modestly smaller than the reported levels from the early period (1969–1985) reported here. However, the relative asymmetry is largely identical. Shaffer credited an earlier study (Brownrigg 1980) with identifying the role of asymmetry in multipliers. The Brownrigg study was of a single plant contraction and closure in Scotland. He reported smaller than expected negative

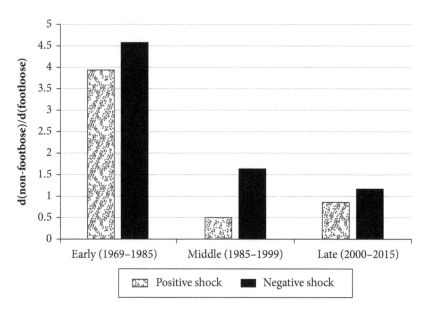

FIGURE 9.6. Asymmetric labor demand shocks in midsized urban places. Rural-Urban Continuum Codes 3 and 4

Source: Data from US Department of Agriculture.

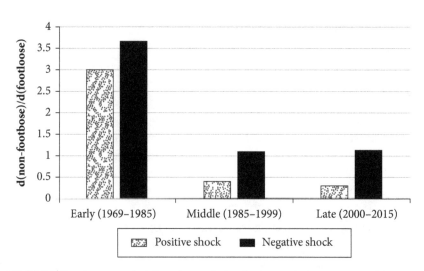

FIGURE 9.7. Asymmetric labor demand shocks in rural places. Rural-Urban Continuum Codes 5 through 8

Source: Data from US Department of Agriculture.

multipliers as compared to the I-O model, which assumes symmetry. These findings compare with one sample period and differ with another in the third existing study of asymmetric multipliers (Shahidsaless, Gillis, and Shaffer 1983).

In another study of multipliers across the business cycle, Nguyen and Soh (2017) report larger multipliers for footloose firms during and after the Great Recession than in the 2002–2007 expansion. This holds both for OLS and the Bartik instrumented multiplier estimated with data from US counties. Interestingly, these multipliers are in the range of the larger multiplier estimates in any of the periods reported in this research. This study was not clearly of symmetry but suggests that business cycle activity affects the magnitude of the employment multiplier. This holds even when instrumenting for national labor demand shocks through the Bartik approach.

Tsvetkova and Partridge (2016) and Partridge, Rickman, Olfert, and Tan (2017) examined multipliers more recently but tested for variation across two time periods in the 1990s and 2000s. Both reported modestly smaller multipliers in the more recent periods, and larger multipliers in the larger geographies.

Bartik and Sotherland (2019) estimated current short-run and long-run multipliers. They reported symmetric multipliers in the range of this chapter (1.1), with larger multipliers for larger geographies and some sectors. This did not compare multipliers over time, or consider asymmetry in this analysis. Nonetheless, this should be viewed as a highly complementary study to the results presented in this chapter.

Finally, I estimated significant differences in multipliers between geographies. Across the geographic samples, multipliers were larger in urban than in rural places. This is consistent with the urban base and agglomerations literature. It is an unsurprising result. For example, Braschler (1972) reported larger manufacturing multipliers in more urbanized areas of Missouri. This type of empirical finding is the common result of most estimates.

To summarize the results of the preceding models: (1) multipliers decline over time; (2) multipliers are asymmetric—generally multipliers are smaller for positive labor demand shocks and larger for negative labor demand shocks; and (3) multipliers are typically larger in urban places than in more rural ones.

Table 9.5 summarizes a selection of the literature on stochastic multipliers. Characterizing the preceding findings against this literature, I find that insofar as research identifies multipliers over time, it has been found that multipliers decline. However, the estimates of multipliers derived in the preceding are larger and decline more significantly over time than found in this body of research. Second, the reported persistent asymmetry in multipliers reported in the preceding is modestly consistent with the two other large empirical studies of the matter. The Shaffer (1983) and the Shahidsaless, Gillis, and Shaffer (1983) papers report

TABLE 9.5. Stochastic estimates of tradable goods multipliers

STUDY	MULTIPLIER VALUE	YEARS	COMMENTS
Hildebrand and Mace 1950	1.248	1940–1947	County-level study of tradable (nonlocalized) employment
Weiss and Gooding 1968	1.8	1955–1960	Private export producing goods in a US county
Moody and Puffer 1970	1.279 to 2.14	1949 to 1966	County-level export (tradable) goods employment
Shahidsaless, Gillis and Shaffer 1983	Increasing; 0.62 Declining; 3.28 Increasing; 0.644 Declining; -0.62	1950–60 1960–70	Study of symmetry between increasing and declining manufacturing employment during two different time periods
Çubukçu 2011	1.229 to 4.853	2000	Turkish districts (subcounty equivalents)
Poppert and Herzog 2003	1.04 to 1.34	1978–1997	Exogenous labor shock (military base closings and openings)
West 1986	1.300 to 2.671	1965–6	Manufacturing multipliers in Queensland, Australia
Moody, Puffer and Williams 1970	1.21 to 5.45	1948–1952	Regionally exporting industries in Kansas counties
Sasaki 1963	1.27	1945–1955	Regionally exporting sectors in Hawaii counties
Biles 2003	1.022 to 1.0104	1995–2001	County subunits in Yucatan, Mexico
Braschler 1972	1.99 and 2.32	1950–1960	Manufacturing multipliers in small and medium sized towns in Missouri
Thompson 1983	1.74 to 1.84	1970s	Philippines subcounty regions
Mathur and Rosen 1974	1.800 to 4.58	1961–1966	Cleveland, SMSA
Moretti 2010	1.73 to 2.89	1980, 1990, 2000	US metropolitan area
Gerolimetto and Magrini 2015	0.618 to 0.629	1980 to 2010	Employment loss and gains, using spatial versions of Moretti (2010) approach
Tsvetkova and Partridge 2016	1.6 to 1.9	1993–2013	Higher in urban locations and in earlier periods
Nguyen and Soh 2017	1.53–1.606/1.68–3.01	2007–9	Employment loss and gains in Great Recession
Partridge, Rickman, Olfert, and Tan 2017	2.1 and 1.6	1990 to 2000 and 2000 to 2010	Two periods, with declining multipliers in more recent (2000–2010)
Bartik and Sotherland 2019	1.1–2.9	1998 to 2016	Geographic and industrial variation to calibrate the use of multipliers by economic development officials

asymmetry, but some inconstant asymmetries over time. Finally, the preceding findings of larger multipliers in more urban places is highly consistent with both strains of theoretical literature on the propagation of labor demand shocks (economic base and agglomeration) and consistent with previous studies that examined this issue.

My findings report a much smaller multiplier over time. While I confirm some earlier analysis on the multiplier size in urban places, the results diverge from the literature in the magnitude of asymmetry of multipliers. This latter result is important because there is little relaxation of the symmetry assumption in most policy work surrounding multipliers. This requires some contextual development as part of a policy discussion of these findings.

Implications for Policy

Employment multipliers are used almost daily in a policy context, applied to estimate the impact of almost any firm relocation, expansion, or contraction. Universities, hospitals, and other employers use multipliers to explain their economic impact on communities, and local government officials deploy these estimates to evaluate tax incentives and infrastructure investment.

Domański and Gwodsz (2010) explained that multipliers can assist in evaluating the benefits or costs of foreign investment or the changes to economic policy in regions. They also outlined the use of multipliers to understand the effects of negative economic shocks such as the contraction of an industry or firm within a region. Place-based policies are often developed or evaluated using these multipliers from IMPLAN, REMI, or RIMS II from the Bureau of Economic Analysis.

This study casts doubt on the use of I-O multipliers across a number of applications. The first of these involves methods of using and explaining existing multipliers.

First, the use of I-O multipliers derived using assumptions of symmetry likely overstate economic impacts of positive labor demand shocks. Therefore, estimates of the benefits of new firm relocation or expansion are overstated in studies of counties located outside of large metropolitan areas (those with more than 250 thousand persons). In evaluating the relative impacts in these locations, researchers should provide empirical estimates of labor demand shocks in recent geographies. Lacking such examples, researchers might scale multipliers consistent with results obtained in this study. These findings also caution against using existing I-O multipliers in performing estimates of negative labor demand shocks on regions.

The policy implications of these findings go beyond the deployment of traditional I-O multipliers for policy analysis. Asymmetric propagation of labor market shocks, declining effects, and urban rural differentials all speak more broadly to the efficacy of traditional place-based economic development efforts that focus on business attraction.

The findings reported in this study argue strongly against a resource allocation mix that favors business attraction policies. There are three compelling reasons against this. First, the benefits of business attraction have been declining over time. Second, outside of a few hundred very large metropolitan areas, the employment benefits of attracting new footloose firms are lower than the costs of losing these firms. Third, the use of symmetric multipliers to assess the benefits of attracting new firms is overstated everywhere except in the largest metropolitan areas.

These observations are more acutely true for small cities and rural locations. The multipliers presented in tables 9.2 and 9.3 along with the graphical depiction in figures 9.6 and 9.7 clearly demonstrate the asymmetry of effects of labor demand shocks. Growth in labor demand among footloose firms does less to improve subsequent footloose employment than negative shocks do to reduce nonfootloose employment. This asymmetry argues against business attraction policies designed to induce positive labor demand shocks associated with footloose employment. There is little upside benefit and lots of downside risk to such employment growth.

To extend these obvious arguments, I appeal to work by Hicks (2016), who evaluated the supply side of footloose business attraction. In this work, Hicks outlined several empirical concerns about the dwindling availability of footloose firms as a source of regional growth. Among the more compelling pieces of evidence is the cumulative decline in footloose firms measured as both manufacturing and nonretail financial services firms (figure 9.8). The declining multiplier effect of footloose employment, combined with declining probability of new firm relocation reduces significantly the benefits from economic development polices targeting the attraction or expansion of footloose firms.

The findings presented in this chapter are also supported by economic theory. Among the dominant predictions of New Economic Geography (Krugman 1991, 2011) is that agglomeration effects are accompanied by thicker labor markets and deeper regional specialization. Having foregone a full-fledged theoretical introduction to these issues in the introduction, I will not explain these issues here. However, it should be clear that agglomerations would be associated with higher multipliers as firms locate to places with more backward (forward) linkages. It should also be clear that thick labor markets might dispel much of the labor market effects of negative labor demand shocks. That is observed in these data for the larger counties (metropolitan areas of 250 thousand or more).

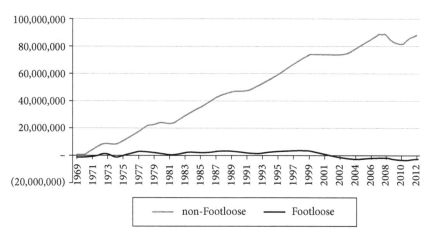

FIGURE 9.8. Cumulative job growth in footloose and nonfootloose firms

Source: Data from Hicks 2016.

These counties would more likely experience both thicker labor markets and more abundant trade linkages. Crowley (2016) has provided a clear explanation of the limitations of multiplier use in the context of incentivizing footloose firms.

Thus, both the geographic and asymmetric findings reported in this chapter are consistent with the general research findings on the impact of agglomeration. The declining footloose firm effects over time are consistent with much of the new economic geography.

Finally, it is important to outline some limitations of this work, along with future directions of analysis. First, the general range of findings reported here is not dependent upon the efficacy of the Bartik instrument because OLS results repeat the relative size changes, the geographic pattern, and the asymmetry of the multiplier. However, any instrument should be viewed with caution, including an instrument that has become a mainstay of the literature. Studies that can evaluate multipliers in a quasi-experimental setting (such as the data deployed in Greenstone, Hornbeck, and Moretti 2010) would be welcomed.

Second, the periods under analysis could be extended, but that change would shift this analysis from the short-term to long-term multiplier because intra-Censal county data are not available prior to 1969. This chapter estimates short-term multipliers, across three periods and across three definitions of urbanization. The degree to which these findings are sensitive to different definitions of urbanization or different periods would be worthy research.

These empirics use manufacturing employment to test footloose employment multipliers. Analysis of exporting multipliers, which would include nonfootloose but exporting firms such as agriculture or mining, would be a useful extension. This work would also be policy relevant, particularly in areas with significant natural resource extraction.

Despite these limitations, the findings that employment multipliers are asymmetric between positive and negative labor demand shocks, declining over time, and higher in urban than in less urban places provide information that is relevant to public officials. These results should cause hesitation in the deployment of I-O multipliers for policy use, particularly for smaller cities and rural areas, and cause considerable reconsideration of policies focusing on attracting footloose jobs to a region.

References

Bartik, Timothy J. 1993. "Who Benefits from Local Job Growth: Migrants or the Original Residents?" *Regional Studies* 27, no. 4 (January): 297–311. https://doi.org/10.1080/00343409312331347575.

Bartik, Timothy J., and Nathan Sotherland. 2019. "Realistic Local Job Multipliers." *Employment Research* 26, no. 2 (April): 1–3. https://doi.org/10.17848/1075-8445.26(2)-1.

Biles, James J. 2003. "Using Spatial Econometric Techniques to Estimate Spatial Multipliers: An Assessment of Regional Economic Policy in Yucatan, Mexico." *The Review of Regional Studies* 33 (2): 121–41.

Braschler, Curtis. 1972. "A Comparison of Least-Squares Estimates of Regional Employment Multipliers with Other Methods." *Journal of Regional Science* 12, no. 3 (December): 457–68. https://doi.org/10.1111/j.1467-9787.1972.tb00367.x.

Brownrigg, Mark. 1980. "Industrial Contraction and the Regional Multiplier Effect: An Application in Scotland." *The Town Planning Review* 51, no. 2 (April): 195–210. https://www.jstor.org/stable/40103712.

Crowley, George R. 2016. *Tax Incentives Job Creation and the Unseen: Is Alabama Giving Away the Store to Attract New Industry?* Troy, AL: Troy University, Johnson Center.

Çubukçu, K. Mert. 2011. "The Spatial Distribution of Economic Base Multipliers: A GIS and Spatial Statistics-Based Cluster Analysis." *A| Z ITU Journal of the Faculty of Architecture* 8 (2): 49–62.

Domański, Bolesław, and Krzysztof Gwosdz. 2010. "Multiplier Effects in Local and Regional Development." *Quaestiones Geographicae* 29 (2): 27–37. https://doi.org/10.2478/v10117-010-0012-7.

Gerolimetto, Margherita, and Stefano Magrini. 2015. "A Spatial Analysis of Employment Multipliers in the US." *Letters in Spatial Resource Science* 9 (September): 277–85. https://doi.org/10.1007/s12076-015-0157-z.

Greenstone, Michael, Richard Hornbeck, and Enrico Moretti. 2010. "Identifying Agglomeration Spillovers: Evidence from Winners and Losers of Large Plant Openings." *Journal of Political Economy* 118, no. 3 (June): 536–98. https://doi.org/10.1086/653714.

Guo, Jiemin, and Mark A. Planting. 2000. *Using Input-Output Analysis to Measure US Economic Structural Change Over a 24 year Period*. Washington, DC: Bureau of Economic Analysis. https://www.bea.gov/system/files/papers/WP2000-1.pdf.

Hefner, Frank L., and Paulo P. Guimaraes. 1994. "Backward and Forward Linkages in Manufacturing Location Decisions Reconsidered." *Review of Regional Studies* 24 (3): 229–44.

Hicks, Michael J. 2016. *Why Have Local Economic Development Efforts Been So Disappointing?* Muncie, IN: Ball State University, Center for Business and Economic Research. https://projects.cberdata.org/reports/DisappointingEconDevt-20160620.pdf.

Hildebrand, George H., and Arthur Mace Jr. 1950. "The Employment Multiplier in an Expanding Industrial Market: Los Angeles County, 1940–47." *The Review of Economics and Statistics* 32 (3): 241–49.

Jones, Paul M., Eric Olson, and Mark E. Wohar. 2015. "Asymmetric Tax Multipliers." *Journal of Macroeconomics* 43 (March): 38–48. https://doi-org.proxy.bsu.edu/10.1016/j.jmacro.2014.08.006.

Krugman, Paul. 1991. "Increasing Returns and Economic Geography." *Journal of Political Economy* 99, no. 3 (June): 483–99.

Krugman, Paul. 2011. "The New Economic Geography, Now Middle-Aged." *Regional Studies* 45, no. 1 (January): 1–7. https://doi.org/10.1080/00343404.2011.537127.

Mathur, Vijay K., and Harvey Rosen. 1975. "'Regional Employment Multiplier: A New Approach': Reply." *Land Economics* 51, no. 3 (August): 294–95. https://doi.org/10.2307/3145096.

McNulty, James E. 1977. "A Test of the Time Dimension in Economic Base Analysis." *Land Economics* 53, no. 3 (August): 359–68. https://doi.org/10.2307/3146126.

Moody, Harold T., and Frank W. Puffer. 1970. "The Empirical Verification of the Urban Base Multiplier: Traditional and Adjustment Process Models." *Land Economics* 46, no. 1 (February): 91–8. https://doi.org/10.2307/3145430.

Moody, Harold T., Frank W. Puffer, and Robert M. Williams. 1970. "An Eight-Region Model." *Growth and Change* 1, no. 4 (October): 20–6. https://doi.org/10.1111/j.1468-2257.1970.tb00122.x.

Moretti, Enrico. 2010. "Local Multipliers." *The American Economic Review* 100, no. 2 (May): 373–77. https://doi.org/10.1257/aer.100.2.373.

Nguyen, Ha, and Jiaming Soh. 2017. "Employment Multipliers over the Business Cycle." Policy Research Working Papers, 8105, The World Bank Group, Washington, DC, June 2017. https://doi.org/10.1596/1813-9450-8105.

Pesaran, M. Hashem. 2006. "Estimation and Inference in Large Heterogeneous Panels with a Multifactor Error Structure." *Econometrica* 74, no. 4 (July): 967–1012. https://www.jstor.org/stable/3805914.

Polak, Jacques J. 1939. "International Propagation of Business Cycles." *The Review of Economic Studies* 6, no. 2 (February): 79–99. https://doi.org/10.2307/2967392.

Poppert, Patrick E., and Henry W. Herzog Jr. 2003. "Force Reduction, Base Closure, and the Indirect Effects of Military Installations on Local Employment Growth." *Journal of Regional Science* 43, no. 3 (August): 459–82. https://doi.org/10.1111/1467-9787.00307.

Richardson, Harry W. 1985. "Input-Output and Economic Base Multipliers: Looking Backward and Forward." *Journal of Regional Science* 25, no. 4 (November): 607–61. https://doi.org/10.1111/j.1467-9787.1985.tb00325.x.

Richardson, Harry W., and Peter Gordon. 1978. "A Note on Spatial Multipliers." *Economic Geography* 54, no. 4 (October): 309–13. https://doi.org/10.2307/143281.

Rickman, Dan S., and Mouhcine Guettabi. 2015. "The Great Recession and Nonmetropolitan America." *Journal of Regional Science* 55, no. 1 (January): 93–112. https://doi.org/10.1111/jors.12140.

Sablik, Tim. 2013. "Recession of 1981–82." Federal Reserve History, (November); accessed January 18, 2019. https://www.federalreservehistory.org/essays/recession-of-1981-82.

Sasaki, Kyohei. 1963. "Military Expenditures and the Employment Multiplier in Hawaii." *The Review of Economics and Statistics* 45, no. 3 (August): 298–304. https://doi.org/10.2307/1923901.

Shaffer, Ron E. 1983. "A Test of the Differences in Export Base Multipliers in Expanding and Contracting Economies." *Journal of Regional Analysis and Policy* 13 (2): 61–74.

Shahidsaless, Shahin, William Gillis, and Ron Shaffer. 1983. "Community Characteristics and Employment Multipliers in Nonmetropolitan Counties, 1950–1970." *Land Economics* 59, no. 1 (February): 84–93. https://doi.org/10.2307/3145878.

Thompson, John Scott. 1983. "Patterns of Employment Multipliers in a Central Place System: An Alternative to Economic Base Estimation." *Journal of Regional Science* 23, no. 1 (February): 71–82. https://doi.org/10.1111/j.1467-9787.1983.tb00784.x.

Tsvetkova, Alexandra, and Mark D. Partridge. 2016. "Economics of Modern Energy Boomtowns: Do Oil and Gas Shocks Differ from Shocks in the Rest of the Economy?" *Energy Economics* 59 (September): 81–95. https://doi.org/10.1016/j.eneco.2016.07.015.

van Dijk, Jasper Jacob. 2017. "Local Employment Multipliers in US Cities." *Journal of Economic Geography* 17, no. 2 (March): 465–87. https://doi.org/10.1093/jeg/lbw010.

Weiss, Steven J., and Edwin C. Gooding. 1968. "Estimation of Differential Employment Multipliers in a Small Regional Economy." *Land Economics* 44, no. 2 (May): 235–44. https://doi.org/10.2307/3159318.

West, Guy R. 1986. "A Stochastic Analysis of an Input-Output Model." *Econometrica* 54 (2): 363–74.

AFTERWORD

Greg Goodnight

This afterword is adapted from the keynote address that Mayor Goodnight gave on May 11, 2018 at the 2018 Small Cities Conference in Muncie, Indiana. The theme of the conference was "Vulnerable Communities," and the papers presented addressed the challenges facing smaller and midsized cities. Goodnight was Mayor of Kokomo, Indiana from 2008 through 2019. Kokomo is in Howard County, about sixty miles due north of Indianapolis. Its economy has been and continues to be based largely in manufacturing with a large share of these jobs producing automobile parts and components for Chrysler and General Motors (GM). In 2000 there were approximately 19,300 manufacturing jobs in Howard County, which accounted for approximately 34 percent of total jobs. By 2009 manufacturing employment had decreased to about 7,900 (18 percent of total jobs). Through the federal government's Troubled Asset Relief Program (TARP) in 2009, Chrysler and GM were recipients of financial assistance (loans), and the federal government took an ownership stake in each company. By the end of 2014 both companies had restructured and paid back the majority of the TARP outstanding loan amounts, and the federal government had sold its ownership stakes in each company.[1] During 2018, the most recent year for which data is available, manufacturing employment in Howard County approached twelve thousand jobs (about a quarter of total jobs in the county).[2] Goodnight's speech provided the conference attendees with a concrete sense of the challenges facing urban leaders attempting to revive a small city that had experienced a substantial decline in its economic fortunes. We include it here as a reminder of how broad policy initiatives such as TARP interact with on-the-ground political realities to shape small-city redevelopment efforts.

When I first ran for Mayor of Kokomo in 2007, things looked much different from the way they would look just a year later in 2008. In 2007, the unemployment rate was around 5 percent. Housing was stable. Our city's most controversial topic was whether or not city government should plant flowers. We had no idea what was to come and what Kokomo would have to do to get through the Great Recession.

In the years leading up to the Great Recession, we were too comfortable. Kokomo had spent years saying nothing was wrong and ignoring the warning signs. We, like too many other midsized cities, rode the wave of relative prosperity, looking only 7 minutes ahead—and sometimes backwards. Never strategizing about what the future would bring, we failed to position ourselves for a changing world.

In 2007, Kokomo was like most other midsized cities in the Midwest, and just like them, we were not prepared. We were not prepared for the brutal downturn in the economy, changing demographics, or the shifting national trends back to broad urbanization. We stuck with the status quo. We did not invest in ourselves. Instead, we handed out bonuses and pay raises to city employees, overbuilt our infrastructure, embraced sprawl, and allowed vinyl villages to pop up. We were fat, happy, and unhealthy—a couch-potato city.

Then, one day, we had a heart attack. And not just a run of the mill, "Take an aspirin once a day," heart attack. It was a knock-you-off-your-feet kind of heart attack. Our three largest employers filed for bankruptcy—simultaneously. Unemployment skyrocketed to over 20 percent. We were forced to deal with years of deficit spending. If that was not enough, in December 2008, *Forbes Magazine* listed Kokomo as the third Fastest Dying City in America. And at that time, it was certainly true. Kokomo was on the operating table, and the doctor was ready to call it.

In 2009, with help from the federal government, the automotive sector was somewhat stabilized. Kokomo was given a second chance at life. Our major employers reorganized, and slowly they began hiring. The immediate danger, at least, seemed to be over, but we still had hard decisions to make.

After this heart attack, we could have easily gone back to our fat and happy ways. In fact, many citizens expected us to return to the couch and kick up our feet. Kokomo could have just blamed the experience on the historic nature of the Great Recession and on the long-term realities facing many Rust Belt cities. Instead, we took our own heart attack seriously. We listened to the experts. We studied urban planners, economists, realtors, demographers, professors, and social scientists. We were determined that Kokomo would incorporate real research and insights and not go back to our unhealthy, crippling habits. We got the necessary treatment, got off the couch, and actually decided to follow the doctor's orders. We had to attract new residents and top talent to the workforce while also streamlining and improving government services.

What I am about to say, you probably already know. Low-skill manufacturing jobs have been declining in cities for a long time. Yet, many cities did not do anything about it. After the Great Recession our community decided that this time, things would be different.

As with most change, it was not easy. I was fortunate to have the backing from our city council, where I had served prior to becoming mayor. From those years on the council together we had learned to trust each other during both good times and bad. So, during the toughest of times, as we started the transformation process I was fortunate to have a partner in our reforms. And while we recognized the likely political fallout of making broad changes in a complacent Midwest culture, we were all willing to stay strong, trust the data, and put aside partisan politics.

It seemed like previous mayors had always been the good guys. They were able hire their friends and family; I had to lay mine off. Instead of giving employees raises and bonuses, we chose to invest our very limited dollars in public amenities. We added features to Kokomo Beach, our public pool. We extended and enhanced our urban trail network to create more spaces for pedestrians and cyclists. To create more community events, we built a downtown concert venue and expanded our farmers' market. Having no public transportation system, we created one, which is now the largest free-to-the-rider bus system in the state. We implemented each of these projects while trying to build back cash reserves to a safe level. Instead of kissing babies at cafes and shaking hands at assembly lines, we had to spend time huddled in meetings about how to make our urban core more walkable and more attractive to outside investment.

There was a moment during my first year in office, in the midst of the Great Recession, when we had to make hard, unpopular but necessary decisions about staffing levels. My entire family was feeling the pressure. Pressure from constant hateful attacks in the newspapers, on talk radio, social media, and even in person when we were just trying to pick up something at the pharmacy. One night, my wife Kelli said to me, "I didn't sign up for this," and I agreed. I wasn't enjoying any of it. To be honest, I was pretty sure I did not want to run for re-election, and in 2009, the public probably felt the same way.

From that moment on, political calculations nearly ceased. I was sure one term was all I was going to get, and that was actually liberating. We were going to do what was required, in the time that we were given, to make Kokomo a better place to live. We were not going to allow Kokomo to fall further behind. You see, it is easy to live a healthy lifestyle immediately following a major scare. Anyone can follow any regimen when death is still looming large in the rearview mirror. The real issue is how to maintain it and create long-term change. Can you keep it up even when you are in better shape, or will you fall back into complacency? In Kokomo, and other midwestern cities, this is the defining challenge that will ultimately determine our survival.

I have been mayor now for more than ten years and have served as president of our state's Cities and Towns Association. I have met local mayors, governors, CEOs, and other decision makers throughout the state and country. So, now after living with these challenges for a decade, I believe success comes down to leadership. You need strong and bold leadership to overcome the naysayers.

Think about it this way—losing weight is easy in theory. You just need to eat less and move around more. Burn more calories than you consume. Eat less sweets. Eat more broccoli. It is that simple. The hard part is the implementation of that plan. It is not eating another doughnut, even though you really, really want it. It is telling your family that you have to pass on going to Martino's for pizza, which is really hard to do in Kokomo, because that is "nationally recognized hall-of-fame pizza." Losing weight and transforming your city is much the same process. It is not about having more data and knowledge. It is about having the focus and follow-through to execute that theory.

As local leaders, most of the time we know what we need to do. The data is there. It is not hard to make calls to other officials, visit other cities, or examine the findings from researchers. Having a plan is easy, but that is not enough. Implementation in the face of naysayers, NIMBYs, Facebook trolls, and so many other factions is the hard part. It is not good enough to just have the right ideas; you must have the will, as leaders, to break through that wall to get results.

This is a daunting challenge. Telling your citizens that we can no longer hope to lure a large factory to our city. That is hard. Telling your residents that quality of life is economic development. That is hard. Redesigning your city and making infrastructure changes that just might inconvenience a pick-up truck driver but make it safer and easier for folks to walk and bike. That is hard. And do not even get me started on trying to have a conversation about "footloose jobs versus nonfootloose jobs" without citizens staring at you blankly, probably thinking, "What does any of this have to do with the 1980s movie starring Kevin Bacon?"

The unfortunate truth is that nearly all action results in criticism. Right after I took office, former two-term Kokomo mayor Steve Daily told me, "If you want a long career in politics, don't do anything. If you want to get re-elected, don't do anything." Let's face it, the Midwest is full of popular politicians who did not do a damned thing. And that is probably why they are loved. This may be the fundamental challenge local leaders face. I have yet to find a single issue where there was not some kind of complaint or backlash. "The potholes on the streets are awful." I agree—so, let us pave the streets. But then I hear, "I'm tired of all this construction!"

A perfect example just happened a few weeks ago. Kokomo is fortunate enough to have an Indiana University regional campus. By now you would think that everyone would agree that Indiana University Kokomo's success is vital to the long-term prosperity of our city. You would also think that everyone could agree IU Kokomo has made enormous progress over the last ten years—adding sports programs, expanding degree offerings, and graduating the largest classes ever two years in a row. In fact, IU Kokomo is the fastest growing IU campus in the state. Yet, when we announced that a private developer, without using any federal, state, or local tax dollars, was going to build student housing next to IU Kokomo, my office got calls from people complaining about it. The Facebook comments were filled with posts such as "IU Kokomo is doing just fine without this–why change?"; "We don't need any more housing!"; "Who is going to live there?"; and "Those college kids are just going to have parties!" And my favorite: "Yeah, I think we need it—but just not there."

So, in those moments, what do you do? How can you create the progress you know you must, while convincing the public that this is the right direction? Steve Jobs once said, "People don't know what they want until you show it to them." This has been key to much of our success in Kokomo. Show results. In a city like Kokomo that is what you have to do. After thoroughly researching, planning, and executing the right idea, it has been my experience that over time, many will come around and support the results. There are several projects that were aggressively fought in the planning stages, but now they have broad support—and a few are even praised on occasion.

In 2010, when we transformed downtown Kokomo into a pedestrian-friendly area, many people fought it. We converted every single street from one-way to two-way. We eliminated all downtown stop lights in exchange for four-way stops. We pulled out every single coin-operated parking meter from the sidewalks. We put in ADA-compliant pedestrian bump-outs at the intersections. And we did not stop planting flower baskets or trees. In fact, we expanded our planting efforts. Some of the very same people who challenged these strategic changes now celebrate them. These changes may seem like the obvious, easy, and uncontroversial thing to do. But believe it or not, I have real scars from these fights. And with social media providing a space and amplifying everyone's voice, we constantly see the misinformed communicating with the uninformed. This blinds us to the truth of what our cities can become.

Local leaders face more challenges than just social media trolls and a changing economy. We are also facing increasing hostility and interference from federal and state government—from prohibiting sanctuary cities to stopping antidiscrimination efforts and preventing referenda on local issues. With all that, local leaders must be focused and determined. These challenges are enough to make any rational person question themselves about wanting to run for office. It is difficult to get quality candidates to run in the first place, but we need them to run. We cannot let the criticism and challenges stop us from being proactive.

We cannot be "just caretakers." We cannot sit on our hands or crawl back onto that couch, just because it is the easy thing to do. We cannot be willing to simply manage the decline of our cities. Progress requires us to do the hardest thing any elected official has to do—tell the people the truth. It is hard because when the truth means making changes that impact people's lives, even in seemingly small ways, it is often ignored or challenged. As psychologist Harry Levinson said, "All change is loss; all loss must be mourned." It is natural to be apprehensive when something that we experience or interact with changes. But after some time, the roots will take hold, the grass will grow again, and the people will come around—or maybe they won't.

Research and data have given us the blueprint to build successful cities. But the data alone won't save our cities. People ignore inconvenient data all the time. Talk to a smoker, and they will not disagree with you or dispute the thousands of peer-reviewed articles and studies about the dangers of smoking. Every smoker knows the health risks. Telling them again is not going to get them to stop smoking. The same is true in local government. It is only when we have leadership with the moral fortitude to fight through all the challenges that we can create the change that is required. Because no one else is going to do it.

On December 3, 2018, I will become the longest serving mayor in Kokomo's history, and since 2008 every council member, Democrat and Republican, has been re-elected. I don't say this to be boastful but to prove that bold and progressive leadership, even in the face of seemingly overwhelming criticism, can be successful.

Bold leadership can yield the largest free-to-the-rider transportation system in the state. It can create one of the most walkable downtowns and bring about dramatic increases in housing construction. It can create a fiscally sound city with the lowest debt per capita of Indiana's largest cities. And, it can build a cash surplus of more than 15 million dollars. Bold leadership can reduce government payrolls while increasing services and rally citizens to your cause. I believe these things because we have done all of them and more in Kokomo. I love Kokomo. I am not ashamed to say that. As leaders and as citizens, it should never be wrong to show pride for your city. Not only for how it is today but for what it can become.

In closing, I ask the researchers and academics here today to keep supplying us with the data, information, and ideas needed to prepare our cities for the future. And to the local leaders attending the conference: trust the data and remember why you became involved in public service in the first place. Improving people's lives is difficult work, but it is deeply rewarding. If you as a local leader will not do it, who will make the hard choices?

I look forward to seeing your work continue and inspire leaders for years to come. Also, I invite all of you to visit Kokomo to see for yourself why I love my city so much.

Notes

1. See Goolsbee and Krueger 2015 for more details on the federal government bailout of Chrysler and GM.

2. Employment data is from US Bureau of Economic Analysis 2018, Regional Data tables.

References

US Bureau of Economic Analysis. 2018. Regional Data, Local Area Personal Income and Employment, Total Full-time and Part-Time Employment by Industry (CAEMP25), Accessed July 20, 2020. https://apps.bea.gov/itable/iTable.cfm?ReqID=70&step=1.

Goolsbee, Austan D., and Alan B. Krueger. 2015. "A Retrospective Look at Rescuing and Restructuring General Motors and Chrysler." *The Journal of Economic Perspectives* 29, no. 2 (Spring): 3–24. https://doi.org/10.1257/jep.29.2.3.

WORKING CITIES CHALLENGE INITIATIVES

TABLE A1. Massachusetts—Round 1 (2014–2017)

CITY/INITIATIVE	DEMOGRAPHICS (2016)	COLLABORATORS (PARTIAL LIST)	10-YEAR SHARED RESULT
Chelsea/Chelsea Thrives	Population: 38,244 Median family income: $53,219 Poverty rate: 16.9%	The Neighborhood Developers (lead), Police Department, City of Chelsea, Roca, Chelsea Public Schools, Chelsea Collaborative, and residents	Improve safety perception by 30% in poorest neighborhood; reduce crime rate by 30%
Fitchburg/ Reimagine North of Main	Population: 40,441 Median family income: $59,307 Poverty rate: 15.1%	Montachussett Opportunity Council (lead), City of Fitchburg, Fitchburg State University, NewVue Communities, Health Foundation of Central MA, Fitchburg Art Museum, and residents	Transform the North of Main into a neighborhood of choice where people want to live, work, play, and invest
Holyoke/ SPARK	Population: 40,280 Mecian family income: $45,598 Poverty rate: 25.2%	Greater Holyoke Chamber of Commerce (lead), Holyoke Community College, City of Holyoke, Bank RSB, Holyoke Creative Arts Center, One Holyoke CDC, Career Point, SCORE, and small business owners and residents	Create 300 new businesses, with 20% Latino-owned
Lawrence/ Lawrence Working Families Initiative	Population: 79,337 Med an family income: $38,681 Poverty rate: 24.2%	Lawrence CommunityWorks (lead), Lawrence Partnership, City of Lawrence, career center, Northern Essex Community College, school district, The Community Group, and residents	Increase parent income by 15% and dramatically increase parent engagement in the public schools

Note: Demographics for Massachusetts—median family income: $90,180; poverty rate: 11.4%

TABLE A2. Massachusetts—Round 2 (2016–2019)

CITY/INITIATIVE	DEMOGRAPHICS (2016)	COLLABORATORS (PARTIAL LIST)	10-YEAR SHARED RESULT
Haverhill/Mt. Washington Alliance	Population: 62,340 Median family income: $75,240 Poverty rate: 10.1%	Community Action, Inc. (lead), City of Haverhill, school district, neighborhood businesses, Chamber of Commerce, Northern Essex Community College, faith community, and resident groups	Mt. Washington neighborhood matches city median on employment, income, school quality, voting, and code reporting
Lowell/ Working Cities Lowell	Population: 109,871 Median family income: $55,999 Poverty rate: 17.2%	Coalition for a Better Acre (lead), City of Lowell, UMass Lowell, Cambodian Mutual Assistance Assoc., Middlesex Community College, health and career centers, housing authority, and residents	Increase by 10%: income, employment, school readiness, and inclusion in the Acre neighborhood
Pittsfield/ Working Cities Pittsfield	Population: 43,632 Median family income: $60,378 Poverty rate: 14.2%	Central Berkshire Habitat for Humanity (lead), City of Pittsfield, Berkshire United Way, Berkshire Health System, Berkshire Community College, career center, faith community, and residents	Increase full-time workforce from 42% to 45% and number of people living above 200% FPL by 1,300, and ensure Pittsfield is inclusive community
Springfield/ Springfield WORKS	Population: 153,991 Median family income: $39,836 Poverty rate: 26%	Economic Development Council of Western MA (lead), Regional Employment Board of Hampden County, MGM, United Personnel, City of Springfield, Springfield Technical Community College, and school district	Increase proportion of residents who are currently employed from 58% to 75%, and improve job retention and wage growth

Note: Demographics for Massachusetts—median family income: $90,180, Poverty rate: 11.4%.

TABLE A3. Rhode Island—Round 3 (2017–2020)

CITY	DEMOGRAPHICS (2016)	COLLABORATORS (PARTIAL LIST)	10-YEAR SHARED RESULT
Cranston/ OneCranston	Population: 80,882 Mediar family income: $79,214 Poverty rate: 6.9%	Comprehensive Community Action Program (lead), Center for Southeast Asians, City of Cranston, library, Police Department, school district, Roger Williams University, Texas Roadhouse, YMCA, and residents	Increase social cohesion by 30%; decrease economic and educational disparities among minority and low-income residents
Newport	Population: 24,570 Median family income: $81,806 Poverty rate: 9.7%	Boys & Girls Club of Newport County (lead), school district, Community College of RI, City of Newport, Housing Authority, East Bay Community Action Program, Newport Health Equity Zone, Chamber of Commerce, and residents	Decrease the poverty rate in Newport by 20%
Providence	Population: 178,851 Median family income: $43,585 Poverty rate: 23.7%	City of Providence (lead), Genesis Center, Dorcas International, Providence Housing Authority, The WorkPlace, Providence Career & Technical Academy, Apprenticeship RI, RI Hospitality Assoc., RI Dept. of Education, and We Make RI	Number of unemployed Providence residents served by the workforce system will mirror the characteristics of unemployed Providence residents

Note: Demographics for Rhode Island—median family income: $75,655; poverty rate: 13.8%.

MT. AUBURN ASSOCIATES—ROUND 1, FINAL EVALUATION RUBRIC

OUTCOME AREAS	INDICATORS	SUBINDICATORS
Expanded and sustained collaborative leadership	WCC team organizations demonstrate distributed leadership, sharing responsibility for achieving the shared result.	
	WCC teams demonstrate preparation for sustaining collaborative, system-oriented work in service of shared result.	
	Existing leadership connections are strengthened, and new leaders identified and engaged.	Initiative resulted in new or deeper relationships among organizations and/or catalyzed changed perspectives among leaders.
		New partners have been welcomed into the leadership of the initiatives.
		Partners place increased priority on working with leaders who represent the racial and ethnic diversity of their cities.
		Stakeholders cite rising, new, talented civic leaders who reflect the diversity of their communities.
	Teams have ongoing collaboration with other networks, collaboratives, or other key organizations active in related systems in the city, formally or informally, on issues that extend beyond the specific WCC result.	
Value and diffusion of core elements	WCC teams see substantial contribution of core elements in progress toward shared result.	Stakeholders note collaborative leadership made a substantial impact on the outcomes achieved.
		Stakeholders note community engagement made a substantial impact on the outcomes achieved.
		Stakeholders note use of data made a substantial impact on the outcomes achieved.
		Stakeholders note that system change made a substantial impact on the outcomes achieved.

(continued)

OUTCOME AREAS	INDICATORS	SUBINDICATORS
	Organizational leaders bring core elements back to home organizations, diffuse into practices and policies.	Partner organizations have changed systems to support stronger collaborations with other leaders or leading organizations in the cities.
		Partner organizations have changed systems to better engage residents.
		Partner organizations have changed systems to better use data.
Engaged residents	WCC partners regularly sought out resident voices and insights when developing strategies	
	WCC teams' strategies directly respond to resident insights.	
	WCC teams demonstrate accountability to residents by directly communicating progress toward shared result.	
External recognition	WCC leaders develop or improve relationships with entities outside the cities, including attracting new outside resources aligned with shared result.	

SAMPLE QUESTIONS, LAWRENCE PARTNERSHIP SURVEY

1. On a scale of 1–10 (with 1 being very weak and 10 being very strong) how strong is Lawrence's civic infrastructure, which is defined by the Boston Fed as "the network of organizations, resources, leaders, and residents that can be mobilized to solve a complex problem or pursue a new opportunity"?

2. To what extent do you agree or disagree with the following statement: If Lawrence faced an unexpected economic, physical, or social shock (such as a loss of major employer or a sudden rise in high school dropout rates), I have a high level of confidence in the civic leadership of Lawrence to respond quickly and capably to the challenge?

3. How would you describe the ability of leaders in Lawrence to resolve conflict so that they are able to work together toward long-term community improvement?

4. To what extent do you agree or disagree with the following statement: The leaders in Lawrence reflect the diversity of city residents?

5. To what extent do you agree or disagree with the following statement: Community leaders effectively raise local awareness and build political will in support of efforts to improve conditions in Lawrence?

6. To what extent are leaders within the following sectors protective of their own resources and knowledge? (Options: public; private; non-profit; anchor institutions)

7. How often is the following statement true: Lawrence's government works with nonprofits and the private sector to address challenges in Lawrence?

8. How often is the following statement true: When a new opportunity is presented, leaders and institutions come together to determine how best to pursue it?

9. How actively do the following sectors work to create opportunities to improve quality of life for low-income residents? (Options: public; private; nonprofit; anchor institutions)

10. How often is the following statement true: Businesses in Lawrence participate in efforts to improve the community?

11. How often is the following statement true: Lawrence's government is responsible and accountable to its citizens?

12. How effective are leaders in Lawrence when it comes to securing and leveraging available resources and assets? This includes governmental and foundation grants, subsidies, tax credits, and even nonfinancial assets like real estate, time, and expertise.

13. How much influence do groups that represent low-income or other marginalized residents have in the planning and decision-making processes?

14. To what extent do you agree or disagree with the following statement: People from all neighborhoods, ethnicities, and income levels have equal opportunities to participate in Lawrence's decision-making process?

Note: Questions were derived from multiple existing sources, including the ACEs and Resilience Collective Community Capacity (ARC3) survey developed by Community Science (http://www.appi-wa.org/wp-content/uploads/2016/07/APPI -White-Paper.pdf) and the Wilder Collaboration Factors Inventory (https://www .wilder.org/Wilder-Research/Research-Services/Pages/Wilder-Collaboration -Factors-Inventory.aspx).

SAMPLE QUESTIONS, SURVEY OF STATE LEADERS' PERCEPTIONS OF CIVIC INFRASTRUCTURE

1. How accountable do you find leaders from the following sectors? (Options: public; private; nonprofit; anchor institutions)
2. How actively do leaders from the following sectors appear to convene all segments and communities in <city>?
3. How has turnover in leadership impacted your own work? (Options: Turnover has not stifled any opportunity or progress; Leadership has fluctuated to the extent that it is difficult to work with this sector; Lack of turnover has been a barrier)
4. Within each of the following sectors, are there leaders that you would consider visionary, that challenge existing assumptions and think innovatively about their community?
5. In the time that you've worked with partners in this city, how often have leaders from multiple sectors (public, private and nonprofit) worked together on projects?
6. For each of the following sectors, is conflict more or less what you would expect? (Options: There is less conflict than I would expect; The amount of conflict is natural, and about what I would expect; There is more conflict than I would expect; There is far too much conflict; I don't know)
7. How challenging is it for you and your partners to work in the existing political environment?

8. To what extent do you feel that residents are authentically involved in local planning initiatives?

9. Which of the following best characterizes the level of cohesion between different neighborhoods and/or groups (ethnic, socioeconomic, religious, etc.) in <city>?

Notes on Contributors

James J. Connolly is George and Frances Ball Distinguished Professor of History and Director of the Center for Middletown Studies at Ball State University. He earned a PhD in American History from Brandeis University (1995). His research examines American urban life, cultural history, and politics from the late nineteenth century to the recent past. His publications include *Print Culture Histories Beyond the Metropolis* (2016, coeditor); *What Middletown Read: Print Culture in an American Small City* (2015, coauthor); *After the Factory: Reinventing America's Industrial Small Cities* (2010/2012, editor); and *Decentering Urban History: Peripheral Cities in the Modern World*, a special issue of the *Journal of Urban History* (2008, editor).

Vikash Dangal is a former PhD student in the Department of Agricultural Economics and Agribusiness at Louisiana State University. He holds master's degrees in agriculture economics as well as analytics. His primary research interests are in regional science and public economics, especially focused on social mobility and racial disparities in children's outcomes. His current research projects include analyzing the variation in intergenerational mobility by race/ethnicity and the effect of childhood environment in future outcomes like income and incarceration in the United States. In addition, he is a tutor of economics and statistics at the Academic Center for Student-Athletes, Louisiana State University.

Colleen Dawicki is deputy director of the Working Cities Challenge, coordinating the competition and supporting nine cities across Massachusetts and Connecticut while leading internal learning and communications for Working Places across New England. In addition to supporting smaller cities through the Challenge, she is pursuing research to better understand the ways in which civic infrastructure can be strengthened to improve outcomes for low-income residents in smaller cities. Before joining the Boston Fed in late 2014, Colleen worked with smaller cities to provide urban policy research and technical assistance as the director of the UMass Dartmouth Urban Initiative. Colleen is also a fellow with MassINC's Gateway Cities Innovation Institute and a member of the School Committee in her small-city home of New Bedford. She holds a Master of Public Policy degree from UMass Dartmouth and a BA in public and private sector organizations from Brown University.

Jennifer Erickson is associate professor of anthropology at Ball State University (2010–present). Her primary research focuses on refugee resettlement, citizenship, race, ethnicity, and gender in small Midwest cities. Her book, *Race-ing Fargo: Refugees, Citizenship, and the Transformation of Small Cities* (2020, Cornell University Press) traces the history of refugee resettlement to Fargo, North Dakota, from the 1980s to the present day, focusing on the roles that religion, race, ethnicity, and sociality play in everyday interactions between refugees and the dominant white Euro-American population of the city. Through the comparative study of white, secular Muslim Bosnians and Black Christian Southern Sudanese, *Race-ing Fargo* demonstrates how cross-cultural and transnational understandings of identity and political economy shape daily citizenship practices and belonging. Prior to academia, Erickson worked in refugee resettlement in South Dakota and for a local women's nongovernmental organization in postwar Bosnia-Herzegovina.

J. Matthew Fannin is the William H. Alexander Professor of Rural and Community Development Economics in the Department of Agricultural Economics and Agribusiness at Louisiana State University and the LSU AgCenter. He has been with LSU since December 2003. In addition to teaching and advising students in regional economics and community development, his academic program includes research and extension components. His research program has included evaluating strategies around rural physician recruitment, rural hospital funding policies, and financial resilience of rural county and parish governments to tropical natural disasters in a changing federal policy environment. His current research focuses on evaluating the role of wealth assets on economic prosperity and social mobility of rural and Micropolitan areas. As a part of this effort, he was coeditor of the book *Rural Wealth Creation*. Dr. Fannin serves as Chair of the Population and Place Analytics Panel with the Rural Policy Research Institute (RUPRI).

Dagney Faulk is director of research in the Center for Business and Economic Research (CBER) at Ball State University in Muncie, Indiana. Her research focuses on regional economic development issues and state and local tax policy. She has worked on numerous Indiana-focused policy studies on a variety topics including analysis of fixed- route bus transit, the regional distribution of state government taxes and expenditures, local government consolidation, and property tax issues. She is coauthor (with Michael Hicks) of the book *Local Government Consolidation in the United States* (Cambria Press 2011). She received her PhD in economics from the Andrew Young School of Policy Studies at Georgia State University.

Greg Goodnight served three terms as mayor of the City of Kokomo, Indiana, from January 1, 2008 through December 31, 2019. During his tenure, Kokomo was recognized both statewide and nationally for achievements including a Harvard University Bright Ideas in Government Award, two Indiana Association of Cities and Towns Community Achievement Awards, the Indiana Chamber of Commerce Community of the Year Award, an Indiana Main Street Association Design of Downtown Public Improvement Award, and the creation of the largest free-to-the-rider fixed-route bus system in the state. He has also served as a guest lecturer at Yale University's School of Management and as a fellow for the Center for National Policy.

Michael J. Hicks is director of Ball State University's Center for Business and Economic Research and the George and Frances Ball Distinguished Professor of Economics in the Miller College of Business. His research interest is in state and local public finance and the effect of public policy on the location, composition, and size of economic activity. Hicks earned doctoral and master's degrees in economics from the University of Tennessee and a bachelor's degree in economics from Virginia Military Institute. He is a retired Army Reserve Infantryman.

William Grady Holt is associate professor, coordinator of the Urban Environmental Studies (UES) Program, and co-chair of Architectural Studies at Birmingham-Southern College. Holt holds a PhD from Yale University with a focus on urban and cultural sociology as well as a JD from Vermont Law School in environmental and energy law. Holt has edited two books, *Urban Areas and Global Climate Change* and *From Sustainable to Resilient Cities: Global Concerns/Urban Efforts*. His new work focuses on the branding of post-Civil Rights American Cities and environmental justice issues with EPA Superfund sites. As a US EPA College/Underserved Community Partnership Program (CUPP) member, the UES Program collaborated with Bessemer, Alabama, on postindustrial redevelopment programs.

Hannah Lebovits is an assistant professor at the College of Architecture, Planning, and Public Affairs (CAPPA) at the University of Texas-Arlington. Her research focuses on the ways that local communities can govern toward social sustainability. She earned her graduate degrees at Cleveland State University and has experience in the nonprofit and public sectors. Her work has appeared in peer-reviewed journals, national and international media outlets, and local newspapers.

Alan Mallach is a senior fellow with the Center for Community Progress and teaches in the graduate city planning program at Pratt Institute in New York. His work focuses on urban revival, social equity and neighborhood change. He has served as the Director of Housing and Economic Development for the city of Trenton, New Jersey, and is the author of *Bringing Buildings Back: From Vacant Properties to Community Assets* and other books. His latest book is *The Divided City: Poverty and Prosperity in Urban America.*

Pamela Schaal is an associate professor of political science and public administration at Ball State University. Her research focuses on the political conditions that enhance our institutional separation of powers and system of federalism, namely more enhanced veto points achieved through divided government. She received her doctorate in political science from the University of Notre Dame. Before returning to academia, Dr. Schaal worked in Washington, DC, for a few think tank contractors including the Urban Institute and the COSMOS Corporation as well as for several members of Congress from both political parties.

Charles Taylor is the managing director of the Bowen Center for Public Affairs at Ball State University. He is also an associate professor of political science and director of the master of public administration program. His research focuses on state and local budgeting and policy. In addition to his academic experience, he worked fifteen years in Missouri local government as an engineer and manager. He received a bachelor of electrical engineering from the University of Missouri and his doctorate in policy studies from Clemson University.

Henry Way is professor of geography at James Madison University in Harrisonburg, Virginia. With a background in cultural and political geography, he researches and teaches urban sustainability, urban design, and urban planning with a geographical perspective. His work particularly focuses on the challenges and opportunities of smaller cities in these areas. As well as pursuing academic work in this field, he is active in the planning community, serving as chair of the City of Harrisonburg Planning Commission for a number of years. At JMU he is also associate director of the School of Integrated Sciences. He received his bachelor's degree in geography from Oxford University in the UK, his master's in geography from Cambridge University in the UK, and a PhD in geography from the University of Kansas.

Emily J. Wornell is a research assistant professor in the Indiana Communities Institute at Ball State University working with the Center for Business and Economic Research (CBER) and the Rural Policy Research Institute (RUPRI). As a rural sociologist and demographer, she specializes in the areas of inequality and population change in rural communities. Her research explores household livelihood strategies; community vulnerability to economic change; community and economic development; and immigration in new and rural communities. Emily also has a strong interest in the intersection of research and policy and in the rural voice in policy decisions, implementation, and evaluation. She regularly works with communities and policy makers to better understand and utilize research to develop more sustainable and efficacious policy.

Index

References to figures and tables are indicated by "f" and "t" following the page numbers.